Media in the Enlarged Europe

In memory of Jim Hall, a great friend, a great mind, a great loss.

Media in the Enlarged Europe
Politics, Policy and Industry

Edited by Alec Charles

intellect Bristol, UK / Chicago, USA

First Published in the UK in 2009 by
Intellect Books, The Mill, Parnall Road, Fishponds, Bristol, BS16 3JG, UK

First published in the USA in 2009 by
Intellect Books, The University of Chicago Press, 1427 E. 60th Street, Chicago,
IL 60637, USA

A catalogue record for this book is available from the British Library.

Cover Design: Holly Rose
Copy Editor: Laura Booth
Typesetting: Mac Style, Beverley, E. Yorkshire

ISBN 978-1-84150-998-3

Printed and bound by Gutenberg Press, Malta.

CONTENTS

Introduction: States of Transition

Alec Charles

The first problem one encounters when compiling a book about the European Union is that organization's apparently interminable transitionality. The EU is in a constant state of flux: its constitution, its institutions and even (indeed, especially) its borders are as inherently unstable as its political, economic and regulatory complexion.

The draft manuscript for this collection was completed in the immediate wake of the Treaty of Lisbon, and, although this agreement appeared at the time to represent an end, or a climax, to years of international wrangling over the European Union's proposals for constitutional reform, and a unanimous commitment to the future of the Union itself, the events of 2008 cast that future back into controversy, doubt and heated dispute.

The advantage of journalistic writing on the subject of the EU is its very ephemerality: a journalist's musings upon the topic are as contemporaneous and impermanent as the currency of the paper they're printed on – or of the web page onto which they're uploaded. The disadvantage of academic writing on this subject is that it is so quickly outdated, while at the same time so bibliographically permanent.

'Here lies one whose name was writ in water.' John Keats – an Englishman who in his own way toyed with the European project (and died toying: three months before that other great Europhile, Napoleon Bonaparte) – had those words engraved upon his tombstone, in the Protestant cemetery in Rome. The problem, of course, is that our words, like Keats's own, do not in fact flow towards the ocean, but – preserved on paper or on stone – may return to haunt us.

The best, therefore, that we can hope is that our texts will at least survive as documents of their times, and not cause too much embarrassment to future readers or to our future selves.

The uncertainty principle that governs the European Union also, inevitably, determines the mass media as a whole. The unpredictability of technological, economic and aesthetic trends has led media studies perpetually to reinvent itself: it is a discipline of indiscipline. However, in the field of media studies, as in the European Union itself, there remains one constant and one certainty: inconstancy and uncertainty. This collection therefore offers itself as a record of, and a meditation upon, one particular moment in the ever-evolving history of European media; but it may also, we hope, reflect European media's permanent condition of transitionality – and, as such, be of interest and value to readers in coming years, months and hours.

Aware of these inconstancies, this collection attempts to see European media in their broadest sense. Europe does not stop at the borders of the European Union – indeed, it might be argued that the European Union does not stop at its own borders – and therefore this collection in part looks beyond those national and cultural boundaries. This collection also views the mass media not only in its more traditional senses, but also looks at newer media technologies and their applications.

The recurring theme that binds all of the diverse papers in this collection is the relationship between European media industries and their social, economic, political and legislative contexts. Crucially, this collection examines not only the impacts of national and supranational policy and ownership upon European media, but also the influences of those media upon their socio-political environments – advancing the notion of a defining and constantly evolving dialogical relationship between the diverse and often antagonistic factors and players involved.

The first part of this collection offers a snapshot of media politics, policies, industries and cultures in the European Union as a whole; the second part presents individual case studies of the history and current state of the mass media in specific European nations – older, newer and prospective members of the European Union.

This collection has evolved out of a conference on 'Media in the Enlarged Europe', which took place at the University of Bedfordshire on 5–6 May 2006. Our thanks are due to all those who participated in that conference, to Professor Les Ebdon, Professor Andrew Slade, Professor Luke Hockley, Professor Garry Whannel, Dr Jim Franklin, Dr Moira Hampson, Peter Dean and John Stephens, and in particular to Professor Alexis Weedon, Director of the University of Bedfordshire's Research Institute for Media, Art and Design, and Professor James Crabbe, Dean of the University of Bedfordshire's Faculty of Creative Arts, Technologies and Science, for their unstinting encouragement and support. Special thanks are also due to May Yao and Laura Booth of Intellect Publishing, and to Dr Jason Wilson of Queensland University of Technology with whom I co-organized the 2006 conference and evolved the concept of this collection.

PART ONE: STATE OF THE UNION

THE ENLARGED AUDIO-VISUAL EUROPE: THE MANY FACES OF EUROPEANIZATION

Hedwig de Smaele

The transition from Communism to post-Communism in the 1990s was accompanied in central and eastern European countries by the emergence of new nation states, new political and economic systems and subsequently new media systems. At the same time, collaboration among eastern European countries, based on a shared ideology and Soviet hegemony, largely disappeared and was replaced by new alliances, mainly with the West. Membership of (western) European institutions such as the Council of Europe and especially the European Union became for many central and eastern European countries a priority to which they geared their reforms. As of writing, ten central and eastern European countries have joined the EU – the Czech Republic, Estonia, Hungary, Latvia, Lithuania, Poland, the Slovak Republic and Slovenia in May 2004, and Bulgaria and Romania in January 2007. The European Union represents, with 27 Member States and several more candidate Member States, indeed an enlarged Europe.

A commonly used concept to discuss the impact of EU membership on the domestic policies and practices of old and new Member States is that of 'Europeanization'. But can we speak of Europeanization in connection with the audio-visual field in the enlarged Europe – and, if so, in what sense?

A return to Europe?
In the period 1945–1989 'Europe' became identified with 'western Europe'. The Berlin wall was *de facto* the eastern border of Europe. Behind it lay the eastern bloc, 'the Other' in political,

economic, ideological and military terms. Researchers studying the European audio-visual field automatically limited themselves to western Europe and the European Union in particular. Eastern Europe was involved, at the most, as a 'third party', not as an organic part of Europe.

The end of the Cold War also ended the concept of Europe defined as West in opposition to East (Kevin 2003: 1). New definitions of Europe – both geographical and cultural or ideological – were formulated in connection with the question of membership of the EU. According to Article 237 of the Treaty of Rome (1957) and Article O of the Treaty of Maastricht (1993) 'any European State [...] may apply to become a Member of the Union.' The word 'European' was not officially defined. Moreover, the European Commission (1992: 11) spoke out against a closed definition of 'Europeanness' that would define for now and forever the borders of Europe. European identity was instead considered a dynamic concept, related to the integration process. Some definition, however, was felt to be necessary. Article O was amended by the Amsterdam Treaty of 2 October 1997 (which entered into force on 1 May 1999). The new Article 49 stipulates that 'every European State which respects the principles laid down in Article 6 (1)' can apply for membership. Article 6(1) refers to the principles of freedom, democracy, respect for human rights and fundamental freedoms, and the rule of law – principles that have been identified by many authors (for example, Arthur Schlesinger in Huntington 1997: 342) as characteristic of European civilization. Since the Copenhagen European Council in 1993 these principles have become known as the 'Copenhagen criteria'. At the Copenhagen Council the European Union set forth in broad terms the conditions for membership. Prospective members need to have a 'functioning market economy' and 'the capacity to cope with competitive pressure and market forces within the Union', as well as 'stability of institutions guaranteeing democracy, the rule of law, human rights, and respect for and protection of minorities'. Next to these political and economic conditions, candidate Member States have to take on the 'obligations of membership' – i.e. they have to take on the 80,000 pages of legislation, directives, regulations and judgements which constitute the *acquis communautaire* (European Parliament 1993). An additional condition for enlargement is, from the EU perspective, the capacity of the Union to absorb new members. The Madrid Council Conclusions (1995) also mentioned the adjustment of administrative structures as important in preparation for accession though not as a condition (European Parliament 1995).

The European Union candidacies of central and eastern European countries, though largely inspired by political, economic and military interests (stability, prosperity and peace in the region), carried an important emotional, even moral, dimension as well. The 'return to Europe' would do away with the 'mistake of Yalta' and symbolized a definitive break with the Soviet past. Acceptance by international organizations, such as the European Union, appeared to the young eastern European states as the confirmation of their independence and the proof of their successful transition (Grabbe and Hughes 1998: 7). The European Union, on the other hand, agreed on enlargement in principle, but showed less enthusiasm in considering enlargement a priority. Bideleux (1996: 241) describes it as significant that the European Union dealt with the enlargement issue as an aspect of foreign policy. Enlargement, in the view of the European

Union, was not allowed to disturb the already far-reaching European integration process (internal market, economic and monetary union, etc.). The starting point for the European Union therefore was the necessary adaptation of central and eastern European prospective members *prior* to membership. As a consequence, the asymmetry and rigidity of the European Union were far greater in the last eastward enlargements (2004 and 2007) than in previous enlargements. Notwithstanding the qualifying conditions of market economies, democracy and the rule of law, the stress was laid almost entirely on on the adoption of the *acquis* as key to the accession process (Kuneva 2001). Although the enlargement procedure was essentially a process of negotiations, the *acquis* – the basis of every negotiation – appeared as non-negotiable. The eastern European applicants could at best influence the pace, but not the content, of reforms. In addition, an extensive system of verification (monitoring the process of harmonization) was set up. This 'logic of control' (Maniokas 2004: 32) made enlargement an exclusively one-way process.

Europeanization as institutional adaptation

The concept of Europeanization takes many forms. Europeanization as a neutrally defined process of 'domestic adaptation to the pressures emanating directly or indirectly from EU membership' (Featherstone 2003: 7) did indeed occur in central and eastern Europe, as it also had in western Europe. Harcourt (2003a), for example, detected substantial convergence at the national levels of the fifteen old Member States in policy paradigms, domestic laws and policy instruments. Europeanization took place both via vertical mechanisms (directives and competition decisions of the European Commission, decisions of the European Court of Justice) and via horizontal mechanisms (suggestion of best practice through European-level policy forums). There are good reasons to assume that policy convergence in central and eastern Europe is even greater – similar, but wider and deeper in scope – than in western Europe. Grabbe (2003: 306–307) lists three such reasons. In the first place, there is the speed of adjustment, the fast adaptation prior to membership, and the fact that these countries start at a much lower point. In the second place, Grabbe points to the openness of central and eastern Europe to EU influence as a result of the process of post-Communist transformation: 'This process has made them more receptive to regulatory paradigms than the EU's Member States were, because EU models were being presented at the same time as central and eastern European policy-makers were seeking a model to implement' (Grabbe 2003: 306–307). Thirdly, Grabbe cites the breadth of the EU agenda in central and eastern Europe, including also economic and political conditions: 'that gives the EU a license to involve itself in domestic policy-making to a degree unprecedented in the current member states' (Grabbe 2003: 307). Dimitrova and Steunenberg (2004: 185) observe, on the one hand, effects that are 'farther-reaching than Europeanization effects in the current member states'. On the other hand, they also point at the danger of 'symbolic' or 'instrumental' adaptations due to conflicting sets of values in central and eastern European countries and the European Union, coupled with the necessity to comply with some of the EU's wishes in order to become full members (Dimitrova and Steunenberg 2004: 190). 'Pressures from the EU promote these sorts of Potemkin-village organizational structures,' writes Wade (1999: 64).

EU audio-visual policy rests on two pillars: audio-visual legislation (in particular the Television Without Frontiers directive [TWF directive]) and funding programs to support the audio-visual industry (in particular the subsequent MEDIA Programmes). Implementation of the first is a condition for participation in the second. Audio-visual legislation is subsumed under Chapter 20 of the *acquis* under the heading of 'Culture and Audio-visual Policy'. The focus, and the sole legal requirement, of Chapter 20 is alignment by the candidate countries with the Television Without Frontiers directive (1989, replaced in 1997, and again under revision). Negotiations concerning Chapter 20 were opened with the central and eastern European countries in two waves: in October–November 1998 with the first, relatively advanced group (the Czech Republic, Estonia, Slovenia, Poland and Hungary) and in May–October 2000 with Bulgaria, Latvia, Lithuania, the Slovak Republic and Romania. On the basis of progress achieved in the legislative alignment process (as monitored by the European Commission on a yearly basis), negotiations were completed with the Czech Republic, Estonia, Slovenia, Poland, Hungary, Latvia, Lithuania and the Slovak Republic in December 2002, and with Bulgaria and Romania in December 2004. There are no transitional arrangements in this area. Legislative alignment, leaving aside the possibility of Potemkin-like harmonization, has been realized.

Harmonization of national media laws in central and eastern Europe took place at almost the same time as the original shaping of those national media laws. Between 1991 and 1996, following the transformation of their political, economic and societal systems, all central and eastern European countries passed new media laws, putting an end to the state monopolization of press, radio, television and film industries, and initiating the moulding of an indigenous media system. As Harcourt (2003b) observed, all these laws reflect hybridization and adaptive borrowing from different western (American, French, German...) models. Complete alignment with EU law, however, caused 'a second wave' of media legislation in central and eastern Europe, following 'the first wave' in the first half of the 1990s. From 1998 onward, but mainly in the years 2000–2002, all the relevant national laws in central and eastern Europe became the subject of numerous amendments and/or replacements by new laws. The changes and replacements were dictated by the 'need' to adapt the different national legislations to the European Television Without Frontiers directive (for a more detailed overview, see de Smaele, 2004).

Europeanization as 'cultural diffusion'

While Europeanization as a process of institutional adaptation is clearly real, Europeanization as 'transnational cultural diffusion' – that is 'the diffusion of cultural norms, ideas, identities, and patterns of behaviour on a cross-national basis within Europe' (Featherstone 2003: 7) – is less evident. Television programmes and films, however, are considered a potential vehicle to spread norms, ideas and identities; and the European Union clearly has the ambition to foster a 'sense of Europeanness' and a 'European identity' as well as an awareness and appreciation of Europe's national cultures via the Europe-wide distribution of audio-visual products (de Smaele 2004: 166–167). However, despite a decade of policy measures to enhance the European cross-national distribution of audio-visual products (for example, the European quota, and financial support for European co-productions), little has changed in this respect. European productions remain nationally produced and nationally distributed. The inflow of U.S. films and TV series has not been diminished, whereas the internal European circulation of television drama remains stagnant (De Bens and de Smaele 2001). European habits of film consumption reveal that audiences watch either domestic productions or American ones, but not those of other European countries (IMCA 2004: 30). A pan-European audio-visual culture has not come into existence. Attempts to make films that reflect a cross-cultural European content (as some Euro-funded initiatives have tried to) remain artificial and end up as weak *Europuddings* (Iordanova 1999), failing in cross-national distribution as they lack even a home market.

Schlesinger (1993: 11) refers to the 'continuing importance of the national level and the resistance it offers to *Europeanization*' [emphasis as original]. The conflict between national and European identities and interests, felt in the old Member States, is a *fortiori* present in the new central and eastern European Member States. The concepts of a European market, European identity, and European culture are difficult ideas for countries that only recently regained national markets, national identities and national culture. The asymmetry, felt by central and eastern European countries, between the old EU and the new EU fuels the idea that the term 'European' mainly refers to 'the interests of others' in contrast to their own national interests. Passages of the Television Without Frontiers directive, implemented in some new Member States only hesitantly or belatedly, invoke the freedom of reception and transmission of television programmes (Article 2) – which primarily benefits such U.S.-controlled and UK-registered channels as CNN, MTV and TNT Cartoon network, channels which were the first to make use of the newly opened eastern European market (Levy 1999: 161) – and the promotion of European works (Articles 4 and 5, the so-called European quota – see de Smaele 2004). 'Europe' is perceived as the outsider and Europeanization, then, inscribes a threat analogous to Americanization.

One market, several markets?
The main characteristic – and at the same time the main weakness – of the European audio-visual market is its fragmentation into numerous small national markets with consequently limited financial means for national productions and low chances of survival for minor producers. Most of the new countries of central and eastern Europe fit this model – with only Poland, and then Hungary and the Czech Republic, as countries with sizeable markets. Productions from small states are often not exportable because they are too culturally specific. In addition, there are extra costs for dubbing or subtitling (for a discussion of the structural handicaps of small countries see Burgelman and Pauwels 1992: 172–173). The European Commission has calculated that 80 per cent of the films made in the 'EU of the fifteen' never leave the country of origin. The same goes for television programmes (De Bens and de Smaele 2001).

Central and eastern European countries also follow this trend. A study by the European Audio-visual Observatory showed that between 1996 and 2001 only 42 films from the countries of central and eastern Europe were distributed commercially in at least one 'old' Member State of the European Union; these films were seen by a total of 2.2 million people in the Union, giving them a market share of 0.054 per cent (European Commission 2003). On western

European television, eastern European films are broadcast only sporadically and outside prime time (De Bens and de Smaele 2001: 61). At the same time, exchange programmes within the region of central and eastern Europe (for example, OIRT) have disappeared, bringing to a halt cross-border circulation within the central and eastern European region (de Smaele 2000). As Iordanova (2002: 33) points out: 'In their drive to get themselves out of the economic ghetto of the Soviet sphere (which they believe also extends over culture), Eastern European countries end up in isolation from each other.'

The dearth of intra-European distribution contrasts with the large market share of U.S. productions, both in cinema and on television. The audio-visual exchange between the European Union and the United States over the last decade shows a trade deficit rising year upon year, mounting to eight billion euros in 2000 – or a deficit of 14.1 per cent (European Audiovisual Observatory 2002: 36–37). U.S. drama production reaches on average 63.4 per cent of audiences of western European television channels (De Bens and de Smaele 2001: 57), and scores even higher on central and eastern European channels (de Smaele 2000: 100). Smaller countries have the greatest difficulties in resisting cheap imports, which are predominantly American.

European co-productions are, at the urging of the European Union, on the increase. European-American co-productions, however, grow even faster (Esser 2006) with European co-productions mainly replacing single-country productions and thus not contributing to an increase in total European production (De Bens and de Smaele 2001: 68). This might be true a *fortiori* for the central and eastern European countries where national film production collapsed in the late 1980s and recovered only slowly throughout the 1990s. Infrastructure, institutions, and funding mechanisms had to be renewed and a new culture of managing the audio-visual sector had to take shape. Participation in the MEDIA Programme, funding by Eurimages (a pan-European funding body which many of the central and eastern European countries joined in the course of the 1990s) and partnership in European co-productions all contributed to the recovery of the eastern European film industries. The new national funding mechanisms of some eastern European countries have even made national subsidies dependent on foreign participation: 'if a production can show it has been granted funding from abroad, it becomes automatically eligible for domestic support' (Iordanova 2002: 518).

Regular cooperation patterns stand out; patterns in which geographical, cultural and linguistic proximities play their parts. France appears as the main partner for Hungary, Romania, and the Czech Republic; Germany is Poland's primary co-production partner; while in the Balkan region one observes a number of regional co-productions involving Greece (Iordanova 1999). Eastern European partners, however, are much more likely to appear as minority producers (Iordanova 2002: 34). Alternatively, they are 'guest countries' for so-called *cross-border productions* – foreign initiatives using (cheaper) local facilities and extras (Steven Spielberg's *Schindler's List*, filmed in Poland, is a classic example).

As this analysis shows, there is a drawback to everything, and every opportunity appears to be a potential threat. In the worst-case scenario eastern European countries end up as minority partners, suppliers of cheap facilities and additional markets for large European players, while their own national production stagnates, is replaced by co-productions, or, at the very least, is not distributed outside their national borders. European support mechanisms such as Eurimages seem to favour the distribution of western European productions (in particular French cinema) to eastern Europe, rather than the reverse (Iordanova 2002: 31–33); while the MEDIA II (1996–2000) and MEDIA Plus (2001–2006) programmes have been found to be most effective in countries with high production capacities, notably France and the United Kingdom (Commission of the European Communities 2004). However, the current MEDIA 2007 (2007–2013) programme has ambitions to correct this situation. If these are realized, the new programme will be more advantageous to central and eastern European countries.

Conclusion

Despite many differences, eastern and western European audio-visual landscapes have a lot in common and are growing closer. In the 1980s Western European countries exchanged the monopolies of public service broadcasters for dual systems comprising both public service television and commercial television. In the 1990s eastern European countries shifted from Communism to post-Communist systems, and from monopolism in broadcasting to dual systems comprising both state (public service) and private television. In January 1993 the western European Broadcasting Union and its eastern counterpart, the International Radio and Television Organization, merged. The audio-visual industry is characterized in most European countries – both West and East – by the proliferation of independent production and distribution companies, while at the same time governments maintain an important regulatory and supportive (financing) role. Both East and West experience similar problems as well as similar solutions. Indeed, 'similarities' and 'commonalities' might be better words to use in the context of the enlarged audio-visual Europe than 'homogenization' or 'Europeanization'.

References

Bideleux, R. (1996), 'Bringing the East back in', in Bideleux, R., and Taylor, R. (eds.), *European Integration and Disintegration. East and West*, London: Routledge, pp. 225–251.

Burgelman, J.-C., and Pauwels, C. (1992), 'Audiovisual Policy and Cultural Identity in Small European States: the Challenge of a Unified Market', in *Media, Culture and Society* 14:2, pp. 169–183.

Commission of the European Communities (2004), *Proposal for a Decision of the European Parliament and the Council. Concerning the implementation of a programme of support for the European audiovisual sector (MEDIA 2007)*, 14 July 2004. Available at: http://europa.eu.int/comm/avpolicy/media/pdffiles/com470_en.pdf Date accessed: 19/8/08.

De Bens, E., and de Smaele, H. (2001), 'The Inflow of American Television Fiction on European Broadcasting Channels Revisited', in *European Journal of Communication* 16:1, pp. 51–76.

de Smaele, H. (2000), 'Oost- en West-Europa: naar een eengemaakt audiovisueel beleid?', in Bilteryst, D., and de Smaele, H. (eds.), *Transformatie en continuïteit van de Europese televisie*, Ghent: Academia Press, pp. 79–107.

de Smaele, H. (2004), 'Audiovisual Policy in the Enlarged European Union', in *Trends in Communication* 12:4, pp. 163–180.

Dimitrova, A. L., and Steunenberg, B. (2004), 'Conclusions: the 'end of history' of enlargement or the beginning of a new research agenda?', in Dimitrova, A.L. (ed.), *Driven to change. The European Union's enlargement viewed from the east*, Manchester: Manchester University Press, pp. 179–193.

Esser, A. (2006), *Audio-Visual Content in Europe: Transnationalisation and approximation*, paper presented at 'Media in the Enlarged Europe', University of Bedfordshire, 5–6 May 2006.

European Audiovisual Observatory (2002), *Yearbook 2002. Film, television, video and multimedia in Europe*, Vol. 1, 5, Strasbourg: European Audiovisual Observatory.

European Commission/Commissie van de Europese Gemeenschappen (1992), 'Europa en de uitdaging van de uitbreiding', *Bulletin van de Europese Gemeenschappen. Supplement 3/1992*, Luxemburg: Bureau voor officiële publicaties van de Europese Gemeenschappen.

European Commission (2003), *Enlargement soon to be a reality. 9 candidate countries admitted to MEDIA programme*. Available at: http://europa.eu.int/comm/avpolicy/media/enlarg_en.html Date accessed: 19/5/04.

European Parliament (1993), *European Council in Copenhagen, 21–22 June 1993. Conclusions of the Presidency*. Available at: www.europarl.eu.int/summits/copenhagen/co_en.pdf Date accessed: 13/5/06.

European Parliament (1995), *Madrid European Council, 15–16 December 1995. Presidency conclusions*. Available at: www.europarl.eu.int/summits/mad1_en.htm Date accessed: 13/5/06.

Featherstone, K. (2003), 'Introduction: In the Name of "Europe"', in Featherstone, K., and Radaelli, C.M., (eds.) *The Politics of Europeanization*, Oxford: Oxford University Press, pp. 3–26.

Grabbe, H. (2003), 'Europeanization Goes East: Power and Uncertainty in the EU Accession Process', in Featherstone, K., and Radaelli, C.M. (eds.), *The Politics of Europeanization*, Oxford: Oxford University Press, pp. 303–327.

Grabbe, H., and Hughes, K. (1998), *Enlarging the E.U. Eastwards*, London: Pinter.

Harcourt, A. (2003a), 'Europeanization as Convergence: The Regulation of Media Markets in the European Union', in Featherstone, K., and Radaelli, C.M. (eds.), *The Politics of Europeanization*, Oxford: Oxford University Press, pp. 179–202.

Harcourt, A. (2003b), 'The Regulation of Media Markets in selected EU Accession States in Central and Eastern Europe', in *European Law Journal* 9, pp. 316–340.

Huntington, S. (1997), *Botsende beschavingen. Cultuur en conflict in de 21ste eeuw.* (original *The clash of civilizations and the remaking of world order*), Antwerp: Standaard Uitgeverij.

IMCA [International Media Consultants Associés] (2004), *Etude du paysage audiovisuel et des politiques publiques des pays candidats dans le secteur audiovisuel. Rapport transversal*, Pour la Commission européenne – DG EAC/59/02. Available at: europa.eu.int/comm/avpolicy/stat/2002/5886_imca/59-02-finalreport.pdf Date accessed: 19/5/04.

Iordanova, D. (1999), 'East Europe's cinema industries since 1989', in *Media Development* 3. Available at: www.wacc.org.uk/publications/md/md1999-3/iordanova.htm Date accessed: 14/11/02.

Iordanova, D. (2002), 'Feature filmmaking within the new Europe: moving funds and images across the East-West divide', in *Media, Culture and Society* 24:4, pp. 517–536.

Kevin, D. (2003), *Europe in the Media. A Comparison of Reporting, Representation, and Rhetoric in National Media Systems in Europe*, London: Lawrence Erlbaum Associates.

Kuneva, M. (2001), 'The Acquis Is Not Enough', Speech at the Federal Trust's Conference on European Union Enlargement: Linking Civil Society, the Citizen, and the State, 21–24 November, Berlin, *Transitions Online*, 12 December 2001.

Levy, D. A. (1999), *Europe's Digital Revolution. Broadcasting regulation, the EU and the nation state*, London: Routledge.

Maniokas, K. (2004), 'The method of the European Union's enlargement to the east: a critical appraisal', in Dimitrova, A.L. (ed.), *Driven to change. The European Union's enlargement viewed from the east*, Manchester: Manchester University Press, pp. 17–37.

Schlesinger, P. (1993), 'Wishful Thinking: Cultural Politics, Media, and Collective Identities in Europe', in *Journal of Communication* 43:2, pp. 6–17.

Wade, J. (1999), 'Priest and Penitent: the European Union as a Force in the Domestic Politics of Eastern Europe', in *East European Constitutional Review* 8, pp. 62–67.

Trends in Television Programming: Commercialization, Transnationalization, Convergence

Andrea Esser

The 1980s heralded a new phase in western European broadcasting. Technological developments and a shift in ideology towards neo-liberal policies brought about a restructuring of television architecture: the public service monopoly was replaced with a public-service/private-commercial duopoly, and television's traditional role of serving the nation was supplemented by the profit objective. Competition increased continuously. Programming, too, was affected.

Above all, America's influence on programming increased. The United States has exported programmes globally since the 1930s and European broadcasters have long glanced across the Atlantic for inspiration, but the years after the mid-1980s saw U.S. influence grow exponentially (Woldt 1993; B](r)ereyst 2001). Limited financial resources forced new commercial channels to fill their schedules with cheap acquisitions in the start-up period. Moreover, the near non-existence of an independent production sector meant that in the early phase of European market commercialization, the heightened need for programming could not be met domestically. The huge U.S. market was not only able to support large volumes of high-cost audio-visual fiction, but, being commercially advanced, it also had long-running series. The latter provided the new broadcasters with an inexpensive means by which to fill large amounts of transmission time. In addition, it was an effective new strategy for securing audiences.

It was not just a reliance on U.S. fiction imports which increased (De Bens et al. 1992; OBS 1997). U.S. production values and styles, such as the personalization of news, were also copied. In TV fiction, according to Alessandro Silj et al. (1988), elements of American serials, such as basic dramatic situations and stylistic devices, came to be absorbed (Frey-Vor 1990: 495). Moreover, stripped scheduling and the lead-in scheme were imported from the commercially experienced U.S. market.

Politicians (for example, Barzanti 1990) and academics (for example, Hamelink 1993) across Europe were anxious that the continent's bastions of national culture would be Americanized and an essential outlet of national identity would be lost. By the mid-1990s this fear had subsided. Academics joined industry executives in pointing out the popularity of local programmes with audiences and the increase in the production and scheduling of domestic content. The localization strategies of such international broadcasters as MTV were highlighted and so were the 'failures' of early pan-European channels. It was concluded that cultural differences were too great to allow transnational, pan-European television to succeed; television was to remain a national matter (see Collins 1992; Hasebrink 1995; Straßer 1995).

However, we may conversely suggest that, with rising competition, markets moved towards increasing commercialization and transnationalization. I have argued in earlier work (Esser 2002) that transnationalization became a defining feature of the development of European television from the mid-1980s onwards, in relation to ownership, channel offerings, consumption and programming. This chapter aims to reinforce these findings with reference to recent developments in programming, highlighting some of the empirical evidence which shows that the amount of content shared transnationally is growing, not declining. As a result, television output has become increasingly similar across borders. This approximation of content takes place not only through the quantity of shared content, but also through transnational programme hits and genre fashions, and through converging production patterns and scheduling practices. An economic analysis reveals that commercialization, and accompanying trends towards transnationalization and convergence, are unlikely to be reversed.

After briefly addressing some terminological and theoretical concerns, this chapter will focus on the particularly significant development of entertainment programming. It has been observed that with television's increasing commercialization and with, as a consequence thereof, the growing competition for audiences, the space that entertainment programmes occupy in television schedules has gradually risen (Biltereyst 2001). The entertainment category moreover is important because, since the mid-1990s, format-based entertainment has come to define television across Europe, especially during prime time. We will first look at the trend for formatted light entertainment, then turn to the vexed issue of the relationship between American and domestic TV fiction, and will conclude with the question as to whether the content convergence of television in Europe also has an element of 'Europeanization'.

Terminological and theoretical foundations

The 'transnational' terminology used in the following pages reflects the complexity of the field and requires some clarification. In light of EU broadcasting policy it is only natural to have an interest in the question of 'Europeanization'. The term's conceptualization, however, is problematic. Firstly, for geographical reasons: should we define Europe along EU borders or those marked out by the Council of Europe? Both have relevance for the development of European television. This paper focuses on the European Union, broadly distinguishing between western European countries and central and eastern European countries, whose development in television now follows that of western Europe but with a time lag and different premises. Secondly, what is meant by 'Europeanization'? Following Kevin Featherstone's (2003: 7) classification of the term's four major academic uses, it may be pointed out that this chapter's interest is specifically in 'transnational cultural diffusion'.

Moreover, whilst of great interest, 'Europeanization' is insufficient to describe the development of audio-visual content within the European Union. As the following pages will show, most programme trends surpass Europe's borders; they seem international, or global, rather than European. Overall, the term 'transnationalization' seems preferable. Broadcasting processes, like those in many other sectors, do not proceed in uniform or evenly distributed patterns. They are complex and irregular entities. For example, different countries in Europe have different production, import and export patterns, depending on their size, wealth and language constitution; and American companies have by far the most impact in the audio-visual distribution sector globally. The term transnationalization disguises these uneven patterns to a lesser extent than 'globalization' or 'internationalization'.

Roland Robertson's theory of globality, defined through processes of *glocalization*, is useful for understanding the complex global-local nexus defining today's television markets, and cultural spheres more generally. According to Robertson (1994), both the original theorization of the globalization process as universalizing and homogenizing and the responses to it, which foreground localization and particularization, have caused a theoretical constriction which detracts from a more intricate reality. Particularization, Robertson points out, developed not *against* but *as part* of internationalizing processes. In other words, globalization involves the 'invention' of locality; it institutionalizes the expectation and construction of local particularism. This is also true for the transnational media: 'An "international" TV enterprise like CNN produces and reproduces a particular pattern of relations between localities, a pattern which depends on a kind of recipe of locality. This standardization renders meaningful the very *idea* of locality, but at the same time diminishes the notion that localities are "things in themselves"' (Robertson 1994: 38).

Hence, we should carefully question the widely held assumption that commerce drives transnationalization and culture sets limits to this by requesting transnational business to cater for essential local sensibilities (see Robins 1997; Straubhaar 1991). Moreover, we must refrain from seeing transnationalization and localization as binary opposites. As the next section will show, the two go hand in hand.

Commercialization, transnationalization, convergence: light entertainment formats
Transnational programme trends are identified in market reports (for example, IP's *Key Facts*, *Screen Digest*) and trade journals (for example, *Broadcast*, *Television Business International*), particularly in the coverage of international programme markets. For example, the IP's *Key Facts* yearbook reported that reality, event and factual television 'continued to thrive' around the world in 2004 (IP Groupe 2005: 35).

Even central and eastern European countries, whose television markets are only just developing commercially, are already displaying the same transnational trends. Thus it was reported that: in the Czech Republic (even though 'original Czech series at prime time were the main weapon') 'the reality show phenomenon finally hit the republic' (IP Groupe 2005: 117); Hungarian television was 'dominated by reality formats' (IP Groupe 2005: 189); Latvia was 'hit by the reality show boom' (IP Groupe 2005: 231); Lithuanian commercial channels were 'filled with light entertainment programmes, such as reality shows, talk shows, soap operas and serials – of both international (mainly North and South American) and local formats' (IP Groupe 2005: 239); and in Slovakia 'in line with European developments, it was reality shows and docu-soaps, which attracted the population most' (IP Groupe 2005: 329).

The light entertainment boom consists of formats developed in one market and then sold internationally, usually for local adaptation. It started in the early 1990s, when talk shows and game shows proved popular with viewers. In the late 1990s this success was followed by formats for reality shows, and in the new millennium by hybrids, such as *Faking It, Wife Swap* or *Changing Rooms* – variations on the traditional genres of observational documentary, game shows and soap drama. A kind of indirect programme import, formats have not only come to constitute a major share of the overall programme offerings of many general interest channels but they also determine prime time schedules and even national Top 10/20 programme rating lists, as the following table shows:

Table 1. Top-rated formats in a selection of European countries, 2004.

Belgium (North)	Slovakia
A Farmer Wants a Wife	*(Pop) Idol*
(Pop) Idol	*Girl in a Million*
Wife Swap	*Who Wants to Be a Millionaire?*
Under Construction	*Wife Swap*
France	**Hungary**
That'll Teach Them	*Who Wants to Be a Millionaire?*
(Pop) Idol	*Megastar (Pop Idol)*
The Bachelor	*The BachelorWife Swap*
UK	**Germany**
I'm a Celebrity Get Me Out of Here	*Who Wants to Be a Millionaire?*
Strictly Come Dancing	*I'm a Celebrity Get Me Out of Here*
Big Brother	*Popstars (rival format to Idol)*
Wife Swap	*The Swan*
You Are What You Eat	
Brat Camp	

Source: Collated by the author from countries' Top10/20 programme lists, IP, *Television Key Facts*, 2005.

The above not only demonstrates top audience ratings for these shows but also reveals that they work exceptionally well in several countries. To give the full picture of their transnational pulling power: by 2006, one of the most successful formats to date, *Who Wants to Be a Millionaire?* (created by British producer Celador in 1998), had been sold to 105 countries, 67 of which had produced local adaptations. In Europe it has ranked among the most popular programmes in Sweden, Holland, Germany, Britain, France, Italy, Hungary, Estonia, Slovakia and Slovenia (Celador 2006; IP 2005).

According to trade publisher *Screen Digest* (2005: 100) the number of formatted shows broadcast between 2002 and 2004 rose by over a third; and this trend shows no sign of letting up. Even formats for comedy shows are now crossing borders. Germany's prime time improvisation comedy *Schillerstrasse*, launched in autumn 2004, had sold to sixteen territories on four continents by 2006. In Europe it had been bought by broadcasters in Belgium, the Czech Republic, Denmark, Finland, France, Italy, the Netherlands, Romania, Spain and the United Kingdom.

Broadcasters appreciate formats not just because they are popular with audiences but because they make economic sense. They offer a proven track record of success in other countries, enable the creation of popular 'domestic' programmes, fuel local production and contribute to domestic production quotas, provide high volume titles, can be produced relatively cheaply, have been proven to work in the long term, and are successful in providing high revenues from spin-offs and merchandising.

It is also interesting to note that differences between local adaptations seem to be diminishing. According to media journalist Peter Keighron there is now greater standardization and less local deviation. Format fees based on a percentage of the production budget (5–15 per cent per episode) and limited consultancy, he reports, are no longer the lynchpin of the business. Today, the value of a reality or other prime time entertainment format lies in selling production expertise, including casting, filming and editing skills (Iosifidis et al. 2005: 153).

Audio-visual content based on formats has become a pre-eminent part of European television. It contributes to the convergence of television imagery and hence of the TV experience (if not necessarily its reception) transnationally.

Fiction programming: localization or transnationalization and convergence?
Undoubtedly there are still notable national differences when it comes to television production and scheduling. In audio-visual fiction there are variations in relation to the types of prime time fiction different European countries invest in (Jezequel and Lange 2000) and the origins of imports (OBS 1997–2005). Despite these traditional distinctions, though, shared trends seem to be the way forward. The European Audio-visual Observatory (OBS) attests to an 'erosion of national differences' in fiction programming, reporting that convergence takes place in relation to production and scheduling, production capacities, serial formulae, standard episode length, genre breakdown, and patterns of exploitation of domestic and foreign products (2001a).

For example, OBS statistics show that the period 1996–1999 saw a marked rise in fiction production in western Europe's five biggest television markets – Germany, Great Britain, France, Italy and Spain. The reasons suggested by the OBS for this upward trend were shared by each country: most commercial broadcasters were now well established and had bigger programme budgets; competition within markets was strong and necessitated investment in local productions; and prices for American fare had risen and made acquisitions from the United States less attractive.

From 2000 onwards conditions for fiction production worsened in all these countries. Given the significant decrease in advertising revenues in 2001 and 2002 and their no-more-than-modest growth since 2003 (OBS 2005: 31; IP Groupe 2006: 42), we must assume that much cheaper (but popular) light entertainment formats provided an economically sensible alternative. It is also the case that in all five countries TV movies were much more badly affected than series. The latter remain popular with broadcasters as they create loyalty, fill schedules, are suitable for prime time and daytime scheduling, and deliver high audience ratings.

We shall now shift our focus from the convergence of programme production and scheduling to the rise in domestic production in the mid-1990s and the simplistic conclusion academics and industry executives drew from this: a trend of localization. If we look at the origins of TV fiction in European schedules, statistical data clearly reveals that in contrast to the 1980s, the 1990s showed a surge in the production and scheduling of domestic programmes on commercial television channels. This was especially true in terms of prime time scheduling, which became increasingly domestic, whilst U.S. content was mainly pushed into off-prime time schedules.

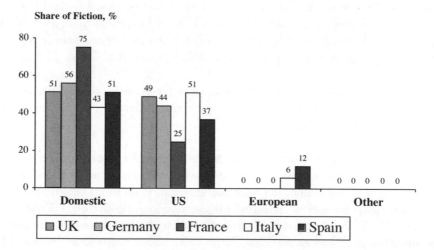

Graph 1. Geographical origin of TV fiction during prime time in Europe's five largest television markets. *Source:* The graph is based on *Eurofiction* data, which measured TV fiction programmed by major networks in the sample week 12–18 March 2000; OBS 2001b.

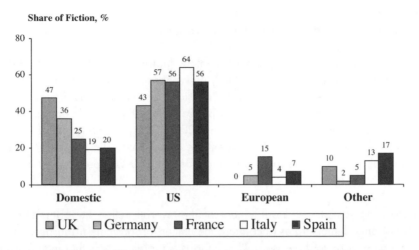

Graph 2. Geographical origin of TV fiction throughout the day in Europe's five largest television markets. Source: The graph is based on *Eurofiction* data, which measured TV fiction programmed by major networks in the sample week 12–18 March 2000; OBS, 2001b.

However, confining themselves to the cultural argument of 'audience taste', few pointed out that prices for U.S. fare had risen (for example, Meckel 1994: 105). Moreover, later OBS statistics show that what was strongly believed to be a linear trend had ceased. In 2000, in three of Europe's major television markets, the United Kingdom, Germany and Italy, U.S. imports were on the increase again. In Germany and the United Kingdom, American content achieved significant leaps that year, from 30 to 44 per cent and from 38 to 49 per cent of all prime time fiction respectively (OBS 2001b).

Graph 1 demonstrates that, with the exception of France and Spain, even during prime time domestic fiction did not feature much more prominently than U.S. fiction. In Italy it was even lower in this sample week.

Figures for the whole day reveal the undisputed dominance of U.S. programmes. Particularly interesting here is France, with the relation between U.S. and domestic fiction being nearly reversed.

The years since have proven that programme developments are much more complex than interpretations in the 1990s admitted. Most notably, they have firmly established that there is no simple linear development of a declining reliance on U.S. fiction.

Europeanization, Americanization, globalization?
Nothing so far suggests a 'Europeanization' of television markets. Whilst such a process is clearly manifested in EU regulation and policy – above all in the Television Without Frontiers directive's 'minimum rules' – one feels obliged to question the development of an inter-European

programme trade – in so far as the TWF directive asks broadcasters under its jurisdiction to reserve a 'majority proportion' of their total transmission time for European works.

A few broadcasters ignore the quota completely (notably BSkyB in the United Kingdom and all cable and satellite channels in Italy); new channels have to adhere to the rule only 'progressively' and 'where practicable' (1997 revision); and the majority of broadcasters across Europe who comply (i.e. schedule at least 51 per cent of content with European origin) achieve this with overwhelmingly domestic productions (CEC 2006). As the graphs on scheduled TV fiction above have demonstrated, the percentage of non-domestic European programmes is minimal. A notable exception is to be found in those smaller European countries which share a language with a larger neighbour.

A diachronic analysis of the development of the overall fiction import pattern in Europe (Graph 3) not only demonstrates once more the limited programme trade between European countries in comparison to their use of U.S. imports – it also reveals that inter-European trade has seen no growth.

This graph shows that the overall quantity of imports and co-productions has grown – something to be expected at times of rising demand. This is also the case for hours imported from within Europe, which have risen from 30,206 in 1996 to 36,092 in 2004. In terms of the overall share of imported and co-produced audio-visual fiction, however, this means a decrease from 11.5 per cent in 1996 to 10.6 per cent in 2004. The nominal decline of U.S. imports in 2001,

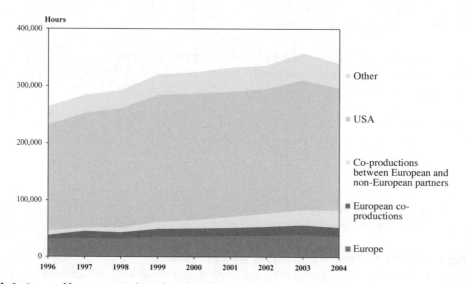

Graph 3. Origin of fiction imports broadcast by TV channels in western Europe, 1996–2004. *Source:* Based on ETS/OBS data, OBS Statistical Yearbooks 2002 + 2005.

2002 and 2004, on the other hand, has been balanced by the high increase in U.S.-European co-productions, which constitute the vast majority of co-productions in the European/non-European co-production category.

Table 2. Origin of Top 10 series in Europe, 2004.

Country	Domestic	Foreign
Old EU countries		
Austria	1	
	2 co-prod with DE	7 DE
Belgium (North)	9	1 NL
Belgium (South)	–	6 FR 3 US 1 GB
Denmark	4	3 US 3 GB
Finland	8	2 US
France	10	–
Germany	10	–
Greece	10	–
Ireland	4	3 GB 3 US
Italy	9	1 US
Netherlands	7	1 BE 1GB 1 US/CA
Portugal	8	1 US 1 DE/AT
Spain	8	2 US
Sweden	4	4 GB 1 DK 1 US
Great Britain	10	–
New Entrants		
Czech Republic	8	1 DE 1 FR
Estonia	4	2 US 2 GB 1 DE 1MX
Hungary	2	6 US 1 GB 1 CZ
Latvia	–	7 RU
		1 MX 1 DE/AT 1 VE/US
Lithuania	1	3 DE 2 RU 2 MX
	(co-prod with RUS)	1 US 1 VE/US
Poland	9	1 GB
Slovenia	5	1 FR 1 DE/AT 1 US
		1 MX 1 VE

Source: Collated by the author, based on information provided in IP, Television Key Facts, 2005.

It is interesting to note, though, that the central and eastern European television markets seem to have much more diverse import patterns than their western neighbours. If we look at the geographical origins of the Top 10 series in EU countries, we can see that, whilst most old EU members only import from neighbours with whom they share a language, from the U.S. and maybe from Britain, the picture is much more varied in the new Member States.

Conclusion

This chapter has tried to challenge prevailing notions of television having remained a national matter, arguing that for all the popularity of local content, persisting national differences and the unaltered weakness of inter-European programme trade, sufficient empirical evidence exists to suggest audio-visual content overall continues upon its trajectory of transnationalization, and that, as a result, television across Europe is undergoing a process of convergence.

Format-based programming also demonstrates that local adaptations do not develop in opposition to internationalization processes, but are in fact part of those processes. Transnationalization and localization should not be viewed as opposite poles but as two trends progressing hand in hand within the single process of 'glocalization'. It might be argued that audiences usually register format-based programmes as home-grown, and are unaware they are shared internationally; and many are inclined to agree with Albert Moran (1998) that local adaptations express the strength of local identities rather than television's trend towards transnationalization. But it cannot be denied that these shared formats imply convergence. If they were to be classified as 'international programming' the amount of 'national' programming would decrease substantially.

With reference to the question of a Europeanization of audio-visual content, we can conclude that both the format trend and programme import patterns hint at 'international transnationalization' rather than Europeanization; and this means different things for different genres. We can still speak (more or less) of Americanization when we look at the trade in fiction. When we look at format-based light entertainment, however, the trade is much more balanced. The United Kingdom, the Netherlands and Scandinavian countries have all proven very successful in selling formats globally (*Screen Digest* 2005: 100.).

Great attention has been paid to economic factors because both transnationalization and convergence are trends resulting from European television's growing commercialization and commercial maturation. Commercial pressures will not ease off but are likely to increase in the foreseeable future. Most of Europe's markets are already defined by fierce competition and increasing fragmentation. In this environment, broadcasters are looking for 'must-see television', for popular brands that deliver large audiences season after season. Internationally proven, long-running programmes not only offer something of a ratings guarantee but also have the necessary marketing clout.

Market fragmentation also brings increasing pressure to programme budgets (Price 2002: 321). As programmes, more than ever, need to be of high production quality in order to be competitive, content must be financed through an extended customer base – achieved through geographically expanded programme distribution and maximum exploitation across the spectrum of distribution platforms.

The growing trend to finance audio-visual content through the international market is clearly visible. The first attempts, accelerating in the early 1990s, were co-productions (Esser 2002: 13–29); more recently, this trend has been given a new impetus by a change in strategy from selling finished programmes to pre-sales (Steemers 2004; Colwell and Price 2005). The move from Europe's traditional 'cost plus' production model (where the broadcaster finances the whole programme and retains all secondary rights) towards the American 'deficit financing' model (where broadcasters pay a substantial fee for the first transmission rights and the producer finances the deficit by selling secondary rights) forces producers and distributors to sign up numerous clients before starting production. This not only concerns much drama production; high-cost documentaries and children's animation are also financed transnationally.

Furthermore, a continuation of the transnationalization of audio-visual content can be expected as a result of the changing structure of channel-scapes. Television markets are increasingly coming to be determined by international broadcast networks such as HBO or Disney (Chalaby 2005; Esser 2002). Although these broadcasters have over the last decade come to adapt their schedules to local viewing habits and to invest in local productions, there remains a strong incentive (profit) for them to exploit existing programme libraries in as many markets as possible. The same is true for transnational broadcasters such as the RTL Group or Scandinavian Broadcasting Systems, which own a myriad of channels across Europe.

There are two final reasons for the continued transnationalization and convergence of television content. Firstly, the implementation of stripped scheduling across Europe has led to a standardization of programme length and serialization. The original problem of fitting imports into local schedules has largely vanished. Secondly, the increasing commonality of programmes, production values and styles has led viewer expectations across Europe to converge. As a result it should become easier to sell content transnationally – to buyers and audiences alike.

In today's television the 'cultural' aspect of content, in both the senses of 'local origin' and of 'citizenship', is of decreasing significance. Much more important in deciding what gets produced and scheduled is a programme's ability to be popular and commercially successful. In this respect we should also rethink the concept of 'Americanization'. As German scholar Peter Ludes pointed out in 1989, instead of viewing Americanization as a nation-specific influence, we would do better to understand it as a form of general commercialization – something that just happens to come from the United States, the world's biggest, toughest and most experienced television market (1989: 43). A careful look at audience ratings suggests that television viewers might have long understood this.

References

Barzanti, R. (1990), 'Audiovisual Opportunities in the Single Market', *MEDIA 92* (Newsletter of the MEDIA 92 Programme) 9, p. 1.

Bil!tereyst, D. (2001), 'Reappraising European Politics to Protect Local Television Content against US Imports', in D'Haenes, L., and Saeys, F. (eds.), *Western Broadcasting at the Dawn of the 21*[st] *Century*, New York: Mouton de Gruyter, pp. 83–108.

Celador (2005), 'International facts and figures on *Who wants to be a millionaire?* Format'. Available at: http://www.celador.co.uk/factsheets/international_factsheet_august_2005_copy1.doc Date accessed: 20/4/07.

Chalaby, J. (2005), 'The Quiet Invention of a New Medium: Twenty Years of Transnational Television in Europe', in Chalaby, J. (ed.), *Transnational Television Worldwide: Towards a New Media Order*, London: IB Tauris, pp. 1–13.

Collins, R. (1992), 'Pan-European Channels Launch Into Phase Two. Learning From Past Experience', in *TBI*, October 1992, pp. 68–70.

Colwell, T., and Price, D. (2005), *Rights of passage. British television in the global market*, Report commissioned by the British Television Distributors' Association and UK Trade and Investment, London.

De Bens, E., Kelly, M., and Bakke, M. (1992), 'Television Content: Dallasification of Culture?', in Siune, K. and Truetzschler, W. (eds.), *Dynamics of Media Politics*, London: Sage, pp. 75–100.

Esser, A. (2002), 'The transnationalization of European Television', in *Journal of European Area Studies*, 10:1, pp. 13–29.

Featherstone, K. (2003), 'Introduction: In the name of 'Europe', in Featherstone, K. and Radaelli, C. (eds.), *The Politics of Europeanization*, Oxford: Oxford University Press, pp. 3–26.

Frey-Vor, G. (1990), 'Charakteristika von Soap Operas und Telenovelas im internationalen Vergleich', in *Media Perspektiven* 8, pp. 488–496.

Hamelink, C. J. (1993), 'Europe and the democratic deficit', in *Media Development* XL, p. 4.

Hasebrink, U. (1995), 'Trennende Gemeinsamkeiten. Europäische Öffentlichkeit scheitert an nationalen Medienmentalitäten', in *Agenda* 21, pp. 16–18.

Iosifidis, P., Steemers, J., and Wheeler, M. (2005), *European Television Industries*, London: BFI.

IP Groupe (2005), *Television 2005. International Key Facts*, Neuilly.

IP Groupe (2006), *Television 2006. International Key Facts*, Neuilly.

Jezequel, J-P., and Lange, A. (2000), *Economy of European TV Fiction*, Strasbourg: OBS.

Ludes, P. (1989), 'Amerikanisierung, Kommerzialisierung, oder Modernisierug der Fernsehmedien in der Bundesrepublik Deutschland', in Gellner, W. (ed.), *Europäisches Fernsehen – American-Blend? Fernsehmedien zwischen Amerikanisierung und Europäisierung*, Berlin: Vistas, pp. 37–52.

Meckel, M. (1994), *Fernsehen ohne Grenzen? Europas Fernsehen zwischen Integration und Segmentierung*, Opladen: Westdeutscher Verlag.

Moran, A. (1998), *Copycat TV: globalization, program formats and cultural identity*, Luton: University of Luton Press.

OBS (1997), *Statistical Yearbook '98*, Strasbourg: OBS.

OBS (2001a), 'European TV Fiction Production in Decline', press release, Cannes, 9 October. Available at: http://www.obs.coe.int/about/oea/pr/pr_eurofiction.html Date accessed: 20/4/07.

OBS (2001b), 'TV Fiction Programming: Prime Time is Domestic, Off-Prime Time is American', press release, Cannes, 9 October. Available at: http://www.obs.coe.int/about/oea/pr/pr_eurofiction_bis. html Date accessed: 20/4/07.

OBS (2002), *Eurofiction 2002*, vol. 5, Strasbourg: OBS.

OBS (2005), 'Eurofiction 2005: Total production of fiction in the 5 largest countries is on the up', press release, Strasbourg, 11 October. Available at: http://www.obs.coe.int/about/oea/pr/eurofiction2005. html Date accessed: 20/4/07.

Robertson, R. (1994), 'Globalization or Glocalization?', in *Journal of International Communication* 1:1, pp. 33–52.

Robins, K. (1997), 'What in the world's going on?', in du Gay, P. (ed.), *Production of Culture. Cultures of Production*, London: Sage, pp. 12–32.

Screen Digest (2005), 'World trade in television formats', newsletter, April 2005, pp. 100–101.

Steemers, J. (2004), *Selling television. British television in the global marketplace*, London: BFI.

Straßer, R. (1995), 'In enger Nähe so fern', in *Filmwoche/Filmecho* 27, pp. 22–40.

Straubhaar, J. (1991), 'Beyond media imperialism: asymmetrical interdependence and cultural proximity', in *Critical Studies in Mass Communication* 8:1, pp. 39–59.

Woldt, R. (1993), 'Internationalisierung des europäischen Programmarkts – Chance oder Bürde?', in Pragnell, A. (ed.), *Europas Medien im Wandel*, Manchester: EIM, pp. 119–133.

Pluralist over Profitable: The Audio-visual Transformation Dilemma in Central and Eastern Europe

Gabriela E. Chira

The transformation of the media in Central and Eastern European Countries (CEECs) has primarily been influenced by complex liberal conditions imposed by the two main European organizations which these countries sought to join after the fall of their authoritarian regimes: the Council of Europe and the European Union. Both imposed clear membership criteria with regard to freedom of expression and the creation of a functioning market economy by the time of accession, including media able to compete in the EU market.

The acceding CEECs clearly needed to fulfil these requirements in preparation for EU membership. This went hand in hand with their 'eagerness [...] to "fit into" the western world' (Sarikakis 2005: 167), an objective promoted by the CEECs' elites even before the end of their authoritarian regimes. In concrete terms, by the dates of their entries into the European Union, these countries needed to comply provisionally with the EU *acquis* (or the *aquis communautaire*) which meant adopting the body of EU law. With regard to the audio-visual sector, this meant adopting the audio-visual *acquis* (or, in EU terminology, fulfilling the Culture and Audiovisual Chapter).

But has this provisional compliance with the EU *acquis* brought about broadcasting pluralism in the acceding CEECs and the enlarged EU of 27 Member States? Such pluralism would secure the production and distribution of high-quality, independently produced television programmes, involving a diversity of points of view which can sustain the empowerment of citizens to participate in informed and rational debates (in Habermasian terms) within society.

In the period under analysis, 1990–2006, the broadcasting sector displayed signs of great dynamism in the region: broadcasting was the most rapidly changing media sector and the most sought after for multinational buyers, as well as for local economic players. State-owned televisions stations embarked upon a soul-searching and profit-hunting period which concluded with an overall reaffirmation of their power at the end of the 1990s. As Peter Gross puts it: 'privatization of the media has resulted in serious competition for state- or government-controlled "public service" broadcasting and in increasingly heated debate over what constitutes "public service", in a rush on the part of governments and political parties to influence and manipulate, if not control, private commercial broadcasting [...] content.' (Gross 2002: 66) In general, western models were privileged. The television sector in general was identified as the chief opinion-former among the media in central and eastern Europe. Moreover, it is the sector which is most strongly regulated by EU legislation, especially through the complex Television Without Frontiers (TWF) directive. It therefore presents interesting features in relation to the CEECs' preparations for EU entry.

Before proceeding to analyze the transformation of the CEECs' audio-visual sectors as their foremost mass media during the pre-EU accession period, we will first look at the definition of mass media and especially of broadcast media in the European Union and specifically in central and eastern European contexts.

Definitions of mass media in the CEECs after 1989

Definitions of the media are multidimensional (Jakubowicz 1998–99): they refer to relations of the media to the state and society, social and cultural values, organizational and technological features, conditions of distribution, reception and use, and the social relationships of senders and receivers. These definitions have direct implications for regulation. For example, the relations of the media to the state and society lead to differentiations between public and private communication, and affect the nature and the scope of regulation. Definitions of the media in the CEECs are also related to different theories (Jakubowicz 1998–99: 1): press theories, normative theories and communication theories. The last sixteen years have brought, on the one hand, profound alterations in media regulation and media definitions in the CEECs, as a consequence of systemic changes, and, on the other hand, uncertainty over regulatory models. This is illustrated by the repeated revisions of the TWF directive.

The changes in the nature of the state and society that affected the CEECs at the end of the 1980s had a major impact on the media. The transformations started immediately after the fall of their authoritarian regimes, but it was only the approaching date of EU membership – a factor political in nature – which brought legislative coherence in the audio-visual field. As the yearly progress reports of the European Commission for each central and eastern European candidate to EU membership show, there is visible progress towards the date of membership for complying with EU law in the field of broadcasting. This was the only strong identifiable incentive and constraint that gave real coherence to the audio-visual legislation in the acceding CEECs.

Changing perceptions of the mass media in the CEECs after EU accession

It is difficult to generate a systematic analysis of the transformation of broadcasting in the acceding CEECs. The most common mode of analysis looks at broadcasting as an economic sector which has been 'reformed', like many other economic sectors, in an attempt to comply with EU conditionality. If we take into consideration the reality theory of media transformation (Jakubowicz 1998–99), from 1990 to 2006 broadcasting's role was to behave in ways which would:

- Bring the societies closer to the western ideal imposed by the elites prior to 1990.
- Enable the 'reform' (de-nationalization, privatization) required by western conditionalities (the Council of Europe and EU membership criteria and the International Monetary Fund [IMF] conditionality for loans).
- Be profitable.
- Establish the media's 'watchdog' role to reinforce the newly fashioned democracies (related to the political Copenhagen criteria – requiring candidate states to create stable institutions guaranteeing democracy, the rule of law, human rights and respect for minorities).

The Community courts contributed greatly to the definition of broadcasting from an internal market perspective. The European Court of Justice (ECJ) first defined broadcasting as a 'service' (in the *Sacchi* decision of 1974, the ECJ offers a definition of the broadcasting message as a 'service', without reference to the content of the television message, or the technical tools used). Later on, the message was considered as a 'good', and the Community principle of free movement of goods was applied to broadcasting communication (decisions *Reti*, *De Agostini*, *Pro Sieben Media AG*, *RTL* and *Bacardi*). Meanwhile, the European Court Human of Rights (ECHR) looked at broadcasting more as a medium which guarantees and reinforces the newly fashioned democracies by playing a 'watchdog' role. The ECJ – taking into account ECHR case law on the application of the European Convention on Human Rights – later adopted the view that maintaining a pluralist audio-visual sector was vital for any democratic society, as suggested by Article 10 of the European Convention on Human Rights. Considering these interpretations, we could conclude that Article 10 – which incorporates freedom of expression into the Community system – guarantees not only an individual right to the freedom of the media but creates an obligation to guarantee the pluralism of opinions and the cultural diversity of media content, in the interests of democracy and freedom of information for all the citizens of the Member States of the Council of Europe, including all EU Member States. Another important development within the Community system was the addition to the Amsterdam Treaty of a protocol stressing that public broadcasting services in EU Member States are directly related to the democratic, social and cultural needs of each society, as well as to media pluralism. Broadcasting seems therefore to be the best indicator of media pluralism in the European Union.

Two factors can help identify whether the likelihood of EU membership created the best conditions for broadcasting pluralism in central and eastern European acceding countries. These are: (1) respect for freedom of expression, as a pillar of the freedom of the media; and (2) the diversity of media content.

Freedom of expression in the European Union

Freedom of expression is closely linked in many legal systems to the protection and proper functioning of democracy, even though it is an individual right. Although an individual right, freedom of expression takes on different attributes in the realm of the media, empowering the media to play a role 'in ensuring that a diversity of viewpoints (political and cultural) are transmitted to those viewing, without domination by any particular group' (Harrison and Woods 2000: 479). Article 10 of the European Convention for the Protection of Human Rights and Fundamental Freedoms guarantees the right to impart information and ideas without interference by a public authority. This imperative is related to the underlying existence of a public sphere, as a place for the interaction of citizens from the same political space in areas such as culture and social debates: 'whilst a democracy obviously depends on an informed citizenry making good political choices, a complex and technologically advanced democracy also relies on citizens having a good understanding and tolerance of their own and others' social and cultural duties and needs – citizenship in a broad sense. Following this reasoning, European audio-visual policy is underpinned by the assumption that the media are a force for good in both the political and cultural sphere' (Harrison and Woods 2000: 479).

In the CEECs, this environment has been created by the adoption of western-style legislation. After the fall of their authoritarian regimes, the desire to adopt western mass media values and to join an uncertain but somehow perceptible European public sphere went hand in hand with meeting the democratic conditionality of the Council of Europe, for these States were eager to join that organization. In the field of freedom of expression, this meant the adoption, at the beginning of the 1990s, of the fundamental freedoms in the Convention, which provides for the right to freedom of expression (including the freedom to hold personal opinions, and to receive and pass on information and ideas).

With regard to the EU norms in the field of fundamental freedoms, the *acquis communautaire* does not provide explicitly for the respect of these fundamental freedoms. The rights and guarantees included in the Convention of the Council of Europe are the ultimate expression of the fundamental values shared by all Member States – including the EU Member States – and the European Union itself. This is one of the founding principles of the European Union. In the context of the ratification of the Constitutional Treaty of 2004, the way in which EU law recognizes fundamental values, rights and freedoms remains a matter of open debate. This debate could bring about:

- ■ The inclusion of the newly compiled catalogue of human rights and fundamental freedoms – the Charter of Fundamental Rights of the European Union – in the Treaties, with the ratification of the Constitutional Treaty; and/or
- ■ A climate for the European Union to adhere to the Convention of the Council of Europe.

But even if the EU does not include the catalogue of fundamental rights and freedoms in the Treaties, and does not sign up to the Convention of the Council of Europe, the respect of fundamental freedoms remains implicit in the EU's legal order, and Member States are supposed to respect them. Article 49 (of the EU Treaty in connexion with Article 6 § 1 of the EU Treaty and its interpretation by the EU institutions) requires Member States to have signed the European Convention on Human Rights by their dates of accession

The new constitutions of the CEECs all include provisions on freedom of expression. But the way they are applied in practice depends on other legal conditions. The survival, until the late 1990s, of protective provisions against defamation, obscenity, blasphemy and racism, as well as the protection of privacy, public morals and national security, undermined media freedom in all the CEECs. For a long time after the fall of their authoritarian regimes, their penal codes still allowed intrusions into press practices under the cover of protecting power (both political and economic) from defamation. As a consequence, relations between the media and political power assumed various forms: the consistently belittling of, and displays of paternalistic attitudes towards, journalists; a systematic lack of response to media revelations of official corruption (Gross 2002); open physical and psychological intimidation 'accusing the media of everything from irresponsibility [...] to being unpatriotic by not toeing the official line or by not being sufficiently nationalistic' (Gross 2002: 60). However, approaching EU membership accelerated the demise of these tendencies. In Romania, for example, the possibility of a prison sentence for 'insult' survived until 2004, when the Penal Code was amended. But the real application of the repeal of the crime of 'insult' came only in 2006 when it was urgently necessary to get the green light from the European Commission for EU entry.

Community involvement in European media policy

The rationale for the European Community (EC) involvement in European media policy was 'originally economic' (Harrison and Woods 2000: 480). Later, as a result of European Parliament advocacy (Sarikakis 2005: 159), the view that the audio-visual sector had a major role to play in promoting the cultural and political integration of the European Union gained ground. However, EU audio-visual policy is still trying to find the best way to achieve this. The three main elements in EC audio-visual policy (Harrison and Woods 2000: 480) are: (1) the adoption of common technical standards for satellite broadcasting; (2) a legal basis for the free movement of broadcasts from one EU Member State to another (further to the existing case law on the free movement of television broadcasts under Article 49 [ex 59] EC – Freedom to Provide Services); and (3) the promotion of the European element in audio-visual policy. The EU's audio-visual policy tries to ensure both the freedom of the audio-visual market and the diversity of content through two policy approaches: an interventionist approach and a free market approach (Harrison and Woods 2000: 480). Most of the rules regulating European broadcasting are defined by the TWF directive from 1989 (first revised in 1997). The directive's core deals with two basic principles related to content: the free movement of European television programmes within the internal market, and the requirement that television channels, where practicable, reserve over half their broadcasting time for European works (broadcasting quotas). The TWF directive also aims, although less decisively, at safeguarding certain important public interest objectives, such as cultural diversity (without defining it), the protection of minors and the right of reply.

But are these requirements able to create and sustain the production and distribution of high-quality, independently produced television programmes, programmes which can promote content diversity, and ultimately a sustainable broadcasting pluralism?

As we have seen, acceding countries were obliged to ensure compliance with the TWF directive's requirements prior to accession by harmonizing their laws and after accession by ensuring full and consistent implementation. How has this worked?

The CEECs' compliance with the provisions of the TWF directive

By their dates of EU accession (1 May 2004 and 1 January 2007), all of these central and eastern European countries had complied with the provisions of the TWF directive. We can assume that this was without exception, as the European Commission's reports before accession stated that the legislation of the respective countries complied with the Community's *acquis*.

The process of compliance was considerably accelerated by the prospect of specific entry dates. Thus, if in 1999 the Commission progress reports made gloomy reading for all the acceding central and eastern European countries in relation to the alignment of their media laws with the TWF directive and the capacity of their administrative and implementation structures to monitor the media effectively, in the period from 2003 to 2006 things improved dramatically. We can therefore safely assume that the incentive for complying with the EU requirements in order to join on schedule was crucial. To take only one example: the Commission's Regular Report from 1999 for Romania found that 'some progress' had been achieved in the Romanian audio-visual area, particularly by the adoption, in January 1999, of the Law amending the 1992 Radio and Television Broadcasting Law and the adoption of a number of compulsory standards by the National Audiovisual Council. However, Romanian broadcasting legislation was 'not yet in full compliance with the audiovisual *acquis*'. In 2002, the Commission felt that Romania '[had] made good progress in the audiovisual area'. With the adoption of the new audio-visual law – a new Framework Law to align with the Television Without Frontiers directive adopted in June 2002 – Romania was considered to be 'well advanced' in terms of its transposition of the *acquis*. Legislation for advertising, teleshopping and sponsorship was adopted in March 2002. The National Audiovisual Council (NAC) was re-organized in 1999 in order to strengthen control, regulation and monitoring in the audio-visual sector. By 2003, the European Commission reported that the 'position of the National Audiovisual Council has been further strengthened by the revised Framework Law, which extended the mandate of NAC members from four to six years to increase its political independence, clarified sanctioning procedures and introduced the possibility of more nuanced and proportionate action'. In October 2003, Romania's Framework Law in the Audio-visual Area was revised and the implementation of legislation continued as appropriate. In 2005, two remaining modifications to the Audio-visual Law, concerning jurisdiction and freedom of reception, were adopted. It is clear that Romania's compliance with the audio-visual *acquis* followed the pace of integration:

as soon as an approaching accession date was considered, Romania's compliance with the audio-visual *acquis* was accelerated.

With regard to content, the only provisions clearly referring to the diversity of content of television programmes in the TWF directive are those relating to the priority given to European works, as opposed to American (mainly Hollywood productions and Latin American soap operas), and to safeguarding certain important public interest objectives which, for the moment, include only sport events, the protection of minors, and the right of reply. The notions of 'priority to European works' and 'cultural diversity' were stripped of all sense because of the lack of concrete measures for enforcement. The positive discrimination offered to European producers is unlikely to increase the quality and the diversity of television content as the '10 per cent of their transmission time or 10 per cent of their programming budget for European works from independent producers' is usually converted into time offered to locally produced soap operas and sitcoms which transpose Latin American formats in an eastern European context. In the CEECs, these programmes are produced in studios owned by the most dominant enterprise in the region's audio-visual sector, Central and Eastern European Media Enterprises (CME). The successful Romanian CME-owned studios, MediaPro, are experts in producing action series, telenovelas, soaps or sitcoms such as *Good Guys*, *Tears of Love* and *Neighbours*. These formats dominate Romania's CME-owned PRO TV's prime time schedule, and are also extremely popular at the Slovakian television station TV Markiza: *Susedia* (*Neighbours*) brought impressive viewing figures (58 per cent of audience share in the autumn season of 2006 and 62.1 per cent in the spring of 2007). In the Czech Republic CME-owned NOVA TV saw *Ulice* (*The Street*) capture audience shares of 52 per cent among 15-to-54-year-olds and over 67 per cent for 15-to-24-year-olds in December 2006, prompting TV NOVA to renew the series and extend the episodes to 60 minutes. Their success convinced CME to produce the series in its Romanian MediaPro studios for Ukrainian and Russian audiences (for Studio 1+1 in Ukraine and St Petersburg-Channel 5 in Russia), initiating a strategy of pan-regional idea exploitation. These recent developments show that from their position as importers of American works (Hollywood productions and Latin American soap operas) at the beginning of the 1990s, CEECs are transforming themselves into *exporters* of light-format, popular television products.

These CEEC-based popular productions comply with TWF directive requirements in that they represent predominantly European works by independent producers intended for a European audience. But it is unclear how they are likely to bring about broadcasting pluralism defined as the production and distribution of high-quality, independently produced television programmes, welcoming a diversity of points of view which can sustain the empowerment of citizens to participate in informed and rational debates within society.

Conclusion
The CEECs reacted very pragmatically to the obligation to incorporate the audio-visual *acquis*, namely the TWF directive, in their legal systems. Although several versions of new laws were discussed over their first years of democracy, it was only as their dates of accession approached that broadcasting laws in acceding countries were roughly aligned with EU standards as

expressed in the directive. As European Commission progress reports show, the prospect of EU accession clearly accelerated compliance with the audio-visual *acquis* and improved the CEECs' capacities to regulate, control and monitor their audio-visual sectors between 2001 and 2006. It is nevertheless unclear how the adoption of the TWF directive (the Community audio-visual *acquis*) may foster broadcasting pluralism. Since EU entry, many CEECs saw their broadcasting sectors characterized by the domination of commercially driven companies, the decline of public service television and the growth in exportation of light television formats (a trend very similar to that experienced in western Europe). The TWF directive seems to have created the conditions for the growth of commercial media production but concerns over the pluralism of media content have been overwhelmed by interests in profits and ratings. It is uncertain how the implementation of the Community's audio-visual *acquis* may have stimulated the production and distribution of high-quality, independently produced television programmes – programmes contributing to broadcasting pluralism – and therefore, more generally, to the stability of democracy in these new Member States.

References

Coman, M., (2004), 'Romanian Television and the Challenges of European Integration', in *Trends in Communication* 12:4, pp. 211–22.

European Convention on Human Rights/Convention européenne des droits de l'homme (1987), Leiden: Martinus Nijhoff Publishers.

Gross, P. (2002), *Entangled Evolutions. Media and Democratization in Eastern Europe*, Washington: Johns Hopkins University Press/Woodrow Wilson Center Press.

Habermas, J. (1991), *Structural Transformation of Public Sphere*, Cambridge: Polity.

Harrison, J., and Woods, L. (2000), 'European Citizenship: Can Audio-Visual Policy Make a Difference?', in *JCMS: Journal of Common Market Studies* 38:3, pp. 471–495.

Jakubowicz, K. (1998–99), 'Normative Models of Media and Journalism and Broadcasting Regulation in Central and Eastern Europe', in *International Journal of Communications Law and Policy* 2, pp. 1–32.

Sarikakis, K. (2005), 'Defending Communication Spaces. The Remits and Limits of the European Parliament', in *International Communication Gazette* 67.

A New European Information Order

Jim Hall

Current laws were framed in the age of print. We need a new framework of rules for the age of electronic communications.

Chris Smith, UK Heritage Secretary, 1995

Upon its introduction to Europe, printing, along with its subsequent developments and forms, was rapidly made subject to regulation and containment, at first by the Church and then by the State. Contemporary states, without exception, continue to understand the regulation of the flow of information, through whatever medium and across all genres and forms, as a primary function of government. A closely related function and one of a lower order is, of course, the protection of private property. The Internet impacts powerfully on both and indeed forces us to reconsider their meaning. For 'despite the fact that no-one controls cyberspace, it is not an ungoverned lawless frontier; many actions in cyberspace have consequences in the real world' (Du Pont 2001: 194–195). With the appearance of the World Wide Web in the early 1990s and the realization that the Internet would no longer be the sole province of the military and a few academics, and that the economy of cyberspace impacted uncompromisingly on the real world, governments, including the European Union and its constituent elements, set about bringing the new information medium to heel.

Very few entirely new information problems were raised by the Internet but its design and premise meant that solutions to old problems, for example around the dissemination of hate speech or abusive pornography, or the security of the private and financial information which comprises so much of contemporary identity, had to be rethought. For some states, including some of the advanced democracies, but notoriously such countries as China, Burma and Iran, there was also the sticky problem of that political information which they preferred not to see in the public sphere.

Even within Europe, during the first decade of the twenty-first century, pretexts such as the 'war against terror' inclined governments incrementally to abandon the generally liberal and market-oriented approach to information regulation that had marked the last decades of the twentieth century. In July of 2005, for example, 16 of the German states tried to revoke the Federal Freedom of Information Act (*Gesetz zur Regelung des Zugangs zu Informationen des Bundes*), which had only been enacted a month before, on the grounds that it would enable access to individual medical records. In the United Kingdom, along with Germany and Luxembourg, the most reluctant of the European states to grant information access rights to its citizens, access can be refused under 210 different statutory provisions. Fig leaves like these mean it is frequently difficult to see exactly where new legislation is directly determined by the electronic communications networks which have developed over the past half-century or so and where other factors come into play. There are several instances of new Internet laws being proposed and introduced where, as in the case of pornography featuring minors, there was already perfectly sound legislation existing which prohibited the dissemination of inappropriate material across all media, including the Internet. In the United Kingdom, for instance, the very representation of children in indecent situations (what the law describes as 'pseudo-photographs': animations, computer-generated images and potentially even drawings) is illegal under the Criminal Justice Act of 1988, predating the first moral panic about 'Internet porn' by half a decade or so. That said, globalization, especially the globalization of crime and terrorism, has produced some novel security problems for the advanced democracies.

Those problems spring in part from a set of tensions, by no means limited to the regulation of the Internet, between national security and the right to personal privacy on the one hand and freedom of expression and civil liberties on the other. Of course these sets of factors are themselves fraught with incongruity; the demands of national security will frequently contravene the protocols of personal privacy, and freedom of expression has been known to ride roughshod over civil liberties. This contradiction is exquisitely caught in the UK Human Rights Act (1998) intended to enshrine the rights contained in the European Convention on Human Rights (1950) into UK law. Article 8 declares that, 'everyone has the right to respect for his [sic] private and family life, his [sic] home and his [sic] correspondence', while Article 10 unequivocally safeguards freedom of expression. The regulation of the Internet, whether it is approached from a national, hemispheral or global level, presents pertinacious, on occasion insoluble, jurisdictional problems. It was not merely her Christian Socialist liberalism that led the EU Information Society Commissioner Viviane Reding to announce in 2005 that she had 'no intention to regulate the Internet' (Reding 2005).

But any notion that self-regulation would be adequate to the task of policing the Internet seems naïve. The public pressure that forced the Hays Code upon Hollywood in the 1930s or 'seals of approval' on the U.S. comic industry in the 1950s seems unlikely to work in our very different moral climate, although 'web seals of approval' have been suggested and even tried in several countries. There is also, of course, the half-way position to regulation, which is the state-sanctioned filtering of content which encourages European Internet Service Providers (ISPs) and search-engines to block illegal content hosted from elsewhere. Such volitional policing of the public sphere, the displacement of regulation from the state to service providers, blurs the state's position on the policing of the Internet and brings problems of its own.

Reding's intention notwithstanding, the simultaneous development of the information age and the removal of frontiers within Europe have conspired to produce a data maelstrom, a potential for chaos, particularly around data protection. Sweden's Data Act of 1973, which regulated the automated processing of files containing personal data (and, incidentally, prohibited the discussion of politics or religion on bulletin boards hosted in Sweden) was Europe's first data protection law. One effect of the subsequent proliferation of data protection legislation was to obstruct the free flow of information, even within the borders of the European Union. The Directive on the Protection of Personal Data 95/46/EC (which eventually came into effect in 1998) was an attempt to bring together diverging data protection laws and produce harmonization within the EU and data-security for its citizens both within Europe's borders and beyond. The legislation is effective and has become a model for many other countries (including Sweden itself in 1998). A further blurring of the EU's policing of the information society is embedded in 95/46/EC where it is suggested that the law should not be applied to journalistic, publishing or artistic activities, and that anyone defining themselves as a journalist or artist would, for the purposes of the legislation, be considered as one. The law was made slightly clearer in 1999 when it was altered to say that minor violations should not be prosecuted, although the Parliament still seemed to be suggesting that the law would be applied on an arbitrary, ad hoc basis.

Of course the jurisdictional difficulties facing the regulation of the Internet include the problem that information on the Internet, as it crosses national borders, is undetectable. Without the imposition of draconian and disproportionate blocking measures such as the jamming (or even, as was proposed to Serbia by the United States during the Wars of Yugoslavian Succession, the destruction) of satellites, information uploaded onto the Internet can appear anywhere in the world. Internet Protocol (IP) addresses contain no guarantees with regard to the physical location of the 'transmitter' of information on the Internet and national borders offer no impediment to the dissemination of ideas or indeed, access to consumer goods. Advertisements for the open sale of prescription-only pharmaceuticals on a '.co.uk' website can originate in a country with very different drug laws. The problem applies equally to ideologies. The most effective centres of dissent against the Burmese junta in 2007 included blogs such as Ko-Htike's and indeed the thousands of video clips of the uprising on YouTube, both disseminated from far beyond the country's borders. The political implications of this are perhaps less disturbing to European governments than they are to states wishing to maintain less porous borders, such as China, Saudi Arabia and Belarus, but they still can be argued to warrant a global approach to legislation. While any state can legislate for the local effects of the Internet, by doing so it will inevitably produce knock-on effects for other nations. While a universal regulation code may well be desirable it is unlikely that every state's imperatives for such a code could be met.

The mobility, not to say ubiquity, of information in both high and late capitalism demanded universal regulation from the start, and, in theory, the instruments necessary for the regulation of the Internet are the same as those which enabled the formation of the International Telecommunication Union in 1865 and the Universal Postal Union (then the General Postal Union) in 1874. The Post Office Acts of the 1880s, which controlled the dissemination of illegal pornographic material in Europe and the United States, for instance, were developed to take account of print publishing and the latest postal technologies, and had generally been drafted in terms which meant that they also controlled any medium used as a carrier for such material. The Internet undeniably made such laws much harder to police but, in the United Kingdom, as a case in point, a relatively minor amendment (1994) to the Obscene Publications Acts of 1959 and 1964 brought the Acts up to date with regard to the electronic storage and transmission of information. Recent decades have seen trends towards the liberalization and deregulation of that body of legislation, but there remains a series of problems which seem uniquely related to communication using the Internet and which have been inclined to reverse that tendency. This chapter will go on to consider some of the problems related to the regulation of information on the Internet. It will begin by outlining the ethical issues facing Viviane Reding's successors as they come to set down the code for a *Corpus Iuris Indicii*.

Ethical issues

Legislation is framed by a complex of ethical conventions and codes which, like the law itself, are culturally and historically determined. This might make the regulation of the Internet, a medium that is at once ubiquitous, apparently protean and emergent, seem more a matter of conjecture than conviction. Nonetheless the important issues would seem to include:

    Freedom of information and the accessibility of information
    The rights of the creator and copyright
    Criminal practices involving information theft and misuse
    Human rights, particularly around abuse, hate speech and incitement
    Privacy
    Monopoly and the regulation of information and media markets

While these issues concern the production and dissemination of information in late capitalism, the Internet and its enabling technologies have brought particular twenty-first-century dimensions to them. The fundamental accessibility of information is a case in point. 'Denial of service', resulting from attacks on web servers intended to make them inaccessible to their users, while it is now recognized as an act of war, is also recognized in many countries as a criminal offence. In Europe it was criminalized in the Council of Europe Convention on Cybercrime in 2005. The legislation is rather clumsily prefigured in the UK's Computer Misuse Act of 1990.

Equally, file-sharing software and other modes of information dissemination on the Internet cast doubt on the very possiblity of copyright legislation now functioning as it was intended to. Both the scale of the problem and the present difficulty of enforcement of copyright on the Internet seem to offer little prospect for any remedy of the problem in the near future. While Napster was brought to heel in 2001, its successors proliferate, using BitTorrent technologies which can download complete movies or whole collections of CDs in the same time that Napster-users took to download a few songs. On the face of it the EU Copyright Directive (2001) gives the entertainment industries the protection they need against peer-to-peer websites but it takes neither the scale of the problem nor its global nature into account. There remain many safe havens for the world's growing population of copyright infringers, but, even if those countries are persuaded to sign up fully to their responsibilities under some global agreement such as the Berne Convention, as Ira Magaziner observed in 1997 (cited in Lohr 2000): 'because of the breakneck speed of change in technology [...] government attempts to regulate the Internet are likely to be outmoded by the time they are finally enacted'.

The creators of copyright material are doubly penalized as their publishers and distributors increasingly insist on blanket licensing agreements whereby authors sign away future rights to intellectual properties with regard to future publication across all other media, including any which may not yet have even been invented. In 2007 the World Intellectual Property Organization (WIPO) attempted to go even further with its Treaty on the Protection of Broadcasting Organizations which attempted to ratify an international agreement over a new deal for broadcasters which would have given them, rather than the creators, intellectual property rights over broadcasts, including material on the Internet. The agreement, which was intended as an addition to existing copyright laws, failed to be ratified, and was, in addition, criticized as being a serious threat to freedom of expression. While the global media conglomerates will certainly return to the fray, Patrícia Akester concludes, in her report on the proposed treaty to UNESCO:

> European case law suggests that [...] the European Court will be likely to favour freedom of expression where users' access to political, artistic, literary or journalistic speech is restricted.

> In these circumstances, the European Court could find the free speech restrictions stemming from the implementation of the Draft Treaty unnecessary in a democratic society, not because the Treaty grants exclusive rights to broadcasting and cablecasting organizations, but because the balance between proprietary interests and users' access interests has not been kept.

Akester's advocacy is at odds with both the WIPO proposal and legislation such as the UK's Regulation of Investigatory Powers Bill (2000), which, while it merely set out to give the police the right to read e-mail on the same basis that they can already read postal mail and listen to telephone messages (with a legal warrant), actually gave the police huge freedoms in tracking Internet use and intercepting e-mail. The full title of the bill, known at the time of its enactment as 'the snooper's charter', is instructive:

> An Act to make provision for and about the interception of communications, the acquisition and disclosure of data relating to communications, the carrying out of surveillance, the

use of covert human intelligence sources and the acquisition of the means by which electronic data protected by encryption or passwords may be decrypted or accessed; to provide for the establishment of a tribunal with jurisdiction in relation to those matters, to entries on and interferences with property or with wireless telegraphy and to the carrying out of their functions by the Security Service, the Secret Intelligence Service and the Government Communications Headquarters; and for connected purposes.

It is the joint issues of surveillance and decryption, driven by new common definitions of cybercrime and the procedures necessary to counter it agreed at the European Council meeting held at Tampere on 1999, which lie at the heart of the Act. While few of these crimes were particularly innovative or new, fraud remains fraud whether it is 'Nigerian Letter Schemes' (as the FBI call them) or a mortgage scam; but the Internet, as we have seen, gave many of them a fresh lease of life.

Internet crime: regulatory concerns

'Cyber-terrorism', Romani Prodi commented in 2002 (in an interview with Andrea Di Maio), 'is seen as a serious problem for Member States, especially in the wake of the terrorist attacks against the United States, and we are acutely aware of its possible implications in terms of civil liberties and security.'

Cybercrime tends largely, although not exclusively, as the list below will illustrate, to constitute crime against property. By the turn of the millennium, most European states had arrived at a system of regulation which is part mandatory and part self-regulatory (on the part of the ISPs). Spain's law of Information Society Services and Electronic Commerce (2002), for instance, led to the immediate closure of several hundred Spanish websites and to many more changing their policies about the content that they would carry. Consumers were to be protected against unsolicited messages and ISPs would be state-registered and would be self-monitoring. Online financial transactions would be treated the same as 'real life' ones in terms of records and responsibilities, and, crucially, ISPs would be required to retain comprehensive activity logs for twelve months. The terms of the law originated in the EU's consumer protection mandate but by the time it came before the legislature it had been expanded to address global terrorism and crimes as diverse as the sexual exploitation of minors and identity theft. Most EU countries had already enacted similar legislation. The instruments the European Union created to tame it remain fairly crude and imperfect but the days of the Wild Web are coming to an end. Those instruments, as we have seen, are largely directed at monitoring web activity in order to detect crimes that are already adequately covered by other bodies of law.

The crimes that such measures are intended to police include terrorism, the sexual exploitation of minors, drug-trafficking, money-laundering, electronic fraud, such as theft of credit-card numbers, computerized piracy, and industrial and state espionage. Without exception these activities, or their analogue equivalents, were all illegal long before 1994 when Tim Berner-Lee's creation of the World Wide Web brought the Internet within the reach of the general populace. Any fears that regulation, or indeed action, military or otherwise, by any one country could destroy the Internet are clearly unfounded. If ISPs become too heavily loaded with filtering and self-regulating responsibilities they will simply raise their charges and their overheads. The Internet will slow down until the technology that underpins it becomes affordable again. The legislation itself, like the laws controlling copyright, will always have to balance regulation, or prescription, against enforcement, or what it is possible to enforce.

References

Akester, P., *The Draft WIPO Broadcasting Treaty and its Impact on Freedom of Expression*. Available at: http://unesdoc.unesco.org/images/0014/001464/146498e.pdf#146498 Date accessed: 19/8/08.

Di Maio, A., 'Interview with the President of the European Commission'. Available at: http://www.gartner.com/1_researchanalysis/focus/eu_qa021102.html Date accessed: 30/4/2006.

du Pont, G. (2001), 'The Criminalization of True Anonymity in Cyberspace', in *Michigan Telecommunications and Technology Law Review 7*, pp. 191–216.

Lohr, S., 'Policing the Internet: Anyone but Government', in *The New York Times*, 20 February 2000.

Reding, V. (2005), 'Better regulation for Europe's media industry: the Commission's approach', speech delivered at *Between Culture and Commerce*, Liverpool, 22 September 2005.

The European Union and the Press

David Hutchison

Newspaper circulations vary remarkably in the countries of the European Union, ranging from 450 copies per thousand inhabitants per day in Sweden, through 310 in the Netherlands, to 90 in Greece and 38 in Portugal; high consumption is much more a northern than a southern European habit (De Bens 2004: 18). Circulations generally are falling throughout the western world. A Staff Working Paper produced by the Commission, which makes the point that within the publishing sector in the 25 Member States newspapers account for 36.8 per cent of that sector and periodicals 31.9 per cent (European Commission 2005: 10), goes on to comment: 'The decline in newspaper circulation in Europe has been ongoing for two decades, with little sign of recovery. Evidence from research suggests that the decline is general across all age groups. Taking into account that circulation has also been falling in the U.S. and Japan, it seems reasonable to assume that this decline is of a structural nature' (European Commission 2005: 22).

It should be noted however that the World Association of Newspapers is rather more upbeat on the matter, and claims 2004 as a positive year, since circulation worldwide increased by 2 per cent, and, in the five-year period ending then, by almost 5 per cent (World Association of Newspapers 2005: 3). But most of the circulation gains have been in Asia, South America and Africa, although the drop in the European Union overall is 0.7 per cent in one year (2004) and 0.4 per cent over the period 1999–2004. Circulation increases in several countries in the five-year period – Austria (3 per cent), Ireland (29 per cent) and Poland (44 per cent), for example – were counterbalanced by declines in rather more countries, with significant drops in, for example, Germany (8 per cent), France (6 per cent) and the United Kingdom (11 per cent).

The current situation then may not be one of significant decline across the European Union taken as a whole, but in major countries that decline is the reality. It is not difficult to enumerate the factors which have contributed to this decline: increased competition from other media, the growth of the Internet and the inelasticity of time devoted to media activity (people do have other pursuits with which to occupy themselves) are among the more obvious causes which can be adduced. In addition, there is the matter of the orientation towards public affairs of many young people: as Williams has commented, '[they] have exerted their spending power on a range of other media and leisure activities, such as popular music, drinking, clubbing and eating out, which are seen as more preferable pastimes than newspaper reading' (Williams 2005: 32). What must be starting to concern newspaper executives is whether there is a plateau on which circulations will bottom out or whether the decline will continue indefinitely. Companies have tried a range of strategies in order to counteract the decline, the most striking of which is the introduction, by the Swedish company Kinnevik, of its free *Metro* daily papers, which have achieved a circulation of more than five million copies per day across Europe (*Guardian*, 28/11/05); these are financed entirely by advertising and the operation is claimed to be profitable, but, certainly from the perspective of a reader of *Le Monde* or *Die Welt*, it is hard to regard *Metro* as anything other than a condensed version of a newspaper proper, and indeed it is difficult not to see it as a dangerous innovation – for if the consumer can have a newspaper with a brief but adequate summary of what is going on in the world free of charge, why should s/he pay money for an expanded version? Online versions of titles seem a rather better way of seeking to compensate for circulation declines, provided adequate revenue can be raised through advertising and subscriber charges.

Concentration of ownership has grown in Europe. As in the United States, where a company like Gannett is one of three dominant players, so in Germany the Axel Springer company has over 20 per cent of the daily market (Kleinsteuber 2004: 80), and in Britain the Murdoch-dominated Newscorp has over 30 per cent of that market by circulation (Tunstall 2004: 263). A similar process has taken place in France, Italy and elsewhere in western Europe (Kelly et al. 2004). The situation in the former eastern Bloc countries is similar; indeed the growth of concentration in the newspaper markets there is startling. Gulyas has calculated that between 1992 and 2003 the two largest groups in the Czech Republic and Hungary increased their shares of the national dailies market from around 30 per cent to over 70 per cent (Gulyas 2006: 82). Gulyas also notes the tendency in these countries for control of media companies in general to pass into foreign hands, with the market share in the daily newspaper markets of non-indigenous companies having reached 70 per cent in the case of Hungary and 80 per cent in the case of the Czech Republic by 2003 (Gulyas 2006: 78). The German companies, Springer and Bertelsmann, and the Norwegian conglomerate Orkla, have been particularly active. Expansion abroad is not only a feature of the eastern European scene. Newscorp, which, depending on how one configures it, is either Australian or American, has acquired publications in many other parts of the globe, while the Gannett company, through its British subsidiary, Newsquest, has been building up a strong position in British weeklies and regional dailies. But the speed with which the eastern European press has been acquired by foreign investors is remarkable.

Another common feature of the ownership pattern throughout Europe, as elsewhere, is cross media involvement. Companies with interests in one medium often have interests in others and indeed in non-media businesses. So, for example, Bertelsmann, which began life in the nineteenth century as a publisher of Bibles, has interests in its home country of Germany in both press and broadcasting, while also owning publishing companies in the United States. The French company Vivendi, until a rapid decline in fortunes in recent years, amassed a range of interests including water companies in France – its base of operations – and Universal Studios in the USA.

Such organizations are not at liberty to buy and sell just as they please. They face domestic and foreign restrictions on their operations. Many European countries have provisions in place to limit concentration within specific sectors and across sectors. In the United Kingdom, for example, when they go on the acquisition trail, powerful newspaper companies can find their proposals subject to public interest tests by government agencies and by the media regulator Ofcom. In Germany early in 2006, the KEK (Kommission zur Ermittlung der Konzentration in Medienbereich), the German regulatory body, blocked a proposed takeover by the Springer group of ProSiebenSat.1, the country's largest commercial broadcaster, on the grounds that the new entity would have too great a potential sway over public opinion. The decision produced a sharp response from Springer's chief executive: 'What [the regulators] have overlooked is a global shift in media competition into digital distribution markets – as though that were some kind of delusion of new economic yuppies gone wild. This opinion is not only false, it's negligent.' (*Guardian*, 11/1/2006)

This line, much favoured by such individuals, emphasizes both the growth of digital media and the international context in which companies now operate, and as such it mirrors some of the thinking at Commission level in the European Union.

Newspapers are financed by sales and advertising. The particular balance varies from country to country and also by type of newspaper, with, for example, the British mass circulation titles traditionally drawing around half of their income from sales, while upmarket titles tend to rely for 60–70 per cent of their revenue on advertising. The average proportion of advertising revenue to total newspaper revenue across Europe is currently 50–60 per cent (European Union 2005: 20). The major difference between the United Kingdom and the European mainland is the existence of subsidies in many countries, subsidies which are designed to bolster publications which might otherwise be put out of business by stronger competitors. Norway and Sweden have the most developed systems of subsidy and offer the same justification, namely that in the interests of pluralism of news sources and opinion, it is civically desirable that public money be provided to sustain titles which the market left to itself would not support. Sweden, with a population of nine million, currently spends 56 million euros annually on its subsidy programme (Swedish Press Subsidies Council 2005). Subsidy schemes are also to be found in countries as different as Austria and France. In addition, many countries offer other aid such as grants and loans for capital equipment, subsidized telcommunications, cheap postal rates and lower rates of VAT than are generally levelled.

The EU approach to date

Much discussion at EU level in recent years has focused on the concentration issue. However, in responding in 2005 to a Commission Issues Paper on Media Pluralism published as part of the ongoing debate about the revision of the Television Without Frontiers directive, the European Newspapers Publishers Association was forceful in its rejection of any suggestion that an EU-wide initiative was needed – 'Regulation of media pluralism is a matter for the Member States [...] which is subject to the subsidiarity principle' (ENPA 2005: 1). In the same paper the proprietors go on to argue that there are many benefits arising from media consolidation, and while there has been an increase in concentration of press ownership in national markets, 'the impact of this concentration must be taken in its relative context' (ENPA 2005: 5). The views of Members of the European Parliament (MEPs) are cited in support of this position, which is intriguing, given that, as Sarikakis points out in her study of the European Parliament's involvement in media policy, that body has constantly pressurized a reluctant Commission to adopt an anti-concentration initiative (Sarikakis 2001). It is certainly true that the Commission did indeed publish a Green Paper on the matter in 1992 and engaged in fairly lengthy consultation prior to publishing a draft directive in 1996, but ultimately, in the face of sustained opposition from media businesses, it decided no action would be taken at the EU level. As Doyle has noted, 'at the collective European as well as at the national level, the perceived economic opportunity costs of restricting indigenous media firms have completely overshadowed concerns about safeguarding pluralism' (Doyle 2002: 166). Early in 2006 the Parliament rather plaintively reminded the Commission that it had 'long demanded' that a Green Paper on concentration of ownership be produced, without much hope, one suspects, of a positive response from Brussels (European Parliament 2006).

Yet there are signs that the Commission does continue to be concerned about the problem. There have been specific interventions under Competition Legislation (Doyle 2002: 167.), and the Staff Working Paper on the EU Publishing Sector has much to say about how the position of the press might be strengthened through improving productivity and efficiency, and sustained by cheap and effective postal services, particularly for periodicals; but the Paper is also concerned with 'the potential of publishing [in promoting] the diversity of opinion and culture that the peoples of Europe need in order to derive the richest benefits from the information society' (European Commission 2005: 5).

Early in 2007 a Staff Working Paper on Media Pluralism appeared. It discusses the current situation across the media, argues – legitimately – that pluralism of ownership does not of itself guarantee pluralism of expression, and insists that even where there is high concentration, if the right regulations are in place and enforced, then it is still possible for there to be internal pluralism. A study was announced which it was hoped would come up with 'concrete indicators' which 'will enable citizens and all interested parties to assess more objectively media pluralism in Member States' (European Commission 2007:17). The resulting document will no doubt be an illuminating one, but it is difficult to be confident that the Commission will be wholeheartedly committed to any action which might thereafter seem necessary.

Despite the reluctance to date to take initiatives on the concentration front, the fact remains that because of the sheer quantity of legislation, there is a significant EU impact on press policy in the Member States. Two examples may be cited here. The Commission called in September 2005 for a media code of conduct designed to ensure that broadcasting and the press do not offer help, deliberately or accidentally, to terrorists. While it is clearly the Internet which is most open to criticism in this regard – and perhaps the terrorism issue is one of the factors which have persuaded the Commission to begin talking about regulating the Internet, as it did in 2005 – the press will be affected by whatever initiative is developed. One can see how in countries with large Islamic populations enforcing any code will be, to say the least, complicated.

The Market Abuse directive, which appeared in 2002, requires that financial journalists who recommend specific share purchases to readers are obliged to make certain that nothing they publish could be open to the accusation that it is misinformation. The sanctions against those found to have breached this law include jail terms, although the European Union did agree to an amendment to the directive, which means that account must be taken in any specific case of the role of self-regulatory mechanisms – such as codes of conduct and press councils – in the relevant states.

The European Court of Human Rights is also having an increasing impact on the press in EU and non-EU countries alike. After several German publications printed pictures of her cycling, shopping and sunbathing, Princess Caroline of Monaco won a ruling in 2004 which drew on Article 8 of the Convention on Human Rights (Privacy), as against Article 10 (Free Speech), to the effect that private photographs taken without the consent of the individual concerned, and in which there is no legitimate public interest, should not be published. It would appear that this ruling was in the mind of a court in Munich in 2005 when it awarded damages to a gay man who was photographed in an intimate embrace at a festival in Würzburg: two years after the festival, the picture appeared in a Munich tabloid purporting to illustrate the gay scene in that city, and as a consequence the man's sexual orientation became known to his family, who up until that point had been unaware of it (*UK Press Gazette*, 7/10/05).

The Commission could legitimately regard such cases as incidental, in that they do not arise because of the existence of any specific press policies promulgated by the Union. However, there is one rather difficult area where, even in the absence of specific policy, it is hard to see how intervention can be avoided. The European Union is an association of democratic liberal states, in which it is to be expected that freedom of the press is a given; Chapter 2 of the Union's Charter of Fundamental Rights refers specifically to 'freedom of expression and information'.

Preserving such freedom became an issue in the early part of 2006. In September 2005 the Danish newspaper *Jyllands-Posten* published a series of cartoons depicting the prophet Muhammad. The paper had commissioned the cartoons on learning that a Danish writer, who was working on a book about the prophet aimed at children, apparently found that he could not persuade artists to produce illustrations, as they feared criticism and possible physical violence, since for large sections of Muslim opinion such depictions are inherently blasphemous.

The paper decided to test the limits of free speech in Denmark by commissioning the cartoons. Many Muslims in Denmark were offended, and then, after being visited by a delegation of Danish imams, several Islamic countries demanded apologies from the Danish government, and a boycott of Danish goods began. Denmark's Prime Minister initially robustly defended the freedom of the paper to publish; when, at the end of January 2006 *Jyllands-Posten* apologized for offence caused, though still insisted that it had the right to publish, the Prime Minister welcomed the apology but did again make the point that he had no power to censor the press. By this juncture papers in other countries had reproduced the cartoons, apparently as an act of solidarity with *Jyllands-Posten*. As the temperature rose, Danish government property in the Middle East was incinerated and in Afghanistan several people died when police opened fire on demonstrators.

The response of several national leaders in Europe, particularly in France and Germany, was supportive of the right to publish, and of the proposition that free speech inevitably means the right to cause offence; the British Foreign Secretary however criticized the re-publication of the cartoons as 'disrespectful' (*BBC News*, 2/3/06). The reactions of EU Commissioners were rather similar to Mr Straw's. The Trade Commissioner, Peter Mandelson, declared that newspapers which republished the drawings had been 'deliberately provocative' and Franco Frattini, the Justice Commissioner, said that *Jyllands-Posten* had been wrong to publish in the first place (*Guardian*, 3/2/06). A more robust response, while acknowledging unambiguously the offence caused, could have drawn attention to the fact that both residents of and visitors to a Muslim country such as Saudi Arabia have no option but to accept aspects of that society – public floggings, amputations and executions, for example – which may not be to their taste, and therefore Muslims in the European Union have likewise to accept the liberal tradition of free speech which may not be to their taste. Furthermore, it could have been pointed out that non-Muslims seeking to worship, let alone proselytize, in a number of Arab countries, face considerable impediments, whereas Muslims in the European Union are at liberty to worship and evangelise at will; the price of a desirable freedom may be the toleration of one which seems rather less desirable.

As the European Union has expanded, it has encompassed countries which do not have strong democratic traditions; indeed, several have emerged from Communist rule with relatively weak civil societies, and have been obliged to satisfy the Union that their democratic credentials are now completely in order. It is to be hoped that the response of the European Union to any future challenges to freedom of expression, whether in the states which have recently joined or in the other member countries, are met with rather more firmness than was evident in the Danish case.

Conclusion

In 2005 the European Union established a Directorate General for Information Society and Media headed by Viviane Reding; it is now responsible for audio-visual policy, which was previously handled by the Education and Culture Directorate, and publishing, formerly the responsibility of the Enterprise Directorate. This seems an eminently sensible change, given the likely pace of convergence. However, it may also have the effect of highlighting the difference between the Commission's moderately interventionist approach to broadcasting and film and its rather more distanced stance towards the press.

It should be obvious that newspapers in Europe currently face a range of problems. In the first place, the huge variations in consumption among the Member States raise issues about the extent to which citizens are fully informed about what is going on in their own countries and in the European Union as a whole. Radio, television and online services are no doubt very valuable in providing basic information, and public service broadcasting systems are much more likely to be trusted as news purveyors than the press. But it remains the case that the presence in a society of a vibrant newspaper sector is vitally important in raising and sustaining the level of public debate. Even though the British mass-market press, for example, often fails miserably to do any such thing, the UK's upmarket sector usually fulfils that role admirably, as do many newspapers across Europe. A low or declining readership of newspapers is not a symptom of rude democratic health. Likewise, the financial pressure which the press is suffering, as other media seek a greater slice of available advertising revenue, can lead to cutbacks in expenditure on journalism, particularly the time-consuming journalism which raises awkward political and social questions. At the same time, increasing concentration of ownership can mean a significant diminution of pluralism of expression.

The response of Commissioner Reding thus far has been to indicate in a speech to a European Publishers Forum at the end of 2005 that she is concerned to ensure that there is in place 'an early warning system in order to signal whether new policy initiatives would damage the editorial or commercial freedom of the media' (Reding 2005). To this end a Media Task Force has been established, and it is this Task Force which has commissioned the independent study on pluralism mentioned earlier. But it is clear that the Task Force is as concerned about employment opportunities as it is about pluralism and freedom of expression, so it remains to be seen whether it is willing to move beyond the perfectly sensible – if limited – objective which the Commissioner has set it, and to consider whether the European Union needs to be much more proactive in its support of the press than it has hitherto been.

References

Council of Europe (2002), *Media Diversity in Europe*, Strasbourg: Council of Europe.

De Bens, E. (2004), 'Belgium', in Kelly, M., et al. (eds.), *The Media in Europe*, London: Sage, pp. 16–30.

Doyle, G. (2002), *Media Ownership*, London: Sage.

European Commission (2005), *Strengthening the Competitiveness of the EU Publishing Sector*, Brussels: Commission of the European Communities.

European Commission (2007), *Media pluralism in the Member States of the European Union*, Brussels: Commission of the European Communities.

European Newspaper Publishers Association (2005), *Response to the Commission Issues Paper on Media Pluralism*, Brussels: ENPA.

European Parliament (2006), *Press Briefing: a knowledge based society open to all*, Strasbourg: European Parliament.

Gulyas, A. (2006), 'European Integration and East Central European Media', in Hojbjerg, L., and Sondergaard, H. (eds.), *European Film and Media Culture*, Copenhagen: Museum Tusculanum Press, pp. 63–90.

Kelly, M., Mazzoleni, G., and McQuail, D. (2004), *The Media in Europe*, London: Sage.

Kleinsteuber, H. (2004), 'Germany', in Kelly, M. et al. (eds.), *The Media in Europe*, London: Sage, pp. 78–87.

Reding, V. (2005), *Reinforcing the competitiveness of Europe's publishing industry*, Brussels: European Commission.

Sarikakis, K. (2001), *The Role of the European Parliament in the Formation of Media Policies*, Glasgow: Glasgow Caledonian University (Ph.D. dissertation).

Tunstall, J. (2004), 'The United Kingdom', in Kelly, M. et al. (eds.), *The Media in Europe*, London: Sage, pp. 261–274.

Williams, K. (2005), *European Media Studies*, London: Hodder Arnold.

An Elusive European Public Sphere: The Role of Shared Journalistic Cultures

Monika Metykova and Paschal Preston

Jürgen Habermas's seminal *The Structural Transformation of the Public Sphere* (1989; German original published in 1962) provides a basis for discussions of the public sphere(s) in contemporary societies. In his historical narrative informed by the Frankfurt School tradition, Habermas traces the development of the bourgeois public sphere and its consequent transformation, suggesting that the bourgeois public sphere reached its peak in the early-to-mid-nineteenth century. Habermas argues that the public sphere emerged as a space in which private individuals came together as a public to use their own reason to discuss, *inter alia*, the power and direction of the state. In this light, the bourgeois public sphere came into existence as a result of struggle against despotic states. The development of competitive market capitalism led to the creation of institutions within civil society that occupied a space distinct from both the economy and the state. These institutions included newspapers, debating societies, salons and coffee houses.

With the further development of capitalism throughout the nineteenth century, the public sphere underwent significant and (according to Habermas) detrimental changes. The decline of the public sphere is connected with developments such as the growth of large or monopolistic blocs of capital, changes in state-society relations and the increased commercialization of newspapers and popular culture. Thus, the rational-critical debate that characterized the bourgeois public sphere at its peak was displaced by several developments, including a shift towards consumption. In Habermas's influential account, the public sphere continues to exist in appearance only and remains modernity's unfinished promise or incomplete project.

Habermas's concept of the bourgeois public sphere and its transformation has been much invoked, discussed and criticized. It has been understood as a key guide for the analysis of the adequacy of contemporary media institutions (for example, Garnham 1990). It has been criticized on at least three grounds (Dahlgren 1991; Fraser 1993). Firstly, although Habermas admits the exclusionary nature of the bourgeois public sphere in terms of class, he neglects the question of gender. Secondly, he remains silent on alternative public spheres (see Negt and Kluge 1993). And finally, Habermas has been criticized for omitting questions of meaning production and social settings.

Despite these criticisms, Habermas's ideal model has remained highly influential. For example, Garnham points out three key components of Habermas's thesis as essential to an understanding of the public sphere(s) in contemporary societies. Firstly, Habermas focuses on 'the indissoluble link between the institutions and practices of mass communication and the institutions and practices of democratic societies' (1999: 360). Secondly, he stresses the 'necessary material resource base for any public sphere' (1999: 360). Thirdly, Garnham praises Habermas for his avoidance of the simple dichotomy of free market versus state control in his distinction of the public sphere from both state and market, a distinction that enables him to discuss the question of threats to democracy from both. Garnham suggests that these arguments have particular relevance in contemporary societies as the emergence of global markets as centres of private economic power undermines the nation state, and new public spheres and political institutions are needed for the control of the global polity and economy.

In contemporary societies the public sphere ideal is closely linked to evaluations of the role and practices of the mass media. Curran, for example, argues that 'the media are thus the principal institutions of the public sphere or, in the rhetoric of nineteenth-century liberalism, "the fourth estate of the realm"' (Curran 1991: 29), as they play a key role in enabling the public to exercise informal control over the state. Carpignano et al. argue that in the debates about mass media, politics and the public sphere 'there is a common ground, a mutual acceptance of basic premises, shared by participating politicians, conservative ideologues, and leftist cultural critics. Its unquestionable truism is that the mass media today are the public sphere and that this is the reason for the degradation of public life if not its disappearance' (1993: 93).

If we are to understand the nature of public spheres in contemporary European societies, we need to relate such high-level concepts to a more empirical inquiry into the institutions and practices of mass communication. In this paper we consider some findings from a recent multi-country research project *Media and Ethics of a European Public Sphere from the Treaty of Rome to the 'War on Terror'* (EMEDIATE). Here we focus, in particular, on whether there are emergent/embryonic elements of a common mediated European public sphere as marked by shifts towards a shared European journalistic culture.

Literature on European media/journalism cultures

Before moving to such empirical registers, we will briefly consider the prevailing research literature addressing the key factors influencing journalistic practices and media cultures in contemporary European societies. Here we find a large and growing corpus of work concerned with the changing nature of the journalistic profession, practices and media products – produced by media and communications studies' scholars as well as by media professionals. In sum, this work tends to identify the following as major factors or forces influencing media products and practices: changing economic conditions (especially ownership changes and increased competition), policies and regulation (for example, an increased pan-Europeanization of media policies within the European Union and a reliance on self-regulation), journalists' employment contracts and working conditions (for example, changes in these related to technological changes), and the changing interplay of journalistic and other elites (for example, journalists' interaction with sources and other influential actors as well as audiences).

Our own research confirms that developments in these areas have had a significant impact on the mediated public sphere over the last two decades. However, our interview findings suggest that, although journalists themselves identify these trends and developments and their impact on their work ethics and routines, they maintain that key journalistic values which guarantee objective, impartial and balanced reporting continue to be maintained.

One major Europe-related theme in the research concerns the way in which journalists deal with European news or current affairs topics and EU-related information. In general, we find that 'European' themes comprise a relatively small research topic in the eleven countries under discussion. Although the number of studies is small, we find several relevant and empirically grounded studies of the manner in which journalists and the media deal with EU news and current affairs information in the researched countries.

The literature review suggests that in terms of media content 'European' issues tend to be addressed through national frames. Generally, news and current affairs genres remain strongly orientated around national frames or epistemic communities. The most popular forms of shared European mediated experiences seem to lie in the realm of entertainment and sport, but even these are occasional or event-specific rather than routine in character (for example, the Eurovision Song Contest and the European Cup). Even when the phenomenon being addressed is a 'common' European or EU-related topic, it is treated and addressed in very specific ways in each national setting. The findings are similar in relation to ownership and EU policy. Whilst there has been an increase in the transnational ownership structures and in pan-EU policy and regulatory frameworks related to the media, this mode of 'Europeanization' has not been replicated at the level of media content production or editorial cultures. There has been a certain growth in the cross-border application of certain programming formats originating in Europe (for example, Big Brother) and in the co-production of films and television programming. The growing array of commercial and cable or satellite television channels (enabled by EU-level and national policy changes) has certainly led to an expanded demand for programming or 'content', but here the biggest supplier and beneficiary has been the U.S. audio-visual sector.

Journalism cultures in contemporary Europe: findings from interviews

In addition to our review of existing research on European journalistic cultures, we have worked with data collected in interviews with a wide range of journalists in the eleven countries which form part of the study. The interviews were designed to include as wide a cross-section of journalists as possible, from as wide a selection of media as possible. The criteria adopted for choosing the interviewees were that they should be mid-career, with reasonable experience, and preferably with a measure of editorial responsibility as editors or 'gatekeepers' (overseeing the actions of others). Table 1 summarizes the number of interviews conducted in the countries under examination.

We will here offer a brief summary of interviewees' responses to three questions: (1) What are the dominant influences today in the culture of journalism?; (2) Is there a 'European' journalistic culture (a set of values, standards – including ethics – and practices reflecting a specific European sense of identity or common purpose)?; and (3) Is there a pattern to the way in which 'European' topics or issues (i.e. issues connected with the governance, enlargement and political agenda of the European Union and the European project generally) are dealt with in your publication or broadcasting station? (See Preston and Horgan 2006.)

When asked about the dominant influences in the culture of journalism today, the most frequent response from journalists in every country was that accuracy was the most important value. Among the many specific values which were articulated, an emphasis on accuracy was common to all. Perhaps this is because this concept embraces so many aspects of the journalist's craft, encompassing factual correctness, comprehensiveness and balance – so that if a journalist is

Table 1. Interviews by country and type of medium.

Country	Total number of interviews	Press	Broadcast	Other
Britain	7	4	3	~
Czech Republic	8	5	2	1
France	9	4	5	~
Hungary	7	3	3	1
Ireland	9	7	2	~
Italy	7	5	2	~
Netherlands	6	3	3	~
Serbia	11	6	3	2
Slovakia	6	4	1	1
Slovenia	10	2	8	~
Spain	10	4	5	1
TOTALS	90	47	37	6

accurate they are more likely to be fair. In general, we found that the following issues comprised the professional values most frequently mentioned: seeking the truth; objectivity; getting as many sources as possible; checking sources; citing sources correctly; balance; strict separation of fact and opinion; and the need for both commentary and analyses to be strictly based on fact.

However, for several interviewees, professional ethics such as these were only half the story. Journalists in the Czech Republic and Slovakia, for example, argued that, in current media organizations, profit and circulation/viewing figures were the ultimate arbiters. Yet even in the face of the economic (and sometimes also political) pressures that journalists face in the course of their work, some of the media professionals interviewed in this study also emphasized that they had major societal obligations. Significantly, the journalists who articulated such views tended to come from countries which had undergone profound political change over the last three decades (for example, Spain and Slovenia). Also, in many cases it was editors working for public service media who felt societal obligations more strongly than others.

Several editors raised the question of whether the media ought to reflect the values of the society in which they operate, or try to shape them. For example, some interviewees in Slovenia argued that the media's job was to stimulate positive values (such as tolerance in society) by reflecting such values. They were of the opinion, though, that while it was possible to shape public opinion, they could not create new values. There were significant differences of opinion on this subject among the Hungarian editors. Of the seven interviewed, five felt that journalism could not influence or change existing values, but could only reflect them. They argued that Hungarian society was currently undergoing a crisis of values, and that this was being reflected in the low quality of the Hungarian media at this time. The other two felt that the onus on journalists was to try to counteract this trend, by emphasizing social solidarity. A similar point was made by the Serbian interviewees, who spoke of the need for journalists to maintain a 'critical distance from the government and state control', and of the media's educational role. A Serbian interviewee expressed the view that journalism is 'crucial to how a community or country forms its values, as journalists play an important role in shaping public opinion' – for good or ill. The notion that journalists ought to take an interventionist approach in the area of public opinion was explicitly rejected by Dutch editors.

Journalists from some post-Communist countries reflected on the changing professional standing of journalists since the fall of Communism. Czech and Slovak media professionals, for example, pointed out that immediately after the Velvet Revolution of 1989 journalists were acting more as citizens than as journalists, as papers promoted political stances and journalists supported the transformation. As one interviewee put it: 'that was revolutionary journalism, it was frequently waving a flag belonging to this or that [...] and this lasted quite a few years. With time this changed, most of the journalists emancipated themselves [...] and often, since everything is so new here, they overdid it in the other direction.' Since then, journalists gradually became professionals; yet, according to our interviewees, this also means that there is a growing number of journalists who are more concerned about their appearances, their salaries and their careers than about upholding journalistic values.

None of the British or Irish journalists interviewed even mentioned the idea of the media as a promoter of values or morals, in strong contrast with their colleagues on the continent. Indeed, they were more likely to emphasize practical issues, particularly the importance of balancing accuracy with speed, rather than philosophical concerns. As a senior editor at the London-based Sky News put it, the dominant imperative in British journalistic culture was 'getting the story first and getting the story right'.

Our research reveals a very pervasive perception amongst the senior media professionals interviewed that there has been a shift in the news agenda towards lighter, more entertainment-based news, which is seen as largely the result of increased commercialization and competition in the sector. None of those interviewed felt that this was a positive development.

The vast majority of journalists interviewed, irrespective of where they were based, felt that there was no pan-European journalistic culture, but rather national journalistic cultures remained dominant throughout Europe. Those who could identify a European journalistic culture tended to do so by comparing journalism in Europe with journalistic cultures elsewhere; but interviewees felt for the most part that the differences within Europe outweighed the similarities. For instance, many of the Slovenian journalists interviewed noted the difference between European journalism and that of the United States, but nevertheless felt that there was no commonality between (for example) the writing styles or story ideas that would dominate journalism in individual European states. Similarly, most of the Hungarian editors interviewed were unable to define any common European journalistic culture, believing national characteristics to be more important, although many then made reflexive references to differences between American and European journalism, although they could not give specific examples of this phenomenon.

Perhaps it is worth noting that while many interviewees perceived a singular lack of any pan-European journalistic culture, some of the senior journalists interviewed were able to identify similarities between certain countries within Europe. For instance, Spanish journalists observed some similarities between the media in Spain and in France, while one Irish foreign correspondent identified increasing similarities between the Irish press and British tabloids – and not in a positive sense. Other Irish interviewees also referred to the similarities between journalism in Ireland and Britain, which is perhaps unsurprising when one considers the common language and relatively high media penetration of British press and television in Ireland.

British journalists were the most vociferous in their rejection of the notion of a common journalistic culture. Many of the British journalists pointed to the media specifically in France and Germany (no other countries were cited) as examples of profoundly different styles. Both were seen as less vigorous, more reserved or boring, and much less likely to deal with controversial stories than were the British media.

Those who believed that there was a European journalistic area can be divided into two groups. Firstly, those who identified it by contrasting Europe with elsewhere. One British print journalist who had himself worked in the United States for a period noted the 'remarkable' attention paid to sourcing by American journalists and their reluctance to use off-the-record material. The second group were those who felt that a certain common culture of journalism (or perhaps of journalists) had developed to an extent around Brussels. Some pointed to initiatives which had been brought about to foster such a culture, such as France Ouest's training sessions, through which journalists are sent for a week to Brussels or Strasbourg to inform themselves of the relevant institutions and personalities.

None of the journalists identified a specific approach or pattern in the coverage of European issues. Many of the interviewees argued that European issues are considered uninteresting and publishing on Europe can present difficulties within media organizations. European issues tend to be too complicated and difficult to explain, and, in order to cover them, many said they must relate to readers' or viewers' everyday lives and invoke some kind of national or regional interest. Journalists in Slovakia, a relatively new EU Member State, also pointed out that Slovaks in general have not internalized the fact that Slovakia is part of the European Union, and thus EU-related issues are seen only in terms of their relation to Slovak issues. Some media in the newer EU Member States (for example, Czech public service television and Slovak public service radio) had once had special programmes or pages devoted to the enlargement process; however, once the process was complete, European topics became part of more general programmes or articles.

Conclusions

What are the implications for a shared mediated European public sphere? Our research suggests that instead of a shared European journalistic culture, a continued salience of the 'national' structure which shapes journalistic and media cultures prevails. Even where core and common EU-related topics are concerned, these still tend to be strongly interpreted and framed through specific national prisms. 'Banal nationalism' continues to play its role in framing media cultures throughout both the 'old' and 'new' EU Member States. This applies despite all of the recent emphasis on cultural (and economic) globalization and the understanding of the European Union as a case of particularly intensified economic integration at world-region level.

References

Carpignano, P. et al. (1993), 'Chatter in the Age of Electronic Reproduction : Talk Television and the "Public Mind"', in Robbins, B. (ed.), *The Phantom Public Sphere*, Minneapolis: University of Minnesota Press, pp. 93–120.

Curran J. (1991), 'Rethinking the Media as a Public Sphere' in Dahlgren, P., and Sparks, C. (eds.), *Communication and Citizenship: Journalism and the Public Sphere in the New Media Age*, London: Routledge, pp. 27–57.

Dahlgren, P. (1991), 'Introduction', in Dahlgren, P., and Sparks, C. (eds.), *Communication and Citizenship: Journalism and the Public Sphere in the New Media Age*, London, Routledge, pp. 1–26.

Fraser, N. (1993), 'Rethinking the Public Sphere', in Robbins, B. (ed.), *The Phantom Public Sphere*, Minneapolis: University of Minnesota Press, pp. 1–32.

Garnham, N. (1990), *Capitalism and Communication: Global Culture and the Economics of Information*, London: Sage.

Garnham, N. (1997), 'The Media and the Public Sphere', in Calhoun, C. (ed.), *Habermas and the Public Sphere*, Massachusetts, MIT, pp. 359–376.

Habermas, J. (1989), *The Structural Transformation of the Public Sphere*, Massachusetts: MIT.

Negt, O., and Kluge, A. (1993), *Public Sphere and Experience: Toward an Analysis of the Bourgeois and Proletarian Public Sphere*, Minneapolis: University of Minnesota Press.

Preston, P., and Horgan, J. (2006), 'Comparative Analysis of WP3 Reports on Editorial Culture' in *EMEDIATE Project: Media and Ethics of a European Public Sphere – From the Treaty of Rome to the "War on Terror"*, project no. CIT2-CT-2004-506027.

Domesticating Europe: Communicative Spaces of the East of West

Inka Salovaara-Moring

The external and internal conditions of the European Union changed dramatically with the membership enlargement of May 2004. In the case of the Baltic States, Hungary, and also to some extent Finland ten years earlier, realignment was accompanied by a profound redefinition of media systems, notions of political culture, geopolitical position and citizenry, a redefinition that had in fact started several decades earlier. This process was also profound for the European Union itself, the borders of which had moved eastwards over a comparatively short space of time. An even more drastic process started in the nation states that were incorporated into the Union. Public discussion of these historic transformations was closely linked to the new Member States' capacities to make sense of this change (Jakubowicz 2007; Sükosd and Bajomi-Lázar 2003; Vihalemm 2002; Slichal 2001; Sparks with Reading 1998; Lauristin and Vihalemm 1997). A crucial part of this sense-making had to do with how media support public discussion and civic society. Consequently, new demands concerning media practices, possibilities for individual participation and the maintenance of national consent on European issues were considered to have a greater importance than ever before.

When the eight post-Communist countries joined the European Union in 2004 (with Romania and Bulgaria joining three years later), this achievement was seen primarily as a consolidation of democratic values and practices across the continent. The change was called the 'return to the West' but more than that it was literally a return to a unified Europe, a return that radically redefined Europe's eastern border.

However, for the most part, those principles and norms that dominated the enlargement process were speed, efficiency and bureaucratic expertise. In many cases, this process provoked harsh criticism for being a constraint on democratic practice, and commentaries on the roles of the media in this process were particularly negative (Raik 2004). In addition, media systems had to adjust to the new situation by sending correspondents to Brussels and getting used to the transnational governance that soon became part of the domestic agenda.

This chapter focuses on the sociocultural processes of, and obstacles to, 'domesticating Europe' on the EU's eastern border through journalistic practices in four new Member States that have recently undergone geopolitical realignment (Estonia, Latvia, Lithuania and Hungary). The first part discusses the spatio-temporal and contextual nature of mediated communicative space. In the second part, the focus is on the individual experiences of journalists through the dual contextuality of their environments, i.e. applying indigenous news criteria to a foreign territory. The central questions are how journalists interact in national and transnational contexts, what kind of relationships they have with their national media, and in which ways the European project is domesticated from Brussels.

Domesticating Europe

The European integration project has made discussion of transnational spaces for cultural and political debate acute. The main questions have been: can there be a common Europe at all without a pan-European public sphere?; where can common values and ideas potentially be formed?; and where can transnational political institutions find their legitimacy? These issues have become especially sensitive after the setbacks of further integration, in terms of enlargement, the European Constitution and the Treaty of Lisbon, and a growing political distrust amongst the general populations of Member States.

The idea of a 'European Public Sphere' has, up till now, appeared as no more than a Bruxellois administrative Panopticon pipe dream aimed at shoring up the creaking European project – rather than as an empirical phenomenon. In reality, Brussels-based journalists have often been the sole connection between national public spheres, audiences and the governing centre of the European Union. This has given them the special role of being democratic 'proxies' between domestic politics and supra-national governance, as well as being placed in a new 'transit' position between home and abroad.

The number of Brussels-based correspondents and journalists may vary annually and the exact size of the cohort is hard to estimate at any given moment. However, according to a rough estimate by the Press Accreditation Centre, the number of journalists accredited to Brussels is around 1,200. In addition to about 20,000 commission officials, 732 MEPs and their assistants, 25 permanent representations to the European Union with their associated national diplomats and specialists, and NATO's political headquarters, Greater Brussels represents a spatial and temporal hub for European bureaucracy, political, economic and military power, and its huge administrative adjunct.

The Brussels press corps have often therefore been compared to the Washington press corps. In both places, a sizeable number of journalists report on decisions being made in the power centre of a federation (see Tunstall 1971; Schack and de Vreese 2006). However, those things that make Bruxellois journalistic circles different are the same things that make Europe different from the United States: a nation-state-based linguistic, historical, and economic diversity that is largely due to a Cold War heritage. Enlarged Europe represents a modern-day Babel in terms of linguistic and cultural difference.

Thus, in relation to this new spatial and temporal context for the formation of the region's communicative spaces, the dual-contextual nature of the EU journalism of (especially) newer Member States can be understood as functioning at (at least) three different levels. Firstly, enduring geographical and historical features produce fundamental constraints on the development of journalistic culture affecting, for example, how nations and their geopolitics are understood as historical processes and what type of function journalism has in nation-

Table 1. The spatio-temporal contextuality of journalistic cultures in the transitional societies.

Level of analysis	Temporal context of journalism	Spatial context of journalism
Structural level	Structural time: From socialism to capitalism; subordination to independence and sovereignty; journalism reviving social memory and national master-narratives.	Structural space: From nation states to transnational governance; journalism as solidifying nations and supporting 'Europeanization'; in between East and West.
Institutional level	Institutional time: New norms of the journalistic profession; adaptation to market(s), changing ownership and policy-lines of the specific print/audio-visual media; new market-based criteria.	Institutional space: National newsrooms with their traditions and politico-economic constraints; new legal frames for press freedom; different media for different publics (linguistic issues and minorities).
Inter-actional level	Inter-actional time: Contingent events and a sense of belonging to a specific generation; choices and decisions concerning professional roles; processes between informal and formal sources, publics and journalists.	Inter-actional space: Informal networks; spatial patterns of interpersonal communication and interaction with political actors, bureaucrats, etc.; feelings of spatial distance and proximity between home and Brussels.

building and identity-politics. Secondly, formal and institutional constraints in terms of political construction and the enforcement of legal provisions generate a specific politico-economic perspective to which journalism has to be adjusted. Thirdly, local spatio-temporal dynamics form informal networks of personal communication and interaction that affect relationships between domestic newsrooms and the reported 'territory', i.e. Brussels.

Journalism as a cultural practice of forming national communicative spaces can be seen through these contextual levels as a social practice and consequently as mediated through history, institutional structures and individuals. Thus, as a social and ideological practice, EU journalism does not reflect or mirror an easily objectified reality. Journalistic practices are socio-economic, historical, psychological, institutional, and even technical accomplishments – especially in the changing contexts of the new Member States. They are produced as discursive spaces within which certain actions are sensible, accepted, or even necessary. As such, they are ideological in nature – but their ideological underpinnings are not solely nor even predominantly structural or political. In the next section the experiences of EU journalists are explored with reference to these structural, institutional and individual levels.

Three levels of journalistic self-understanding: structural, institutional and individual levels intertwined

There is strong evidence that political history strongly affected how the present generation of journalists was recruited. Brussels is the location of a new and often relatively young, but already experienced, group of journalists who can work in English in addition to their own mother tongues. This is especially notable in the cases of journalists from the newer Member States, where the generational shift within their profession was crucially significant after the collapse of the Soviet regime. In many cases, as a cohort, these journalists formed the first 'European generation' in their respective countries in terms of linguistic skills (English often being the lingua franca), cultural contacts, and a notably different mindset:

> The tragedy of Estonian journalism, or maybe it is a blessing, is that they hired very many very young journalists back in early 1993 like myself. I had graduated but many hadn't, they were offered responsible positions, good salaries and they started working basically 24 hours a day and they didn't have time to complete their educations. These people, they didn't speak languages, they have educated themselves through their work but weren't really able to cover foreign affairs and they didn't have any knowledge of English. (Estonian journalist, Tallinn)

> When the change came there were suddenly tens of newspapers and television channels and everybody just decided to become journalists because they were needed everywhere. Easy as that! We did not have any education or experience and it was called 'children's journalism' or 'baby journalism.' We were playing at being journalists like children and then we became journalists. (Latvian journalist, Brussels)

Many of the old journalists are gone. If they didn't choose to leave themselves, they were removed. The world was so different during the Soviet time that they couldn't have adjusted to these new rules. Think about my father; he worked according to five-year-plans in a state-owned factory. There is a big leap from there to becoming a western capitalist and entrepreneur. (Latvian journalist, Riga)

As a result of historical conditions, and formal and informal networks, individual journalists tended to display similar attitudes, in terms of basic values and an understanding of the importance of the European Union. Individually, journalists often held very specific opinions with notably Euro-optimistic flavours. These tended towards strong political and economic pragmatism and a fairly consensual understanding of the importance of EU integration from an economic perspective:

Of course, in principle, I'm for the EU – sure. Statistically I fall into that democraphic: educated, city-dweller, young – of course, I understand that for all this population slice, of course, in principle the EU is good and NATO is also fine and necessary. (Lithuanian journalist, Brussels)

We [journalists] are typical in one sense: the elite are much more Euro-optimist than the overall population and I would say that most journalists belong to the elite and they mostly share the Euro-optimism. That is not a 100 per cent rule, but it is pretty much a rule. Political and journalistic elites share the same opinions. (Latvian journalist, Riga)

In general, Brussels correspondents have tended to report on EU issues from their national perspectives and every news piece 'had to be sold' to the domestic newsroom by conforming to the national agenda. At the domestic institutional level the European Union seemed to become a non-issue because it was considered distant and to be lacking in news value, and was not seen as a common project of both the elite and the general population. The problem for national foreign newsdesks was that the domestic audiences did not normally seem to be as interested in the EU agenda as in domestic politics. EU issues appeared to be non-issues that did not sell and were not considered particularly 'sexy' within the industry. Sometimes, when these stories were translated for national audiences, 'they could not see the wood for the trees' – a good story might well have focused on domestic political conflict but on a larger scale its significance was infinitesimal:

Our news is often boring; it is lacking in drama and suspense. Perhaps we should learn about Russian journalism and not be so politically correct. Russians tell the story and although they are not always so strict with the facts, they are at least entertaining. (Latvian journalist, Riga)

Newspaper journalists behave as if they were on TV, they are interested in drama, in visually attractive news, rather than in process – but if they send someone with our money then it tends to be to some kind of disaster zone: flood or tsunami. But they don't want to cover the European Constitution or something that has to do with a process that is not so attractive visually but important. (Estonian journalist, Tallinn)

Sometimes the important news is buried under the trivia. Commissioner Margot Wahlström's EU image campaign takes all the space, and at the same time there is the process where a certain type of fuel will be banned within EU and that will have long-lasting effects on the ecological conditions on this continent. Nobody notices this piece. (Hungarian journalist, Brussels)

Journalists as 'symbolic producers and translators' were affected by a professional sub-culture, with all its norms and codes, both written and unwritten. They also seemed to interact in a specific social organization of Brussels-based correspondents, with its own goals and rules. Many of the journalists denied a cultural detachment from their domestic scenes but the spatial distance from 'home' was articulated in other ways. There seemed to be not only a comprehension gap between journalists and their domestic audience, but also a lack of any domestic understanding of the importance of 'Europeanization'. The problem was more that EU news very seldom fulfilled national news criteria. Thus, the biggest obstacle to domesticating Europe had little to do with a shortage of information:

Before the referendum there was quite a lot of money allocated to this issue and a lot of information published and the media got very well paid from that. Before the referendum, it was a goal to get into the EU, get better turnout and votes. Right now, it is not so interesting. It continues but there is not such a goal to achieve. It is more a routine and from the other side the influential people lose interest in the EU. Because of the EU, prices for fuel were going up, and for this and that people were not satisfied. (Latvian journalist, Riga)

The European Union is not a big story any more – to tell you the truth. Nothing comes out of the European Union, no big things are happening here – it's always the same. So you can't see that something is starting and somebody is pushing the whole European Union ahead. So it's quite everyday, wheels going slowly round and round and round – that's it. (Hungarian journalist, Brussels)

Most journalists reported frustration with the way that their audiences' lack of EU knowledge undermined their work. Since most national political systems differ from the EU system, it was difficult for the journalists to cover issues adequately. Often they saw themselves as simply forced to approach a topic from the most basic perspective. The biggest problem, however, was that the lack of genuine interest in EU matters was accompanied by a wealth of easily stirred up scepticism. The domestic political sphere was often criticized for its failure to comprehend the EU's relative importance on the international scene:

Perhaps people are interested in EU matters but they don't seem to understand the issues. I don't know what I could have done during the last ten years to make them understand more. I have constantly written by explaining simply how this regulation or Constitution or whatever will affect them. I simply don't know. (Finnish journalist, Brussels)

On the one hand there is a lot of information, a lot – like an ocean. On the other hand they don't know what to do with this information, with this enormous amount of information – not the only the ordinary people but people at the TV channel and papers. They don't know how to handle it because they don't know how the whole thing is working. So when I say in five sentences what's going on, sometimes my TV channel calls me back – I have to give three pages of explanation just for them to understand those five sentences because they don't know how to handle that, you see. And ordinary people – what do they see? They see their government. (Hungarian journalist, Brussels)

Common people don't care and they are not interested in EU matters. The EU is definitely an elite issue. Sometimes I feel guilty that I misinform people. Hungarian MEPs are not as important as Hungarian people think they are. This is the playground of the big countries, also journalistically. If Barruso wants to talk to some journalists, he calls the *Financial Times*, the BBC and CNN. One Hungarian daily is not very important – or Hungary in general. (Hungarian journalist, Brussels)

According to these correspondents, producing and domesticating Europe was an ideologically and historically important task, and there was a certain drive to widen the level of political discussion and deliberation, and to emphasize its importance at a national level. Many of the journalists reflected upon their immediate responsibility in fostering the European 'domestication' process. On one hand, they reflected on their roles as proxies for democracy: as actors located between Brussels and a home scene trying to convey the importance of EU matters and to widen the public's horizons. On the other, they reflected on themselves as good citizens and felt responsible towards their domestic situations: having to balance what they could see, what they could say and what would be (mis)understood in their domestic frames. European coverage was understood as a form of cultural solidarity and a collective mode of accommodating a changing cultural and political environment – both back home and, through that, within the European Union:

I must tell you that our role here in the European Union is not so good because we are here and we tell the news to the people in Hungary. So the EU exists through us and maybe our eyes are not so good, you see. So the people, the Hungarians, they only read what the correspondents say to them, they never wanted to have the information directly from the European Union for themselves – then they could judge whether it is good or not. So we have a special role which I don't like. I like people to go online – if they read the paper they get what we send them. On the other hand, although the European Union speaks about communication, how it's important to reach the people – they do just the opposite. (Hungarian journalist, Brussels)

To be a correspondent for a big newspaper in your country is a responsibility. So, on a good number of occasions, I remember I was, if not censoring myself, controlling myself. 'Maybe this argument would be far-fetched, too critical; it is not worth being so critical this time.' Things like that. You have to take into account things like what the person (politician, MEP) you are writing about will have to experience; but you just can't. Fortunately for my reputation and readership but unfortunately for my relationships here with individual people, I have a tendency to be too critical, to be too sarcastic, too ironic. You can't do that to the detriment of people all the time. (Hungarian journalist, Brussels)

The intimacy felt towards the political community by the journalists was part of a broader responsibility towards a domestic community, and concern about how that related to the new economically unified space. An Estonian diplomat aptly defined the size of democracy in terms of intimacy and responsibility: 'Estonia is so small everybody is related to everybody, if not related to each other then acquainted with each other. It is like a family.' A nation state as a set of relations within a given national community also adds a corporeal and emotional dimension – structures of feelings, memory and moral imperatives – to be taken into account when exploring the evolving journalistic cultures in the newer Member States. Thus, quite often journalists' reflections on their roles in the process of deepening integration were informed by historical, institutional and individual re-evaluations of the media's role as a mediator between the public and political elites.

Cultural geographies of European journalism
Marx once noted that men don't make their history as they please or under circumstances chosen by themselves but under circumstances directly encountered, given and transmitted from the past. This scenario also applies to the production of contemporary Europe. Cultural geographies of public communication, i.e. national communicative spaces, can be understood as spatially and historically defined sociocultural practices that are modified as part of the collective understanding of the historical legacy and possible future of a specific nation within a larger constellation.

Changes in media systems in the newer Member States have been part and parcel of the general process of what may be called systemic social transformation. What has seldom been studied, however, is how newly recruited journalists themselves see the process of integration. In general, social, economic and political life is absorbed by journalists in a process of interpretation of the values, beliefs, fears, ambitions and typical ideologies of the time. The work of a journalist is also embedded in larger patterns such as historical and political transformations over which an individual has only limited control or no control at all.

In this context, journalists act by creating, translating, and organizing the symbolic exchange across central political and economic discourses between their locations and national newsrooms. At the same time, they participate – willingly or unwillingly – in a process of the modification of different values, democratic ideals and political aspirations, reconstructing their surroundings and larger geopolitical entities in accordance with the economic interests of their newspaper or radio or television station. This type of exchange of values is not only material but also symbolic in relation to norms and cultural structures (Salovaara-Moring 2004, 2006).

However, the dynamics of national communicative spaces are often based on cultural intimacy and the constraints of the media system itself. These constraints seem to be in opposition to the evolving transnationalism and cosmopolitanism that many Brussels-based correspondents seem to represent. This may be due to the lack of a new type of geographical imagination in the general population that would transcend national borders and would inherently acknowledge a spatially broader political concern, creating a vital national interest in EU-issues within domestic settings.

Going one step further on from the traditional notion of the Habermasian public sphere, new EU-journalism could be understood as a type of social technology of transnational citizenship. Its distinctive institutional and symbolic forms emerge in response to a set of imperatives constructed in changing power-matrices in order to govern the habits, desires, fears and passions of dispersed European populations. By translating and giving meanings to such abstract constructions as 'state', 'democracy', 'Europe' or 'identity', journalists modify perceptions of these concepts under the very specific cultural geography of a given population. This is what makes journalism not only information but also a confirmation of the new cultural values, stereotypes and norms of a national community.

At the moment, the processes of 'Europeanization' through the experiences of journalists can only be studied through an evolving tradition which attempts to make sense of the relationships between the supranational and the national. Therefore, journalistic genealogies are like palimpsests of their respective countries, pages that have endlessly been written upon, erased and used again. Earlier historical structures can still faintly be seen through more recent layers of journalistic cultures. Perhaps somewhere there, in between the layers, a new generation or new type of transnationalism in journalism is coming into being. This could represent one way to maintain a sense of solidarity when the Union encounters its next serious challenge.

References

Barnett, C. (2003), *Culture and Democracy. Media, Space and Representation*, Edinburgh: Edinburgh University Press.

Delanty, G., and Rumford, C., (2005) *Rethinking Europe: Social theory and the implications of Europeanization*, London and New York: Routledge.

Ekiert, G., and Hanson, S. (2003), 'Time, Space and Institutional Change', in Ekiert, G., and Hanson, S. (eds.), *Capitalism and Democracy in Central and Eastern Europe*, Cambridge: Cambridge University Press, pp. 15–48.

Gavin, N. (2001), 'British Journalists in the Spotlight: Europe and Media Research', in *Journalism: Theory, Practice and Criticism* 2:3, pp. 299–314.

Jakubowicz, K. (2007), *Rude Awakening. Social and media change in Central and Eastern Europe*, Broadway: Hampton Press.

Raik, K. (2004), 'EU Accession of Central and Eastern European Countries: Democracy and Integration as Conflicting Logics', in *East European Politics and Societies* 18:4, pp. 567–594.

Salovaara-Moring, I. (2004), *Media Geographies. Regional Newspaper Discourses in Finland in the 1990s*, Saarijärvi: Gummerus.

Salovaara-Moring, I. (2006), 'Fortress Europe: Ideological metaphors of media geographies', in Falkenheimer, J., and Jansen, A. (eds.), *Geographies of Communication: Spatial Turn in Media Studies*, Göteborg: Nordicom, pp. 107–125.

Schack, R., and de Vreese, C. (2006), 'Between Risk and Opportunity. News Framings and its Effect of Public support for EU Enlargement', in *European Journal of Communication* 21:1, pp. 5–32.

Schudson, M. (2003), *The Sociology of News*, London: W.W. Norton.

Sparks, C., with Reading, A. (1998), *Communism, Capitalism and the Mass Media*, London: Sage.

Sükösd, M., and Bajomi-Lázar, P., eds. (2003), *Reinventing Media. Media Policy Reform in East-Central Europe*, Budapest: Central European University Press.

Tunstall, J. (1971), *Journalists at Work. Specialist Correspondents: Their News Organizations, News Sources, and Competitor-colleagues*, London: Constable.

Vihalemm, M., and Vihalemm, P., eds. (1997), *Return to the Western World: Cultural and Political Perspectives on the Estonian Post-communist Transition*, Tartu: Tartu University Press.

Vihalemm, P., ed. (2002), *Baltic Media in Transition*, Tartu: Tartu University Press.

THE EUROPEAN UNION AND ITS 'PROMOTIONS DEFICIT': POLITICAL COMMUNICATION AND THE GLOBAL WARMING ISSUE

Neil T. Gavin

The European Union currently faces a set of important and worryingly convergent challenges. These can be grouped as 'political challenges', 'engagement challenges' and 'media-related challenges'. The first of these revolves around the issue of the management of the EU's internal politics, and is particularly salient in a situation where the European Union may have enlarged beyond its capacity to cope. The draft constitutional treaty sought to address some of the procedural difficulties involved, but foundered in the referenda in France and the Netherlands; its resurrection in the Treaty of Lisbon fared as badly at the hands of Irish voters. This is particularly unfortunate at a time when the European Union faces a range of structural and policy problems that will require concerted effort if they are to be confronted effectively. They include the accession of Turkey and Croatia, the response to global warming and carbon emission control, the EU's position on energy security, and its contribution to the resolution of tensions in the Middle East.

These problems assail the European Union at a time when it faces growing challenges revolving around EU citizen engagement or, more precisely, lack of engagement. There is some weakening of support for its core institutions (Føllesdal 2006) and an increase in support for non-mainstream parties that often have an anti-European agenda (Koopmans and Erbe

2004). Turnout at European elections is in a worrying decline in a number of Member States – a function, it is suggested, of the perception that these represent 'second order' contests. And, despite the fact that a high proportion of EU citizens claim an awareness of EU matters, Bruggemann (2005) reported that fewer than 40 per cent had heard of the Convention on the EU Constitution, and a substantial proportion could not name the full complement of EU Member States. Moreover, in some quarters there is little by way of a shared sense of European identity, and indeed little prospect of one developing (Gavin 2000). Finally, the related issue of the 'democratic deficit' is still a problem, despite some recent attempts to rehabilitate the European Union and reassert its democratic credentials (Moravcsik 2002; Mény 2003; Lord and Magnette 2004; Schmidt 2004).

On top of these difficulties, the European Union faces a range of media-related challenges, a significant problem since they are heavily implicated in the way citizens come to orient themselves towards the European Union (Gavin 2007a). First, there is the so-called 'communication deficit'. This suggests that there is insufficient attention to European issues, and as a consequence there is a failure to generate an appropriately well-developed pan-European public sphere (Meyer 1999; De Vreese 2003; Anderson and McLeod 2004). Democratic accountability and citizen engagement suffer accordingly. This is particularly worrying in circumstances where important political developments – such as the Convention – can struggle to find space on the airwaves (Gleissner and De Vreese 2005). The problem here is compounded by what some see as a journalistic deficit (Campbell 2006). Here the primary focus is on journalistic practice. European issues are considered insufficiently newsworthy to command from media organizations the attention and resources they need or deserve – a problem compounded in Britain by the unwillingness of some domestic politicians to make EU issues an agenda priority.

Political communication analysts are heavily exercised by the sort of coverage the European Union gets as a result of these cumulative deficits (Anderson and Weymouth 1999; Gavin 2001b). But there has also been a fair bit of attention paid to the assessment of the difficulties experienced by the journalists who work the European newsbeat, either in Brussels or from their domestic capitals (see Morgan 1995; Baisnée 2002; Firmstone 2004; Gleissner and de Vreese 2005). This literature suggests that they often work under considerable pressure to conform to domestic news imperatives. They do so, often with inadequate resources, and with limited training for (or orientation towards) the complexities of Europe and the politics of Brussels. Journalists can struggle to force onto the agenda an issue that is seen by editors and sub-editors as complex, and abstracted from direct domestic considerations, occasionally dull and often laced with jargon. To compound the problem in getting across Europe's story, there is also a corresponding body of research dealing with the image-management capacities (or, rather, 'incapacities') of the Commission, European Parliament and the Council of Ministers (Tumber 1995; Meyer 2000; Anderson and McLeod 2004; Smith 2004; Bruggemann 2005). These studies suggest that the orientation towards effective communication by the European Union, European Parliament and Commission has been characterized by indifference, mismanagement and incompetence. There has been, in short, a *promotions deficit* (Gavin 2007a) that is every bit as dangerous as the communications deficit or journalistic deficit.

Addressing the 'promotions deficit'

The problems outlined here go some way towards an explanation of the bad press the European Union gets in Britain – an explanation which is not solely focused on the intervention of hostile newspaper proprietors (Anderson and Weymouth 1999). But while the pressures of the journalistic job are unlikely to change anytime soon, the European Union (and the Commission in particular) is experiencing a metamorphosis in its political communication organization and strategy, and seems to be waking up – albeit belatedly – to the fact that it has a serious problem (Bruggemann 2004).

What do these EU initiatives amount to? Peter Mandelson's elevation to the Commission may not have been decisive, but it placed a proven communicator at the heart of EU affairs, alongside other key officials noted for their communication competence, notably Margot Wallström. Mandelson showed that he seemed to appreciate the true nature of the problem: 'effective communication is not about "spin": it is about making sure in the first place that the Commission has sensible, well-thought-out policies that address real needs' (*The Times*, 18/9/04). And if reports are to be believed, the Commission is taking communications a great deal more seriously than it has hitherto.

Formally, the Commission has produced an action plan on communication, a 'Plan-D for Democracy, Dialogue and Debate', and a White Paper on communications policy (CEC 2005a; CEC 2005b; CEC 2006). From these documents, it is apparent that the Commission has finally come to acknowledge the centrality of communications: 'This Commission has made communication one of the strategic objectives for its term of office, recognising it fully as a policy in its own right' (CEC 2005a: 3). Communications considerations are to inform every aspect of Commission activity, from crisis-planning and 'rapid rebuttal', through to policy-planning and execution, and, indeed, all forms of engagement with the EU citizenry. The communications apparatus in Brussels is to be completely reorganized and more closely integrated with Representations in the respective Member States. The Representations are to be beefed up by contracting in audio-visual, Web and PR specialists. They are to coordinate with European Parliament offices, and will be involved in the evaluation of communication activities. Individual Commissioners will act as 'ambassadors' for the European Union and, after the appropriate media training, are to help increase the profile of EU affairs. Importantly, this communications approach is to be informed by feedback from the public (in the form of surveys and focus groups), with Commission messages firmly connected to the preoccupations and interests of EU citizens, and conveyed in a way the public understands. The resultant media commentary is to be monitored systematically. The journalists who write EU-related stories are also a target of the strategy. Training and visitors' programmes will be laid on for these important 'multipliers', serving – so the Commission hopes – to make European affairs more comprehensible to commentators. Most significant of all, this strategy recognizes that this requires money, and lots of it. Therefore, substantial resources have been set aside for a budget that rolls through from 2006 to 2013 (CEC 2005a: 37–38).

The change in orientation represented in these initiatives looks profound. However, amongst observers of the process of the reconstitution of the EU's political communication machinery, there is little by way of assessment of the inherent *limitations* that are likely to condition the results (de Vreese 2003; Smith 2004). So it is the nature of these limitations, and the implications that follow, that form the basis of the following analysis.

It is probably too early to say whether the EU's overall strategy is yielding significant results. However, there are important *operational*, *structural* and *contextual* obstacles that will severely limit what the Commission's grand communication plan can achieve. On the operational front we could, for instance, take the notion that Commissioners act as 'ambassadors' for the European Union. It is all very well that an ambassadorial Commissioner should visit countries which are not their own, but they may be virtual strangers there. And if they *are* known, they are likely to carry the burden of their past associations or affiliations – Peter Mandelson surely being a case in point. Furthermore, will such 'ambassadors' have the time or energy required to engage in the sort of dialogue with journalists at national or sub-national levels that would help put the best gloss on EU affairs? This is an important consideration in a country like Britain where a great deal of EU-related journalism is undertaken *at* the national level, *by* nationally located journalists (Firmstone 2004). The Commission clearly has some ground to make up here, given that the EU's existing communications competence is not rated terribly highly by domestically situated reporters across Europe (Firmstone 2004: 41–42).

But the idea of 'Commissioners-as-ambassadors' is perhaps the least ambitious aspect of the Commission's communication strategy. In operational terms, there are challenges which are even more problematic. The Commission has set aside a substantial budget, but this will need to be spread between Brussels and all 27 Representations. It will have to pay for re-structuring and extra staff, for PR-related contracting out, and for the monitoring of media content and public opinion. All of this will put a substantial strain on what is still a finite budget. Furthermore, we know that financing, coordinating, and implementing a communications strategy at *national* level is difficult enough, as New Labour's third term experiences attest. But doing this across a wide range of different countries, each with unique political and media environments, will need a step-change in effort and resourcing beyond that envisaged in the current action plan. Moreover, any exercise in pan-European outreach has to be seen in the light of evidence suggesting that the Commission is playing a rather belated game of catch-up. For some time now, political actors at national government levels have been aware of the need to operate strategically across a range of European countries, seeking to affect how issues play in the media of other Member States in order to influence policy agendas and affect EU decisions (Meyer 2000:167–68). The Commission, in this respect, is something of a late starter, and has much ground to make up.

These operational issues are, nevertheless, the least of the problems faced by the European Union in framing an effective communication strategy. Structural considerations are a more serious impediment and are, inevitably, less tractable. First and foremost, the European Union is a complex set of interlocking institutions and, therefore, does not have the sort of centralized, monolithic architecture that lends itself to the carefully orchestrated, disciplined and effective control of communications (Scammell 1995; Kavanagh 1995). The Commission may be a strategically situated part of the EU structure, but is not a 'lead institution', at least in a sense that would be meaningful in PR terms. A core problem here is that the Commission's new communication policy is, essentially, a single-institution initiative. While it encompasses coordination and cooperation with other EU institutions (notably the Parliament), this cannot be enforced and will not necessarily be forthcoming. The Commission's relationships with the European Parliament and the nation states that constitute the Council leave more than ample room for conflict or friction over strategy, policy development and implementation, all of which augur badly for concerted and effective political communication.

The shifting interplay of institutional, political and national interests inherent in the EU's structural arrangements make it particularly difficult for the Commission to frame a coherent and agreed 'message' that all can subscribe to, all can stick to and all can consistently drive home in a coordinated fashion – almost the defining features of a successful image management strategy (Scammell 1995; Kavanagh 1995; Lees-Marshment 2001, 2004a and 2004b). Indeed, this will be doubly problematic where national-level governments can act independently in communication terms and externalize to the European Union, or to other Member States, responsibility for those aspects of brokered decisions that impact negatively on their domestic publics (Obradovic 1996; Kevin, 2003: 131). Consequently, any message will almost certainly have to be rather vague, general or abstract. But, if it is, it may be bland to the point of meaninglessness, and will almost certainly lose the punch necessary for effective communication. For instance, *The Guardian* newspaper has reported Margot Wallström's declaration that the European Union needs to transform itself economically, and that twenty million unemployed people in the EU is 'a "totally unacceptable" figure.' (14/10/05). The aim is laudable and the message superficially attractive, but when we get down to brass tacks, the real question will be how, precisely, Wallström's vision is to be achieved – through what mechanisms and policies. Such details are likely to be a good deal more difficult to distil into a message that is easily communicated.

Even if more specific means and ends can be agreed, the complex and institutionally interconnected decision-making procedures of the European Union present what would be formidable communication challenges even for an institution that could count on a powerful and centralized PR apparatus. Firstly, the EU structure is hard to glamorize, and equally difficult for journalists to describe, personalize and relay effectively. This is on top of the fact that TV journalists struggle to represent the European Union, the Commission and the Council in a way that is visually interesting. Furthermore, the sort of delicately brokered deals, play-offs, compromises, flexible implementation speeds and linkages that characterize much of EU policy-making do not produce policy packages that lend themselves to clear and pithy encapsulation. And even if they did, it is likely to become increasingly difficult to translate any resultant messages into a language or idiom that would be understood and appreciated in a uniformly positive way across the whole of an enlarged EU. Meyer (2000: 206) is undoubtedly correct when he states that, 'the Commission's relevant publics vary not only along socio-economic and political lines, but also by nationality. What may be unproblematic and desirable to one national public, may spark an uproar for another one.'

Meyer's subsequent comment – that this makes the Commission all the more dependent on its communication apparatus to address national and sub-national sensitivities – is also a valid point. But it seriously underestimates the depth of the problem faced, and the structural difficulties at its heart. Indeed, one could go as far as to suggest that such structural impediments almost necessitate that the Commission's strategic planning places much more emphasis on PR machinery (or on information dissemination: Bruggemann 2005) than on the sort of message that is to be promoted – a near fatal flaw in communication terms. It may well be the case, as one prominent British journalist put it, that 'Europe needs a bold new story – and [...] new ways to tell it' (The Guardian, 22/3/07). But it remains to be seen whether the Commission is equipped to invent such a story, or tell it in the way it will need to, if it is to convince a discursively 'polyglot' citizenry.

Finally, there are a number of contextual factors that make the evolution of an effective communication strategy less, rather than more, likely. A range of current or impending political and economic problems will test the structures of the European Union, and accentuate some of the problems in the Commission's communications plans. These include the nature of involvement in Iraq and Afghanistan, the framing of an enduring settlement in Palestine, and an international, post-Kyoto approach to global warming. There is, of course, ample room for agreement and compromise on these issues, as Smith (2006) quite rightly reminds us. But they will continue to be controversial and newsworthy, and to highlight important policy differences between Member States, alongside significant clashes of interest. Closer to home, a different set of issues continues to test the European Union. Some are primarily political (like the reframing of the debate on an EU Constitution), but others involve a more incendiary mix of political and economic considerations, where the national, sub-national and regional sensitivities of Europe's constituent countries will be at their keenest (Eriksen and Fossum 2004). These include energy security against a background of 'peak oil' and high energy demand, the settling of budgetary arrangements and the related issue of redistribution, the role of the Common Agricultural Policy (CAP) in the context of ongoing World Trade Organization (WTO) negotiations, and the level of liberalization necessary to confront the EU's economic problems.

The European Union and the climate change discourse

One of the more important of these challenges will be framing a policy response to climate change and carbon emissions. If the European Union needs to send a positive rhetorical message which has broad appeal across a range of constituent national populations, and resonates with current sensibilities, the issues of global warming and its mitigation look like likely candidates. It is a clear and imminent threat, and the target for mitigating intervention is equally clear. The control of CO_2 is also within the EU's competence, in terms of legislative initiatives and their associated policy statements. Additionally, action on greenhouse gas emissions would allow the European Union to distinguish itself from other, less proactive nations – notably America and China – and present itself as a leader in the drive towards a post-Kyoto settlement. However, even this strong discursive position need not necessarily or straightforwardly translate into favourable or complementary coverage. The way that the EU's strategy on climate change and greenhouse gas emissions plays in the media of one of its largest and most significant members – Britain – is a case in point, and it exemplifies some of the problems at the heart of the EU's ongoing communication difficulties. On the plus side, the European Union is obviously capable of generating pretty positive headlines across a wide spectrum of media. From the left leaning, pro-European *Guardian* newspaper, the EU's decision to draw air travel within its carbon emissions trading scheme, generated the headline, 'Europe to include airlines in battle on climate change' (21/12/06). And upon the EU's agreement in March 2007 to set in place ambitious emissions targets, Britain's principal public service broadcaster reported, 'EU agrees on carbon dioxide cuts: European Union leaders at a climate change summit in Brussels have agreed to slash carbon dioxide emissions by 20 per cent from 1990 levels by the year 2020' (BBC, 9/3/07). And on the same occasion *The Economist* could announce 'Winds of change: The EU unveils bold plans to tackle global warming' (9/3/07).

But the range of reports that preceded and followed these rather fleeting headlines, highlights the inherent image-management problems of the European Union, and outlines the difficulties it will have in portraying itself in a positive light – difficulties which stem in no small part from the way its structure and procedures condition both its policies *and* the manner in which they are reported. Before the compromise deal was struck, *The Guardian* could headline a report 'Grand plan for a low-carbon Europe goes up in smoke: European Commissioners at loggerheads over how to shape legislation' (24/1/07), a story revolving around German sensitivities to the impact of targets on the domestic car market: 'A senior German source in Brussels highlighted the rifts, saying: "If we force a target of 120g per kilometre on each new car we would have to close Daimler-Chrysler, Audi, BMW and Porsche and that's not possible. We have to make Europe the leader in green technology while boosting output and jobs."'

Such dramatic and newsworthy examples of communicative indiscipline are an intrinsic and recurrent part of EU political reality (Gavin 2001a), and are almost guaranteed to draw attention. They make news – just not 'good news'.

Similar sensitivities re-expressing narrow and potentially divisive national-level interests were also signalled on the day before the agreement of March 2007 on climate change – 'Nuclear question splits EU climate talks' (*The Guardian*, 8/3/07) – where it was reported that: 'At his swansong summit outgoing French president Jacques Chirac insisted that he would only agree to binding energy targets if nuclear power were included and proposed that 45 per cent of the mix come from non-fossil fuel sources. France gets 80 per cent of its power from nuclear power plants.'

Proposals on the inclusion of nuclear power did eventually figure in the final summit package. But this is a feature that will not play well to citizens in many Member States where nuclear energy is highly controversial (notably Austria, Ireland, Sweden and Germany). It highlights the difficulty in framing compromises which will have broad appeal across the continent. Furthermore, the way this developing story was reported highlights another problem for the European Union – making its activities transparent and easily translated by journalists into a language that is comprehensible and accessible to its citizens. In this instance the BBC, in the report already quoted, continued: 'The statement on renewable energy sources allows flexibility in how each country contributes to the overall target for the EU. Poorer Eastern European countries, which are more dependent on heavy industry and carbon-heavy coal, had argued they would struggle to make the investment in wind farms and solar power necessary to meet binding targets. *The final text allayed their fears by stating that "differentiated national overall targets" for renewables would be set, "with due regard to a fair and adequate allocation taking account of different national starting points"*' (9/3/07) [my emphases].

The complex intricacies of policy represented here, though important, are hardly likely to set the imagination of the average citizen alight. They are intrinsically difficult to render meaningful, relevant and interesting to an audience – a problem that is not entirely unknown, as experience with the Draft Constitution also attests (see Gavin 2007a: 155–56).

But perhaps more damaging still, in the aftermath of the March 2007 EU summit, the competing (and what look like contradictory) priorities of the European Union in the domains of emission control and trade liberalization were prominent even in the Europhile *Guardian* newspaper. The headline 'Europe back open skies deal with America: Transatlantic travel expected to soar 50 per cent and passengers to save £7.7bn as transport ministers give unanimous approval to remove restrictions' (23/3/07) was followed almost immediately, and rather unsurprisingly, with 'Open skies deal will undo curbs on CO2, say Greens'. The opening to the latter report stated that 'Environmental groups warned yesterday that the open skies treaty to liberalize transatlantic flights could undermine efforts to combat climate change' (24/3/07). Here the rhetorical and communicative gains from the EU's policy initiatives on climate change are all too easily turned into what look like a discursive retreat. Delicately brokered deals in one policy domain all too readily and publicly conflict with the goals of policy in another, and in ways that are highly likely to attract adverse publicity, even if climate change is not high on the media agenda (Gavin 2007b).

Finally, a report on the implications of the emissions-capping deal struck in March 2007 reflects the problems the European Union faces in reconciling its varying goals, while at the same time presenting itself in the most favourable light. *The Guardian* (28/3/07) reported that the 'European Union's climate change goals will cost €1 trillion: Report outlines daunting task of CO2 targets.' This story shows that even in a domain where the European Union might make political capital out of its positioning and policy, the associated headlines can be negative, even in the pro-European press. Importantly, stories like this reflect upon the 'output' or 'performance' legitimacy of the European Union (Beetham and Lord 1998; Lord and Beetham 2001), and are particularly problematic where financial considerations are prominent, and where so much is at stake. The issue here is not just about degraded legitimacy as policy chickens 'come home to roost'. It concerns an equally important but more general orientation toward the European Union – the issue of European identity. One of the ways in which citizens may come to identify with the European Union is through direct material gain from involvement in 'Europe' (Wallace and Smith 1995: 134). But it has been observed elsewhere that a European identity will not develop spontaneously. Citizens need to become aware of the benefits the European Union brings, and the media have a role to play here (Gavin 2000). But as the preceding examples demonstrate, this role need not be a positive one. The economic down-side of EU policy is equally likely to receive prominence in reports even in sympathetic newspapers, as this example and others show (Gavin 2001a). There is a danger that the 'output legitimacy' of the European Union will be eroded as a result, but so too may the public's identification with the institutions involved.

Political implications

Current conditions, therefore, present formidable presentational challenges to the European Union. They are likely to continue to expose recurrent lines of tension, in a manner likely to command attention in the media. Where these conditions do not lead to the sort of open disputes that the media are all too happy to pick up on (as we have illustrated), they may well be settled by a range of ungainly compromises, especially in a context where divergent perspectives or preferences are at stake, and where the interests of 27 countries have to be accommodated. Yet any associated compromises or packaged arrangements may be difficult to encapsulate in 'media-friendly' terms, or they may have strongly negative discursive dimensions, as we saw in the global warming example. These problems are bad enough as they stand, but will be exacerbated further if new entrants join the European Union – especially where a whole new range of cultural sensitivities and political sensibilities enter the equation, as they may well do in the case of Turkey.

This will be all the more problematic in a situation where, as Meyer (2000) has noted, the scandals that rocked the Commission in the late 1990s caused the whole Brussels press corps to become more adversarial and tenacious in its investigations. Baisnée (2002) confirms this observation when describing how an aggressive 'anglophone' approach to EU journalism has become much more widespread. Consequently, in this type of atmosphere the problem of selling the European Union to an increasingly sceptical European public will be all the more difficult. The European Union that these journalists will be reporting has grown to encompass 27 countries and is set to include more. This will make significant clashes of interest more likely, and more difficult to accommodate, since the procedural difficulties that the Draft Treaty on the Constitution and the Treaty of Lisbon sought to address are still outstanding. The issues the European Union needs to address are increasingly 'global' in nature and, therefore, more complex and difficult to manage. On top of this, many argue that the EU's ambitions are too modest and that its competences must grow accordingly. As a result of these accumulated developments, the communicative difficulties outlined in the preceding analysis are set to become *more* rather than less problematic, and even the most professional, accomplished and well-organized political communicators would struggle in such circumstances. The danger for the European Union is that these interrelated problems are not straightforwardly amenable to remedial action. The prognosis here is grim, but at least the European Union is taking steps to address its 'promotions deficit', and is no longer pretending, as it used to do, that the problems do not exist. Whether this altered stance will change things in sufficient time to limit the damage remains to be seen.

References

Anderson, P. J., and Weymouth, A. (1999), *Insulting the Public? The British Press and the European Union*, London: Longman.

Anderson, P.J., and McLeod, A. (2004), 'The Great Communicator? The Mass Communication Deficit of the European Parliament', in *Journal of Common Market Studies* 42:5, pp. 897–917.

Baisnée, O. (2002), 'Can political journalism exist at the EU level', in Kuhn, R. and Neveu, E. (eds.), *Political Journalism: New Challenges, New Practices*, London, Routledge, pp. 108–28.

Beetham, D., and Lord, C. (1998), *Legitimacy and the European Union*, London: Longman.

Bruggemann, M. (2005), 'How the EU Constructs the Public Sphere: Seven Strategies of Information Policy', in *Javnost-The Public* 12:2, pp. 57–74.

Campbell, V. (2006), 'A Journalistic Deficit? A Comparative Content Analysis of British Television News Coverage of the 1994 and 2004 European Election Campaigns, in *Journalism Studies* 7:4, pp. 593–609.

CEC (2005a), *Action Plan to Improve Communicating Europe by the Commission*.

CEC (2005b), *The Commission's Contribution to the Period of Reflection and Beyond: Plan-D for Democracy, Dialogue and Debate*.

CEC (2006), *White Paper on a European Communication Policy*.

De Vreese, C.H. (2003), *Communicating Europe: Sixth Output from the 'Next Generation Democracy – Legitimacy in Network Europe' Project*, Brussels: British Council.

Eriksen, E.O., and Fossum, J.E. (2004), 'Europe in Search of Legitimacy: Strategies of Legitimation Assessed', in *International Political Science Review* 25:4, pp. 435–59.

Firmstone, E. (2004), *Final Case Report on the Communication Strategies of the Media: United Kingdom ('The Transformation of Political Mobilisation and Communication in European Public Spheres' Project)*.

Føllesdal, A. (2006), 'Survey Article: The Legitimacy Deficits of the European Union', in *The Journal of Political Philosophy* 14:4, pp. 441–68.

Gavin, N.T. (2000), 'Imaging Europe: Political Identity and British Television Coverage of the European Economy', in *British Journal of Politics and International Relations* 2:3, pp. 352–73.

Gavin, N.T. (2001a), 'Media Coverage of the Single Currency in Britain: An Assessment of Television News in the First Year of the Euro', paper presented at the 2001 ECSA conference, Madison, Wisconsin.

Gavin, N.T. (2001b), 'British Journalists in the Spotlight: Europe and Media Research', in *Journalism: Theory, Practice and Criticism* 2:3, pp. 299–314.

Gavin, N.T. (2007a), *Press and Television in British Politics: Media, Money and Mediated Democracy*, London: Palgrave Macmillan.

Gavin, N.T. (2007b), 'Global Warming and the British Press: The Emergence of an Issue and its Political Implications', paper presented at the 2007 EPOP conference, Bristol.

Gleissner, M., and de Vreese, C.H. (2005), 'News about the EU Constitution: Journalistic Challenges and Media Portrayals of the European Union Constitution', in *Journalism* 6:2, pp. 221–42.

Kavanagh, D. (1995), *Election Campaigning: The New Marketing of Politics*, Oxford: Blackwell.

Kevin, D. (2003), *Europe in the Media: A Comparison of Reporting, Representation, and Rhetoric in National Media Systems in Europe*, Mahwah, NJ: Lawrence Erlbaum Associates.

Koopmans, R., and Erbe, J. (2004), 'Towards a European Public Sphere? Vertical and Horizontal Dimensions of Europeanized Political Communication', in *Innovation* 17:2, pp. 97–118.

Lees-Marshment, J. (2001), 'The Marriage of Politics and Marketing', in *Political Studies* 49:4, pp. 692–713.

Lees-Marshment, J. (2004a), *The Political Marketing Revolution: Transforming the Government of the UK*, Manchester: Manchester University Press.

Lees-Marshment, J. (2004b), 'Mis-marketing the Conservatives: The Limitations of Style over Substance', in *The Political Quarterly*, 75:4, pp. 392–97.

Lord, C., and Beetham, D. (2001), 'Legitimizing the EU: Is there a 'Post-Parliamentary Basis' for its Legitimation?', *Journal of Common Market Studies* 39:3, pp. 443–62.

Lord, C., and Magnette, P. (2004), 'E Pluribus Unum: Creative Disagreement about Legitimacy in the EU', in *Journal of Common Market Studies* 42:1, pp. 183–202.

Mény, Y. (2003), 'De la Démocratie en Europe: Old Concepts and New Challenges', in *Journal of Common Market Studies* 41:1, pp. 1–13.

Meyer, C.O. (1999), 'Political Legitimacy and the Invisibility of Politics: Exploring the European Union's Communication Deficit', in *Journal of Common Market Studies* 37:4, pp. 617–39.

Meyer, C.O. (2000), *Towards a European Public Sphere? The European Commission, the Media, and Political Accountability*, Cambridge (Ph.D. dissertation).

Moravcsik, A. (2002), 'In Defence of the 'Democratic Deficit': Reassessing Legitimacy in the European Union', in *Journal of Common Market Studies* 40:4, pp. 603–24.

Morgan, D. (1995), 'British Media and European Union News: The Brussels News Beat and its Problems', in *European Journal of Communication* 10:3, pp. 321–343.

Norris, P. (2000), *A Virtuous Circle: Political Communications in Postindustrial Societies*, Cambridge: Cambridge University Press.

Obradovic, D. (1996), 'Policy Legitimacy and the European Union', in *Journal of Common Market Studies* 34:2, pp. 191–222.

Ofcom (2004), *The Communications Market 2004*, London: Ofcom.

Scammell, M. (1995), *Designer Politics: How Elections Are Won*, Basingstoke, Macmillan.

Schmidt, V.A. (2004), 'The European Union: Democratic Legitimacy in a Regional State?', in *Journal of Common Market Studies* 42:5, pp. 975–97.

Smith, A. (2004), 'European Commissioners and the Prospects of a European Public Sphere: Information, Representation and Legitimacy', paper presented at the 2004 'Citizenship and Democratic Legitimacy in Europe' Conference, University of Stirling.

Smith, M. (2006), 'European Foreign Policy in Crisis? EU Responses to the George W. Bush Administration', in *European Political Science* 5:1, pp. 41–51.

Tumber, H. (1995), 'Marketing Maastricht: The EU and News Management', in *Media, Culture and Society* 17:3, pp. 511–19.

Wallace, W., and Smith, J. (1995), 'Democracy or Technocracy? European Integration and the Problem of Popular Consent', in *West European Politics* 18:3, pp. 137–57.

THE OTHER FRONTIER: MEDIA ASSISTANCE BY INTERNATIONAL ORGANIZATIONS

Friederike von Franqué

The use of the media to support political objectives is probably as old as the media themselves. Governments have tried various methods to gain influence over media communications. Their methods have included public relations, public diplomacy, propaganda, and assistance to media and journalists in development aid.

Public relations, public diplomacy and propaganda can be summed up as content-focused methods. All three rely on persuasive communication techniques. In foreign aid, however, a new method was introduced: under the umbrella of development assistance, external players fund and support local media institutions, and, in doing so, influence media landscapes. This approach began in the late 1960s with the funding and financing of radio stations in Africa. Thanks to the growing proliferation of cheap transistor radios in developing countries, coverage and speed of dissemination could be much enhanced, the costs of programming lowered and often poor local transportation infrastructures circumvented.

Today's modes of media assistance as yet have no coherent nomenclature. Although 'media assistance' is the most common term for this activity, terms like 'media development' or 'the promotion of free and independent media' can also be found in the documentation of implementing organizations and governments. The Amsterdam-based Non-Governmental Organization (NGO) Press Now (2005: 8) defines 'media development' in the following terms:

'Media development' means activity undertaken to help media outlets work according to the professional and ethical standards which are today expected in, and of, democratic societies. Media development can include a range of actions directed at media organizations themselves, or at their political, economic, legal and regulatory contexts.

It is true that most media assistance activity today is embedded in democracy-promotion programmes. But media assistance can be used for a variety of purposes and does not necessarily assert a normative agenda. It is apparent that not much is known about the political motives of the institutions that fund media assistance, only about the stated objectives of their programmes, although it may be supposed that media assistance is mostly intended to promote democracy. However, this chapter's research into media assistance in Bosnia-Herzegovina and Kosovo exposed other motives – ones which often superseded the promotion of democracy.

The 'range of actions' to which the Press Now definition refers has been detailed by Price et al. (2002) and Price and Thompson (2003). First, there are 'positive' actions, which include financial, material, technical, symbolic or consulting assistance. Recipients could be local media institutions, for example newspapers, publishing houses, radio stations and peripheral media institutions like journalism associations, ombudsmen and media research institutes. Lange (2003) estimated that about 40 per cent of the financial assistance went into training, 34 per cent into direct assistance of individual media companies, and 26 per cent into associations, media centres and legislative reforms.

The second category involves 'negative' actions. These activities aim to prevent the dissemination of certain content, or of content by certain providers. They include such tactics as the assertion of political pressure on local authorities to act against broadcasters or newspapers, technical tactics (such as the imitation, disruption or blocking of broadcasting signals), or even such military tactics as the destruction of transmission or printing sites.

Media intervention in post-Communist Europe and the Balkans

The end of the Soviet Union and the EU accession process fostered a wave of media assistance in the post-Communist countries. Since implementation strategies and funding levels depend on local cultural, social and political contexts, media intervention varied within the different post-Communist countries. Precise figures on funding levels are difficult to identify: incoherent definitions, changing terms and fluid project lines make it difficult to distinguish media assistance resources from other activities. The current calculations can therefore only be rough estimates. Howard (2003: 8) calculated the worldwide funds for media assistance between 1992 and 2002 as one billion U.S. dollars. He used data from Ellen Hume (2004), who estimated U.S. media assistance resources during that period as about 600 million dollars. Price et al. (2002: 40) cite a United States Agency for International Development (USAID) employee who estimated the amount spent by his organization for 'information assistance' between 1991 and 2002 at 260 million dollars. Expenditure on media assistance has risen sharply since the mid-1990s, with the beginning of the international presence in the western Balkans. In the fiscal year 2004 alone, the amount spent for the development of independent media through USAID and the U.S. government totalled 40 million dollars. USAID accounted for most of these resources, around 60 per cent of which went to Europe and Eurasia (GAO 2005: 2).

The most prominent targets for media intervention were the European post-conflict countries. During this period, Bosnia-Herzegovina and Kosovo probably received the lion's share of international media assistance resources. Again, precise funding levels are difficult to identify. The European Commission alone spent 11.25 million euros on media assistance in Bosnia between 1991 and 1999. An additional four million euros were channelled through the Community Assistance for Reconstruction, Development and Stabilization (CARDS) programme (Lange 2003). The European Initiative for Democracy and Human Rights (EIDHR) budget devoted 2.44 million euros to the promotion of 'pluralist citizenry' and 'freedom of expression and human rights' between 1996 and 2004. The latest report finds that international interim authorities and other international players spent at least 87.1 million euros in Bosnia-Herzegovina and 58.6 million euros in Kosovo on media support between 1996 and 2006 (Press Now 2007: 13).

These funds are being channelled through a variety of institutions. These organizations fall into three groups: donors, implementation organizations and contractors. The smallest group is that of the donors. In general, these are multilateral institutions (such as the European Commission), governments (such as the Dutch, Swedish, Swiss, Norwegian, Danish, German, French, Finnish and British ministries of foreign affairs and their embassies), private foundations (such as the Soros Foundation, the Open Society Institute, the Knight Foundation, the Westminster Foundation) and industry organizations (such as the European Broadcasting Union). Implementation organizations act on behalf of, or with the support of, the donors. These are governmental development organizations (such as USAID, the Department for International Development [DFID], Press Now and Deutsche Welle) and, to a lesser extent, public foundations (such as Friedrich Ebert Stiftung and the National Endowment for Democracy) and military organizations (such as the North Atlantic Treaty Organization [NATO], the Stabilisation Force [SFOR] and the Kosovo Force [KFOR]). Media development institutions can be located at the contractors' level: operational NGOs (such as IREX ProMedia, MedienHilfe, Norwegian Peoples Aid and the Instititue for War and Peace Reporting [IWPR]), advocacy NGOs (such as the Swedish Helsinki Committee, Article 19 and Human Rights Watch), private companies (such as Chemonics Ltd) and universities (for example, the American University). It is for the most part the donors who decide where and how they want to spend their money, and it is therefore they who shape media development strategies.

In Bosnia-Herzegovina, the most important players – that is, the biggest donors – were the European Union, USAID (originally represented by the Organization for Transition Initiatives), and, to a lesser extent, the Soros Foundation. The U.S. State Department, the OSCE Missions in Bosnia-Herzegovina and Kosovo and the Swiss Ministry of Foreign Affairs, although not offering similar levels of funding, also played decisive roles in the region's media reconstruction.

General objectives and implementation strategies

The general objective of western aid to the post-Communist countries was to support the transition from authoritarian rule to market-driven liberal democracies. One of the West's methods involved the promotion of independent, accessible and professional media. A significant number of practitioners, politicians and scholars believe that free media helped to liberate those Communist countries from authoritarian rule: Samuel Huntington, for example, gives global communications the credit for that wave of democratization, because of their ability to foster a political 'snowball effect'. The former chair of the Reuters Foundation, Richard Nelson, has argued that the media represented the decisive influence in the collapse of the authoritarian regimes in eastern Europe (Nelson 1997). Bringing 'free media' to eastern Europe therefore seemed to be an extension of an idea that had already proven effective in the democratization of that region. Independent media were indeed essential for the dissemination of political information and campaign messages in the elections that were to be held in these newly democratic states.

Three implementation strategies were adopted: pluralization, regulation and professionalization. The pluralization strategy aimed at establishing more choice in printed products, and radio and television stations. Former state-controlled media markets were to be transformed into market-driven, liberalized environments. With more on offer in media institutions and products, so it was assumed, a greater diversity of viewpoints and representations would be developed.

Within the donor community, two different concepts were applied. Firstly, institutions of European providence focused on minority media, to give formerly neglected social groups voices and platforms within diverse democracies. Secondly, European donors spent considerable sums in supporting public service broadcasters as providers of diverse and inclusive content.

Meanwhile, American donors attached greater importance to funding the commercial media. While knowing that not all of these new media outlets would be sustainable, the American strategy calculated that, through a market-driven consolidation process, professionalism and high-quality content would survive. To keep the market model free from other competition, American donors strongly opposed the European support of public service broadcasting. In media markets with only small total advertising revenues, each additional competitor would diminish the chances of sustainable income generation for commercial providers. In Bosnia-Herzegovina and in Kosovo, a dual media system was installed, a system that included public broadcasters alongside commercial services, but only at the cost of severe opposition from American donors.

The regulation strategy, by contrast, sought to influence the legal and institutional environment for media workers and media organizations. Legal protection for journalists, professional codes of conduct, media appeals boards and transparent complaint processes were considered essential to establish an independent and professional media system able to resist political pressures. International institutions drafted media regulations, initiated and supported press councils, and worked on anti-defamation laws.

The third strategy was professionalization. With the professionalization of journalists and media workers, external players hoped to improve the sustainability of media outlets and their standards of reporting. Some programmes aimed specifically at lessening ethnopolitical tensions through reducing bias in reporting; some aimed at strengthening the watchdog role of the media through the promotion of investigative skills in legal, political and economic reporting; other training projects aimed to contribute to democratization and peace-building by educating journalists about the democratic role of the media and the specific rights of journalists. Other training courses focused on improving the sustainability of media outlets. Senior staff were trained in the business and management aspects of modern media organizations. Perhaps unsurprisingly, business-minded American donors concentrated their efforts in this latter field, while European donors only involved themselves in similar projects at a later stage.

Most of the media funding resources for Bosnia-Herzegovina and Kosovo went into journalistic training. This was partly a consequence of the political economies of the donor community, where short-term projects have more chances of approval, where objective results have to be achieved, and where the mere number of journalists trained is often taken as proof of the efficiency of the project. It was also, in part, a result of a belief common among external players that journalists could be 'immunized' against biased reporting or editorial politics simply by learning professional codes of conduct. The fact that journalists have to manoeuvre through environments weighted with sometimes violent manifestations of political oppression was often overlooked.

The Europeanization of the media?
Some post-Communist countries have now become members of the European Union. Meanwhile, in Bosnia-Herzegovina and Kosovo international interim administrations, military organizations and international NGOs continue to influence local media systems. But, when we observe the media transformations in these post-Communist societies, can we speak of a westernization or even an Europeanization of their media?

It is true that new media institutions are in place and processes have been implemented to protect and regulate media environments – processes modelled upon western democratic norms. A case study of Bulgaria shows that transformations in the media were accelerated by the country's adaptation to international regulations and institutions: the UN Charter, the Covenant on Civil and Political Rights and the Covenant on Economic, Social and Cultural Rights, as well as the country's ratification of the European Convention on Human Rights and accession to the Council of Europe in 1992 (Zankova 2005:7).

However, it appears that the most significant influence upon the transformation of media systems in central and eastern Europe was not related to regulatory convergence so much as to economic imperatives. The democratization process in the media of central and eastern Europe was to a large extent merely a privatization process. Huge media corporations (such as Ringier in Switzerland, the Westdeutsche Allgemeine Zeitung Mediengruppe [WAZ] in Germany, and the Marieberg Group and the Modern Times Group in Sweden) have acquired large sections of the media of these post-Communist countries. While these acquisitions may not immediately or directly have affected such areas as news reporting, it remains clear that the new owners follow profit-oriented editorial strategies – rather than finding economic inspiration in the ideals of democratic pluralism. The consequences of this commercialization and the limitations it may impose upon media freedom can be observed in western and eastern democracies alike.

This liberal media market was, to some extent, an objective of the western media intervention strategy. However, it is hard to measure the effects of international media assistance, development or intervention in this process. It may be some time yet before we can judge the significance of this influence, and specifically how 'European' that influence and its effects may turn out to be: if such a thing as 'Europeanness' indeed exists.

References

GAO (2005), U. S. General Accounting Office, 'Independent Media Development Abroad. Challenges Exist in Implementing U.S. Efforts and Measuring Results. Report to the Chairman, Committee on Foreign Relations, U.S. Senate', Washington, DC.

Howard, R. (2003), 'International Media assistance. A Review of Donor Activities and Lessons Learned', in Conflict Research Unit', *Working Paper Series* 19, Den Haag, Clingendael: Netherlands Institute of International Relations.

Hume, E. (2004), 'The Media Missionaries. American Support for Journalism Excellence and Press Freedom around the Globe. A Report for the John S. and James L. Knight Foundation', Washington, DC.

Lange, Y. (2003), 'Overview of Media Support to Southeast Europe in 2003', Brussels: Media Task Force, Stability Pact for South Eastern Europe.

Nelson, M. (1997), 'War of the Black Heavens: The Battles of Western Broadcasting in the Cold War', Syracuse, N.Y.: Syracuse University Press.

Press Now (2005), 'Media Development by OSCE Field Missions', Amsterdam: Press Now.

Press Now (2007), 'Ten Years of Media Support in the Balkans', Amsterdam: Press Now.

Price, M., Davis Noll, B., and De Luce, D. (2002), 'Mapping Media Assistance', Oxford: Centre for Socio-Legal Studies.

Price, M. E., and Thompson, M. (2003), 'Intervention, Media and Human Rights', in *Survival* 45:1, pp. 183–202.

Zankova, B. (2005), 'The Media in Bulgaria during Communism and their Transformation into Democratic Institutions', Budapest: Open Society Archives at Central European University.

Brand Europe: Moves Towards a Pan-European Identity

Rudiger Theilmann

There is no doubt that brands and branding are well-established marketing concepts which have received increased attention in recent years. Nor is there any doubt that culture, society, education, politics and many other spheres of our lives are increasingly inscribed within the dictates of commercial rules. It not difficult to see that a marketing concept such as branding may be applied to spheres beyond those for which it was originally intended – those of tangible consumer goods (Blichfeldt 2005: 388). It is, for example, well accepted that celebrities are considered to be brands and can even be ascribed a certain brand value (Kotler 2003). The concept of branding has consequently been applied to countries and destinations, accompanied by a growth in self-promoting activities, such as place-branding conferences and seminars, the appearance of new publications and journals, and nation and city brand rankings (Anholt 2003). Still the question remains as to whether the application of branding strategies to places is well-grounded or is merely a vague trend based on false logic. Current discussion about place-branding lacks reflection as to whether it is possible to build and manage place brands, or, more specifically, whether places can be branded as consumer products. As Blichfeldt (2005: 388) finds, 'the applicability [of the branding concept to places] seems questionable due to the fact that new phenomena may be fundamentally different from the substantive domain in relation to which branding as a theory has evolved'.

This chapter aims to tackle three main points. Firstly it will discuss whether places can be branded in the way that tangible consumer products are branded. A discussion of this question should begin with a look at related concepts and practices in the field. Place-branding may be a concept which is in the process of rebranding itself. Related concepts, such as public diplomacy, tourism promotion, the marketing of cities or regions, image campaigns and the use of flags and banners as equivalents to logos, suggest that ideas of branding are already well-established in terms of places. However, the use of these specific terms leads the way to a more elaborate view of place-branding. Places might not be branded in the way consumer products are, but place-branding might be viewed as a concept in its own right, distinct from the traditional product-branding concept. Thus, in elaborating the differences between these two areas, the second aim of this paper is to define specific features of place-branding, features which underline the idea that place-branding is indeed a concept in its own right rather than merely the application of the concept of consumer-product-branding to places. Finally, this paper will examine whether European nations and regions – and indeed the European Union as a whole – can be branded in these terms.

A preliminary distinction should be made between the objects and purposes of place-branding. Szondi (2007: 9) distinguishes between destination-branding and country-branding: 'The aim of destination-branding is to attract visitors and boost tourism while country-branding promotes economic, commercial and political interests at home and abroad.' The discussion of place-branding has further to consider the various objects of branding – countries, nations, regions and cities – and the factors which are vital in the branding process.

But above all a clarification of the concept of branding is needed – one which shall underlie all further discussions of the branding process.

Branding as audience experience

Following a shift in the understanding of marketing communications from a focus upon 'promoting to' towards an emphasis upon 'communicating with' (Fill and Hughes 2006: 4), branding may be considered as an audience experience. This is an outcome-centered view which underlines the role of the audience in the branding process. It implies that the audience experience is nurtured by a variety of sources which might go beyond the marketing activities of a corporation or indeed of a place. A place brand in this context is not something that is imposed on tourists only by means of advertising and other forms of communication (Keller 2003). Blichfeldt (2005) proposes that place brands are distinct from consumer brands in terms of their manageability, since in the case of place brands the major sources by which the audience experience is shaped are beyond the control of marketing professionals.

One should therefore focus on the factors in the branding process which shape the audience experience. Three main sources of audience experience can be identified: mass media, direct experience of the branding objects, and the brand communication strategies of the place-marketers (see Keller 2003; Esch 2005).

Sources of the place-brand experience

While traditional brand campaigns involve marketing messages directly disseminated by marketing professionals, mass media coverage offers a picture which is mainly composed by journalists. The mass media create a reality of their own which is mainly based on news values, audience expectations and the needs or interests of other related players (McQuail 2005).

By contrast, branding based on direct experience involves perceptions which audiences themselves create in their own contacts with the brand objects. In the case of place-branding, those are primarily founded upon the experiences of tourists, investors or businesspeople. These, to a significant extent, include contacts with local residents. Word-of-mouth communication with family members, friends and colleagues is also included in the category of these direct experiences (Blichfeldt 2005: 390).

These approaches differ in their manageability – the extent to which marketers can determine and control the brand experience. It can be assumed that marketing communications is the most planned and manageable aspect of branding. Mass media coverage about a place can be influenced through public relations activities and depends on the working patterns of journalists as gatekeepers (McQuail 2005). By contrast, the audience experience of a place through direct, unmediated contact appears to be the least manageable aspect of branding.

Blichfeldt (2005: 397) argues that local residents represent a core element in place-branding, and that any contact with them contributes to the brand experience. These residents represent a largely unmanageable factor. Olins (2002), however, focuses on the argument that destination-marketers can motivate and inspire (and manipulate) residents and thus control the place-branding process. However, we may consider possibilities for the control of local residents to be somewhat limited, if we view place-branding as an audience-centred concept which sees the audience and residents as autonomous rather than as passively influenced by governmental institutions or other organizations (Fill 2006).

These approaches are not necessarily independent. Direct experiences of a place can, for example, be based on a marketing strategy. Reality can be constructed through marketing or public relations activities. For example, new buildings can be an element within a marketing strategy. Another example would be events or even pseudo-events – events which are created for the sole purpose of attracting media attention – for example, press conferences (Boorstin 1961). Any cultural or sporting event, such as the Olympic Games or a Football World Cup, involves an element of place-branding as it shapes the public and global perception of a country. Any PR stunt creates a reality which can be directly experienced by the public and is also an object of media coverage. For example, according to a recent study, the image of Germany among U.S. citizens has significantly improved as a result of the impact of the Football World Cup 2006 (*Spiegel Online*, 17/4/07). News representations of peaceful fans celebrating the football festival together, accompanied by the official slogan – 'A time to make friends' – have created an overwhelmingly positive image for the nation as a whole.

Another example of the interdependence of these three approaches in creating the image of a country is Larry Charles's film *Borat* (2006) – a text which paints a picture of Kazakhstan somewhat removed from reality. The film's release was followed by an official 40-million-euro branding campaign: an attempt by the Kazakhstani government to create a more realistic view of their country. However, it was the film itself which stimulated a broad media discussion about Kazakhstan. This case shows that branding factors are not independent and might stimulate, or conflict with, each other; it also shows how much impact a single branding event (such as a film) could achieve, uncontrolled by any official national promotional organization or by the government itself.

Differences between consumer product and place brands

Marketers assume leading roles in consumer-product-branding. This is firstly due to the fact that consumer products are created by specific corporations and are themselves part of the marketing process (Kotler 2003). Hence direct brand experiences of consumer products are more manageable than experiences of places, since consumer products offer marketers greater possibilities of control than places and their residents may. Furthermore, products rarely produce so many newsworthy stories as do countries and cities, in that countries and cities are complex entities composed of diverse elements, actors and events (Blichfeldt 2005: 392). Hence countries or cities can achieve permanent and more prominent media coverage than consumer products.

The main difference between consumer-product-branding and place-branding is the way in which consumer-product-brands are marketing-driven, whereas place-branding is more audience-driven. Does this mean that place branding campaigns are not effective? It certainly appears that promotional campaigns play a more indirect and complementary role in place-branding than they do in consumer-product-branding.

Towards place-branding as a concept in its own right

The importance of direct audience experiences in place-branding suggests that there should be a focus on offering 'reality experiences' directly to audiences – and to the mass media. These can include sporting or cultural events – such as hosting the Olympic Games or holding the position of the European Capital of Culture.

The idea of offering experiences of reality is based on three main factors: value is provided for the audiences by events which meet their interests; indirect effects such as mass media and word-of-mouth coverage are stimulated; and positive associations from the experience are indirectly related to the object of branding – the country, region or city.

Much of the reality experience cannot be controlled. However, there is a potential for spill-over effects by which events might create a positive spirit among the citizens of a country or city – which result again in more positive direct experiences for visitors (Olins 2002).

A similar approach in contemporary branding is the concept of brand entertainment. Although it originates in consumer-product-branding, it shares its fundamentals with the concept of place-branding. Brand entertainment is 'best defined as where a brand creates consumer entertainment that would have not existed without that brand and where consumers choose their involvement' (Dawson and Hall 2005: 27). Such cases create a reality in which the audience plays an integral part through participation in programmed events. This is not a direct promotion of products or brands: 'Brand entertainment is based on experiences rather than exposure to traditional marketing communications' (Dawson and Hall 2005: 28).

The diversity of unmanageable brand-drivers (such as local residents) will lead to a diversity of audience experiences. Thus it might be concluded that there can be no clear and simple brand image of any place. There are as many different perceptions as there are different audience experiences. Nevertheless, the culture of a country might be considered an umbrella under which different audience experiences are related to a consistent brand image. In this sense place-branding campaigns might serve as frames which help audiences make sense of, and form clearer pictures of, their strands of episodic experiences (Esch 2005).

The diversity of audience experiences is also related to the segmentation of audiences. Audiences might be segmented according to their various interests in a place. This starts with the distinctions between tourists, investors, businesspeople and visitors with ties to friends or family. Brand experiences in this context are based on the various interests or purposes of the relevant audiences. Thus, a country or city might have a specific tourism image and a different business image. Audiences may also be segmented according to the sources of their experiences of a place. There might be audiences who gain their perceptions only from the mass media, whereas others may experience a place directly.

One conclusion drawn from the diversity of audience experiences is that place-branding should support the process of creating clear images by dividing branding objects into more specific entities. A country can be divided into regions or cities which might appeal to more homogeneous audiences and hence lead to more specific and consistent brand experiences. An example would be the *Deutsche Burgenstrasse* (German Road of Castles) which offers a very specific kind of experience. Paris, London, Rome and Venice also represent unique experiences and are very valuable place-brands – unlike, say, Birmingham, Essen, Lyon or Warsaw, whose branding is virtually indistinguishable from many other cities.

In order for audiences actively to seek experiences of a place, a certain level of existing knowledge of that place is a prerequisite. But in cases in which very little of such knowledge exists, a promotional campaign might stimulate audience experience. Provocative campaigns may be particularly influential in this respect. The film *Borat* first created an awareness of Kazakhstan and then stimulated further interest through the subsequent mass media discussion. It may have stimulated interest in general news about the country and in its image campaign – and may even have finally led some to visit Kazakhstan.

Another specific context for place-branding is a situation of change in a country or city – in terms either of the transitions of countries from one political system to another (as in the case of eastern European countries at the beginning of the 1990s) or of the regeneration of cities (see Hall 2004; Dzenovska 2005). In such cases brand campaigns mainly have the function of re-branding: 'They can change negative or false stereotypes associated with the country and its people' (Szondi 2007: 10). The branding efforts of eastern European countries have, for example, focused on disassociating themselves from being seen as 'eastern European' – a term once synonymous with command economies, the Cold War and political oppression. However, this has led to a similarity in their branding campaigns which raises the question as to whether they have created unique and indistinguishable brands. Belonging to Europe and being at the 'centre' of Europe have been considered particularly positive brand assets which most of these countries share (see Table 1). But would a common campaign have made more sense in their attempts to create a new eastern European brand in order to distinguish those countries from their counterparts in the West? Indeed, U.S. American Secretary of Defence Donald Rumsfeld's description of these countries as representing a 'New Europe' (January 2003) created a powerful and frequently quoted brand name which would put to shame the efforts of most place-branding gurus.

Overall audience experiences can appear remarkably similar. This is directly reflected in efforts that individual (or not-so-individual) countries may make to promote themselves. This might not be a problem in so far as different individuals – tourists, businesspeople, etc. – might have different and unique reasons to visit or experience a specific place. But, as in the field of consumer products, clear distinctions help to support specific choices. If brands become indistinguishable, they lose their value.

Yet the similarity of places and of their promotional campaigns may allow the creation of more transnational brands: brands which unite such similar places and distinguish them from more distant and different places. One such example would be a European brand, developed in order to attract visitors and investors more coherently, consistently and convincingly than the competing marketing activities of the multitude of European countries and regions which often advance similar arguments as to why they are the best sites for business location and investment (Esch 2005). In the age of globalization places are becoming increasingly similar – for

Table 1. Straplines of European countries. Source: Frasher et al. 2003: 40.

Country	Strapline
Malta	'The sun, the sea and 7,000 years of history'
Cyprus	'Irresistible for 9,000 years'
Hungary	'The essence of Europe'
Czech Republic	'In the heart of Europe'
Slovenia	'The green piece of Europe'
Slovakia	'A small country with a big heart'
Poland	'The heart of Europe'
Lithuania	'Centre of Europe'

example in terms of the standardization of legal norms, the convergence of economic systems, and the global availability of news.

'A well educated workforce' with 'good language skills' and a 'dynamic population' are often cited as catchphrases for investors. Indeed, almost every country in Europe could – and actually does – emphasize these qualities (Szondi 2007: 18). The branding campaigns of central and eastern European countries particularly focus on these stereotypes. Similarity and competitiveness with western European standards have become benchmarks for their campaigns – and might finally (paradoxically) create strong, independent country brands. The similarity of campaign messages results in an overall perception of being part of Europe, a perception which underlines the idea that a pan-European brand makes sense.

The similarity of European countries increases the challenge for place-branding to focus on specific brand features – to offer uniqueness within homogeneity. The German campaign *Deutschland – Land der Ideen* (Germany – Land of Ideas) focuses on the inventiveness and world-renowned quality of German industry. It is a re-branding of the successful 'Made in Germany' campaign. However, alongside other industrial countries of the western world, 'Made in Germany' has now lost something of its outstanding uniqueness. Within this context a pan-European brand might profitably focus upon the common features of European countries and, furthermore, consider the diversity within Europe not as disadvantageous but as an additional brand asset.

References

Anholt, S. (2003), *Brand New Justice: The Upside of Global Branding*, Oxford: Elsevier Butterworth-Heinemann.

Blichfeldt, B. S. (2005), 'Unmanageable Place Brands?', in *Place Branding and Public Diplomacy* 1:4, pp. 388–401.

Boorstin, D.J. (1961), *The Image: A Guide to Pseudo-events in America*, New York: Atheneum.

Dawson, N., and Hall, M. (2005), 'That's brand entertainment', in *Admap* 2, pp. 27–30.

Dzenovska, D. (2005), 'Remaking the nation of Latvia: Anthropological perspectives on nation branding', in *Place Branding* 1:2, pp. 173–186.

Esch, F. (2005), *Moderne Markenfuehrung*, Wiesbaden: Gabler.

Fill, C. (2006), *Marketing Communications: engagement, strategies and practice*, Harlow: Prentice Hall.

Fill, C., and Hughes, G. (2006), 'Remixing marketing communications: perspectives on the role and value of the promotional mix', paper presented at the Academy of Marketing Conference, London, July 2006.

Frasher, S., Hall, M., Hildreth, J., and Sorgi, M. (2003), *A Brand for the Nation of Latvia*, Oxford: Said Business School.

Gallarza, M., Saura, I. and Garcia, H. (2003), 'Destination image – towards a conceptual framework', in *Annals of Tourism Research* 29:1, pp. 56–78.

Hall, D. (2004), 'Branding and national identity: The case of Central and Eastern Europe', in Morgan, N., Pritchard, A., and Pride, R. (eds.) *Destination Branding: Creating the Unique Destination Proposition*, Oxford: Elsevier Butterworth-Heinemann.

Keller, K. (2003), *Strategic Brand Management – Building, Measuring and Managing Brand Equity*, Upper Saddle River: Prentice Hall.

Kotler, P. (2003), *Marketing Management*, Upper Saddle River: Prentice Hall.

McQuail, D. (2005), *Mass Communication Theory*, London, Sage.

Olins, W. (2002), 'Branding the nation – The historical context', in *Journal of Brand Management* 9:4–5, pp. 241–248.

Szondi, G. (2007), 'The role and challenges of country branding in transition countries: The Central and Eastern European Experience', in *Place Branding and Public Diplomacy*, 3:1, pp. 8–20.

RELIGIOUS IDENTITIES IN THE EUROPEAN MEDIA: A LEGAL PERSPECTIVE

Russell Sandberg

The abolition of blasphemy laws in England and Wales by section 79 of the Criminal Justice and Immigration Act 2008 was seen by many as the inevitable consequence of the decline and inadequacy of those laws (for a full account of the process of the abolition, see Sandberg and Doe 2008). This chapter examines the history of those laws within the context of European principles of freedoms of religion and of expression, and asks whether the current alternative to legislation – regulation by pressure group – is legally or democratically appropriate.

* * *

Laws both enable and constrain personal identity. The ways in which laws enable and constrain religious identities, in particular, have proved controversial in recent years (see, for example, Hill and Sandberg 2007, and Sandberg and Doe 2007). This is especially true in relation to the regulation of how the media portrays religion. In October 2005, a Danish newspaper with a circulation of less than 150,000 readers published twelve cartoons portraying the prophet Muhammad and making a variety of criticisms of Islam. By March 2007, these twelve cartoons had led to a dozen deaths in Afghanistan, the torching of an embassy in Lebanon and threats of beheading on the streets of London. In January 2005, in the United Kingdom, two million people watched *Jerry Springer – The Opera* broadcast on BBC 2. The plot of the musical saw Springer shot by a guest and taken to Hell, where he meets the Devil and previous guests from the show who take on the personae of various Christian characters such as Christ, God, Mary,

Satan and Eve. Prior to the screening, the BBC received a record 55,000 complaints and, when details of the home addresses of several BBC executives were placed on the Christian Institute's website, several executives had temporarily to leave their homes and one executive actually received a death threat (see *Private Eye* 1152, 17/2/06).

Although it was clear that much of the protest amounted to an orchestrated campaign by certain comparatively small religious groups, the clash between freedom of religion and freedom of expression was certainly back on the agenda. Indeed, the basic conflict between these two rights had never really gone away. Does the right to religious freedom include the right not to be offended and conversely does the right to freedom of expression include a right to say things that may offend? These two statements cannot both be true and so a compromise must be reached. Both rights are protected as Articles 9 and 10 respectively of the European Convention on Human Rights (ECHR). All EU Member States are members of the Council of Europe and are signatories to the ECHR. Article 9 of the ECHR protects right to freedom of thought, conscience and religion and the right to manifest religion or belief. Article 10 protects the right to freedom of expression, the freedom to hold opinions and to receive and impart information.

The clash of freedoms

Under the ECHR, freedom of religion and freedom of expression are both qualified rights. Under Article 9, although the right to freedom of thought, conscience and religion is absolute, the right to manifest religion or belief is qualified by the fact that the right to manifest only extends to manifestation 'in worship, teaching, practice and observance'. The right to manifest under Article 9 is also qualified by a limitation clause: the right to manifest and the rights under Article 10 are qualified by Articles 9(2) and 10(2) respectively, which both provide that a State can limit the right if that limit is 'prescribed by law', has one of the legitimate aims outlined in the Article, and is 'necessary in a democratic society'. One human right may also limit another human right. The European Court of Human Rights has recognized that freedom of religion may be limited by freedom of expression and that freedom of expression may be limited by freedom of religion. The freedom to manifest religion does not include a right to be exempt from all criticism and the exercise of freedom of expression carries with it duties and responsibilities including 'a duty to avoid expressions that are gratuitously offensive to others and profane' (*İA v Turkey*, Application no. 42571/98, 13/9/05).

Of course, whilst it is possible to identify extreme situations where freedom of religion should trump freedom of expression and vice versa, it is more difficult to determine where the line ought to be drawn between the two. For instance, where there is clear hatred towards religious groups, then there is a very strong argument that freedom of religion should trump freedom of expression. Conversely, where religious institutions are the objects of gentle satire, there is a powerful case that freedom of expression should trump religious liberty. However, in a range of factual situations that arise between these two extremes, it is difficult to determine the extent to which one right should be prioritized over the other. This chapter seeks to explore the current balance reached between the two human rights of religious freedom and freedom of expression by legal systems with reference to England and Wales as a case study. This choice is deliberate. Until comparatively recently, concepts of freedom of religion and freedom of expression were not explicitly recognized in English law. This was because England and Wales does not have a formal written constitution and did not recognize the ECHR as part of domestic English law. However, as a result of the Human Rights Act 1998, the ECHR has largely been incorporated into English law. This chapter will examine the effect of this change to determine the effect of European legal standards.

The historical legacy

Historically, the focus of English law was upon protecting the sanctity of religious beliefs rather than balancing competing human rights. The English law of blasphemy was originally policed by church courts but became enforced by the ordinary criminal courts from the seventeenth century onwards. Its purpose was to protect the faith of the established Church of England since that faith was regarded as 'the root of society's political and moral behaviour' (House of Lords Select Committee on Religious Offences Report 2003: 46). A crime against the faith was a crime against the social order since 'it was to seriously threaten the very fabric of political and moral society and had to be punished severely' (House of Lords Select Committee on Religious Offences Report 2003: 46). In short, it was a crime against society. Blasphemy was akin to treason. This was clear in one of the first blasphemy cases to be heard by a secular court: the case of *Taylor* (1676). The case involved a mentally disturbed man by the name of Taylor who had cried out that 'Jesus Christ was a bastard, an impostor and a cheat.' The Chief Justice held that 'such wicked blasphemous words were not only an offence to God and to religion, but a crime against the laws, state and Government' and that 'to reproach the Christian religion is to speak in subversion of the law'.

Blasphemy was originally both a statutory and a common law offence. As a result of the Criminal Law Act 1967 it became only a criminal offence at common law. In England and Wales, a person cannot be convicted of a crime unless the prosecution have proved beyond reasonable doubt that the defendant caused or was responsible for a certain event or a certain state of affairs, known as the external element or *actus reus*, and that the defendant had a certain specified state of mind in doing so, known as the mental element or *mens rea* (Ormerod 2005: 34). The *actus reus* and *mens rea* vary for each offence. In relation to the crime of blasphemy, the *actus reus* was that the defendant has published 'blasphemous' material in any form (Edge 2002: 227). This included material written, verbal or performed. To be 'blasphemous', the content of the material would need to have been be in conflict with the tenets of the Church of England and couched in indecent or offensive terms likely to shock and outrage the feelings of the general body of Church of England believers. It is unclear, however, whether the offence extended beyond the Church of England to protect Christianity generally. Although some cases (such as *R v Gott* 1922) speak of blasphemy protecting 'the Christian religion', other cases (such as *R v Chief Stipendiary Magistrate ex parte Choudhury* 1991) suggest that other Christian groups were only protected 'to the extent that their fundamental beliefs are those which are held in common with the established Church'. The reason behind this is that the Church of England is 'established by law, and is therefore a part of the constitution of the country' (*Gathercole's Case* 1838; see Doe 1996 and Hill 2007). This view has been used by the Supreme Court of Ireland to hold that the crime of blasphemy can no longer be prosecuted in Ireland since Ireland no longer has an established church (*Corway v Independent Newspapers (Ireland) Ltd* 1999). However, although the same argument could have been made in relation to Wales (see Addison 2007: 123), the fact that England and Wales share the same criminal law jurisdiction means that the disestablished Church in Wales has been protected provided that the blasphemous act would have conflicted with the tenets of the Church of England. This means that protection may even have extended beyond Christianity where the alleged blasphemy offended against a belief shared by another group and the Church of England. For instance, in the case of *Williams* (1797), it was held that an attack on the Old Testament was blasphemous notwithstanding the fact that it may be interpreted as an attack on Judaism. The court reasoned that the Old Testament is so connected with the New Testament that any attack on the Old Testament invariably attacked Christianity itself.

What is certain is that, in the words of Ahdar and Leigh (2005: 367), the offence did not protect religious beliefs as such but rather proscribed 'attacks on those beliefs expressed in highly offensive ways'. In the case of *Ramsay and Foote* (1883), the editor of *The Freethinker*, a self-confessed 'anti-Christian organ', which published several hundred comical Biblical sketches, was held not guilty since 'the mere denial of the truth of Christianity is not enough to constitute the offence of blasphemy'; therefore 'if the decencies of controversy are observed, even the fundamentals of religion may be attacked without the writer being guilty of blasphemy'. The *actus reus* of blasphemy required not simply the expression of unorthodox views concerning religion but rather the expression of such views in an offensive way (*Bowman v Secular Society Ltd* 1917). The *mens rea* of the offence was that the defendant must intend to publish the material complained of (*R v Lemon, R v Gay News* 1979). There was no requirement that the defendant had an intention to blaspheme; it is sufficient for the prosecution to prove that the publication had been intentional and that the matter was blasphemous.

The fall and rise of blasphemy

The offence has been rarely prosecuted. During the twentieth century, there were only four reported cases (House of Lords Select Committee on Religious Offences Report 2003: 10). The first two (*Bowman* and *Gott*) occurred in the first quarter of the century and reiterated the historical exposition of the offence. Following these cases, there was not another reported case on blasphemy for almost sixty years. The offence was described as a 'dead letter' (Denning 1946: 46). During this period, blasphemy was not restrained by force of law but was rather curtailed by the fears, anxieties and sensitivities of individuals (see Webster 1990). The Sixties and Seventies saw a number of 'moral panics' concerning pieces of art alleged to be blasphemous (for the classical description of a 'moral panic' see Cohen 1972: 9). In 1967, the entire print-run of Siné's *Massacre*, a French cartoonist's book of anti-clerical cartoons, some of which had a sexual theme, was burnt on the grounds of blasphemy. In 1976, opposition from public officials and pressure groups meant that the Danish film-maker Jens Jorgen Thorsen was unable to make his planned film on the sex life of Jesus in Britain. Most famously, in 1979, cuts were forced to *Monty Python's Life of Brian* (Terry Jones, 1979) and a picketing campaign by Mary Whitehouse led to many town councils banning the comedy (Hewison 1981: 66–67).

In 1951, the UK government ratified the ECHR, which became part of international law but not domestic law. Although English courts made reference to Articles 9 and 10, Convention rights were not legally enforceable in such courts (Hill and Sandberg 2007: 491). Indeed, it was not the ECHR which caused the revival of the offence of blasphemy in an English courtroom but rather the actions of Mary Whitehouse. In 1979, she successfully brought a private prosecution against the editor and publishers of *Gay News*. The newspaper had published an illustrated poem, 'The Love That Dares to Speak its Name' by James Kirkup, describing acts of fellatio and sodomy committed on Christ's body immediately after his death. It also suggested that Jesus had committed promiscuous homosexual practices with the Disciples and other men. The prosecution for blasphemy succeeded at all levels of courts. The House of Lords held that the publication had been intentional and that the matter was blasphemous (*R v Lemon, R v Gay News*). Although the defendants took the case to the European Commission on Human Rights, it was deemed inadmissible (*Gay News Ltd v United Kingdom* 1983)

Almost a decade later, Penguin Books published Salman Rushdie's *The Satanic Verses*. The publication was followed by public order disturbances and a *fatwa* was issued by Ayatollah Khomeini against Rushdie. It was alleged that the depictions of God, Abraham, Muhammad and Muhammad's wives vilified their behaviour and that the teachings of Islam were ridiculed as containing too many rules and as seeking to control every aspect of day-to-day life. The courts at all levels held that legal action on grounds of blasphemy could not be sustained since the passages complained of were not blasphemous since they did not amount to a scurrilous attack on Christianity (*Choudhury*). There was no finding as to whether in fact the book was blasphemous of the Islamic religion. An appeal to the European Commission was deemed inadmissible (*Choudhury v United Kingdom* 1991). However, in another case, that of *Wingrove v United Kingdom* (1997), the European Court of Human Rights upheld the English position. It held that the refusal of a film certificate by the British Board of Film Classification on grounds that the content of the film would be found blasphemous was a justified limitation to freedom of expression under Article 10(2).

The death of blasphemy

By the time of the abolition of the offence of blasphemy under the Criminal Justice and Immigration Act on 8 May 2008, the fact that the offence had not been prosecuted in an English court for almost thirty years had already led many commentators to conclude that the law of blasphemy was now moribund (Addision 2007: 124). However, recent years have witnessed a clear return to the moral panics of the Sixties and Seventies. The furore surrounding *Jerry Springer – The Opera* and the Muhammad Cartoons in *Jyllands Posten* show that whilst blasphemy is not policed by law, it is increasingly enforced by pressure groups. The blasphemy law had been both questioned and superseded by the Human Rights Act (1998), which largely incorporated the ECHR into English law. English courts are now under an obligation to interpret United Kingdom legislation so far as is possible in compatibility with the ECHR and must take into account (though not necessarily follow) the decisions of the European Court at Strasbourg. English courts now need to balance explicit rights to freedom of religion and freedom of expression.

This would affect any possible (though, one suspects, improbable) future calls to return the offence of blasphemy to the statute books: in addition to meeting the requirements of English common law, any prosecution must now be justified under Article 10(2). Although previous European decisions upheld prosecutions for blasphemy, it is worth noting that previous rulings were not unequivocal: as the House of Lords Committee on Religious Offences in England and Wales commented, 'the Court's decision in *Wingrove* that there was not "as yet [...] sufficient common accord" to mean that the English law of blasphemy was in breach of the European Convention does not mean that it will not rule otherwise in the future' (House of Lords Select Committee on Religious Offences Report 2003: 48). Other Convention rights question whether a workable law on blasphemy would now be possible. Many commentators have concluded that a prosecution under any such law would fail since the law would be in breach of Article 7, which provides that the content of criminal offences must be certain. As we have seen, the *actus reus* is uncertain in relation to whether it applies to the Church of England or Christianity. The Irish Supreme Court in Corway and the House of Lords Select Committee on Religious Offences in England and Wales have separately come to the conclusion that a prosecution is unlikely to succeed since it is impossible to say of what the offence of blasphemy consists (House of Lords Select Committee on Religious Offences Report 2003: 48). Furthermore, Article 14 (which prohibits discrimination in the enjoyment of Convention rights) might also be fatal to the offence since, as we have seen, the offence largely excludes non-Christian groups from its protection (House of Lords Select Committee on Religious Offences Report 2003: 48). The dilapidation and impossibility of the blasphemy offence has become a legal fact.

The historical focus of blasphemy laws upon the importance of the established faith has been largely replaced by a new ECHR-inspired focus along the lines of balancing competing human rights. Furthermore, the failure of the blasphemy laws has also meant that other criminal offences have been enacted to regulate speech and actions that may offend religious believers. In addition to a number of general public order offences used in this context (such as sections 4, 4A and 5 of the Public Order Act 1986 and the use of Anti-Social Behaviour Orders), specific religious hate crime legislation has been enacted. The Crime and Disorder Act (1998), as amended by the Anti-Terrorism, Crime and Security Act (2001), provides that the punishment of ordinary criminal acts be enhanced when the offence has been committed by reason of prejudice or hatred towards the victim on the grounds of religion (see Edge 2003; Oliva 2007). The Racial and Religious Hatred Act (2006), by contrast, creates a series of new substantive offences relating to stirring up religious hatred (see Hare 2006; Goodall 2007; Jeremy 2007). These offences seem to buttress the ECHR-inspired model of balancing competing human rights by explicitly outlawing the most extreme cases where freedom of expression is trumped by freedom of religion.

Conclusion

Norman Doe has contended that such European Court decisions on the balance between freedom of religion and freedom of expression have become a 'common source' for the laws of European countries (Doe 2004: 314). Drawing upon a collection of essays that seek to elucidate the portrayal of religion in the media laws of fourteen different European countries, Doe elucidates what he perceives to be the sixteen 'principles of media law on religion common to the states of the European Union'. Doe's first and third principles are of particular interest. His first is as follows: 'There is a right to freedom of expression and the exercise of this right may be subject to respect for freedom of religion.'

Although it is not stated that the exercise of the right to religious freedom may be subject to respect for freedom of expression, the limits on religious freedom made by freedom of expression are present by implication. The principle infers that the limit upon the right to freedom of expression made out of respect for freedom of religion is exceptional. Similarly, although Doe's third principle explicitly focuses on the restriction on freedom of expression by freedom of religion, the converse situation is also implicitly recognized. The third principle reads: 'In its coverage of religion, the secular press must respect religion, it must portray it accurately, and it must not offend religious feelings, particularly when offence may cause breaches of public order. Different religions should enjoy equal protection against offensive publications.'

At a general level, English law follows Doe's principle: the sense that religious freedom and freedom of expression are regarded as two competing human rights which need to be balanced is now entrenched by law, and new offences determine this balancing act in the case of the most serious public order offences. However, in terms of the precise details, the inadequacy and eventual abolition of the blasphemy law have left a legal vacuum that seems to be policed extra-legally by public pressure and by protest groups following moral panics. The lack of legal redress may serve to restrict rather than reinforce free speech. Policing blasphemy by public pressure is potentially problematic, since the most active pressure groups may not be representative of society as a whole. Fear may lead to greater self-censorship than ever before. Whilst laws may enable and constrain personal identity, they have a democratic basis upon which they do so. The same is not true of rule by pressure group.

References

Addison, N. (2007), *Religious Discrimination and Hatred Law*, Oxford: Routledge.

Ahdar, R., and Leigh, I. (2005), *Religious Freedom in the Liberal State*, Oxford: Oxford University Press.

Cohen, S. (1972), *Folk Devils and Moral Panics*, London: MacGibbon and Ree.

Denning, A. (1949), *Freedom under the Law*, London: Stevens.

Doe, N. (1996), *The Legal Framework of the Church of England*, Oxford: Clarendon.

Doe, N. (2004), 'Religion and Media Law in Europe: A Comparative Study', in Doe, N. (ed.), *The Portrayal of Religion in Europe: the Media and the Arts*, Peeters: Leuven.

Edge, P.W. (2002), *Legal Responses to Religious Difference*, The Hague: Kluwer Law.

Edge, P.W. (2003), 'Extending Hate Crime to Religion', in *Journal of Civil Liberties* 8, pp. 5–27.

Goodall, K. (2007), 'Incitement to Religious Hatred: All Talk and No Substance', in *Modern Law Review* 70, pp. 89–113.

Hare, I. (2006), 'Crosses, Crescents and Sacred Cows: Criminalising Incitement to Religious Hatred', in *Public Law* 2006, pp. 521–535.

Hewison, R. (1981), *Monty Python: The Case Against*, London: Eyre Methuen Ltd.

Hill, M. (2007), *Ecclesiastical Law*, Oxford: Oxford University Press.

Hill, M., and Sandberg, R. (2007), 'Is Nothing Sacred? Clashing Symbols in a Secular World', in *Public Law* 2007, pp. 488–506.

House of Lords Select Committee on Religious Offences (2003), *Volume I – Report* (HL Paper 95-1).

Jeremy, A. (2007), 'Practical Implications of the Enactment of the Racial and Religious Hatred Act 2006', in *Ecclesiastical Law Journal 9*, pp. 187–201.

Oliva, J.G. (2007), 'The Legal Protection of Believers and Beliefs in the United Kingdom', in *Ecclesiastical Law Journal 9*, pp. 66–86.

Ormerod, D. (2005), *Smith and Hogan Criminal Law*, Oxford: Oxford University Press.

Sandberg, R., and Doe, N. (2007), 'Religious Exemptions in Discrimination Law', in *Cambridge Law Journal 66*, pp. 302–312.

Sandberg, R., and Doe, N. (2008), 'The Strange Death of Blasphemy', *Modern Law Review* (forthcoming).

Webster, R. (1990), *A Brief History of Blasphemy*, Southwold: Orwell Press.

THE MEDIATED 'UMMAH' IN EUROPE: THE ISLAMIC AUDIENCE IN THE DIGITAL AGE

Yasmin Ibrahim

In today's global landscape the concept of the 'Ummah' or the global Muslim community is represented and mediated through modern technologies. This paper analyses how new broadcast technologies are creating and constituting a new form of mediated 'Ummah' or an imagined Muslim community in the European context. The Islamic audience in the media age can transcend territorial boundaries to feel for its wider communities in different locales. This paper analyses the role of ICTs (Information and Communications Technologies), particularly satellite broadcasting, in reconstructing the Ummah and the consequences of this 'mediated Muslimness' for diasporic communities in Europe.

* * *

Six-year-old Aisha has accompanied her father from Birmingham to participate in the peace march in London. She tells the presenter that she is here because 'people have been drawing cartoons about the prophet'. The presenter responds that the little girl will grow up to be a 'good sister, *Insha' Allah* [as Allah wills]'. The Islam Channel, a satellite channel based in London, is broadcasting live coverage of the peace march against the cartoon controversy. The mood that the TV station portrays is a solemn one highlighting how the peace march had garnered support from Muslims in far-flung locations. It is a contrast to the earlier angry outbursts in London against the caricatures of the prophet Muhammad printed in Danish newspapers, where protestors had carried placards inciting violence and murder against the offenders.

The Islam Channel is one of the many media forms which have emerged on the scene to provide a counter-discourse to the western media's representations of Muslims. It is a free-to-air satellite channel which believes that broadcasting offers a powerful means by which to change some of the negative perceptions about the Muslim community. It hopes to give the *Ummah* (or the global Muslim community) an alternative platform through which to discuss Muslim issues and to encourage non-Muslims to engage in constructive dialogue with them.

On 30 September 2005, the Danish newspaper *Jyllands-Posten* published editorial cartoons depicting the prophet Muhammad. The cartoons set off a wave of protests both in the Muslim and non-Muslim worlds where reactions ranged from peaceful protests to the burning of the Norwegian Embassy in Damascus and the Danish General Consulate in Beirut. Palestinian gunmen hurled pipe-bombs into a French cultural centre in Gaza City, and in Jakarta several hundred demonstrators rampaged through the lobby of a building housing the Danish Embassy (MacAskill et al. 2006). In London more than 500 people led by the extremist group al-Ghuraba (formerly al-Mujahiroun) marched to the Danish Embassy carrying banners inciting Muslims to 'massacre' those who insulted Islam. The cartoon controversy inevitably put the spotlight back on the Muslim community. The media coverage from September 2005 to January 2006 brought the various expressions of anguish and discontent of the Muslim *Ummah* into our living rooms. The media depictions to a large extent reinforced the 'Otherness' of the Muslim world and the constant narratives and images of Muslim dissatisfaction were captured through these media discourses.

The modern and postmodern world is a mediated one, where time and space can be compressed through information and communications technologies. The immediacy of a crisis happening far away can be experienced through technology. This chapter explores how new and old information and communication technologies are constructing a mediated *Ummah* and how this has consequences for today's volatile political landscape. The role of the media in representing the world temporally, spatially and through soundbites and visual images has been a significant effect of modernity. Media artefacts as sites of cultural and knowledge production can mediate how societies experience the world beyond. They help transcend boundaries and spaces to bring the outside world within one's grasp. The media also represent a space where political and cultural or symbolic power can coincide.

The role of technology in texturing the experiences of the mind is an argument mooted by Marshall McLuhan. He contends that technologies such as television can become an extension of the mind where a medium is instrumental in shaping the perceptions and experiences of its audience. The media's ability to temper and texture the experience of the mind through technology highlights the role of ICTs in mediating our environment and our perceptions of the world. Silverstone (2002: 761) describes the process of mediation as a 'transformative process in which the meaningfulness and value of things are constructed'. With this argument Silverstone (1999) fully implicates the media in creating a framework for ordering the everyday and suggests its capacity for meaning-making as an elemental construct for re-framing its interface with the wider world.

The Concept of the Ummah

The *Ummah* refers to an ideal state – an all-encompassing unity of Muslims that is often invoked but never completely realized. In its most rudimentary definition, it refers to a community of believers bound by the tenets of Islam, a community which confers a religious solidarity and fraternity upon Muslims who may be dispersed spatially. With the development of modern technologies such as print and broadcasting, there has been a de-coupling of time and space, making remote communities visual realities within media landscapes (Giddens 1990). This visualization and mediated realism may reinforce the notion of community. In this sense, the *Ummah* can be both a global and local entity. At the local level, it can assume different degrees of hybridity in tandem with its social and political contexts.

The *Ummah* has also been viewed as a transformative concept. As witnessed by the transformation of the Arab tribes into a community of Arabs, and with the expansion of Islam into non-Arab regions, it encapsulates the transformation of different groups of Muslims into a community of believers (Rahman 1983; Watt 1955). In today's landscape, it has come to represent and embody an Islamic community. The subscription to this community is not based on any other criterion but faith. A sense of belonging to this Islamic community can be established without territorial embeddedness or loyalties. It offers possibilities for the formation of hybrid cultural and ethnic identities locally, while being intrinsically bound to an idealized spiritual fraternity globally. The *Ummah* over the years has evolved into a form of social consciousness marked by one's individual relationship with God, and hence provides a framework for global religious communion while accommodating cultural diversity among different communities.

The representation of Muslim issues through western electronic media then creates new forms of crisis in terms of identity and representation for the *Ummah*. Although Muslims share a sense of being part of a global *Ummah*, the intensity of this feeling varies significantly across Muslim communities (Hassan 2003). Worldwide communication links highlight both the commonalities as well as the differences among Muslims. Thus the mediated *Ummah* is a point of identification as well as diversity and hybridity in dispersed Muslim communities. While the unity of the *Ummah* is based solely on its spiritual and religious ethos, the politically polarized contemporary context provides opportunities to reinforce its connections and solidarity through ICTs and to develop a new sense of agency and collective global identity.

The technologically mediated Ummah

In relating the role of ICTs to the construction of a mediated *Ummah* there is a need to accommodate the process of mediation that happens within the everyday and its role in electronically constituting a sense of community through wires and soundbites. The representation of the *Ummah* is connected to the 'globalized' nature of contemporary existence. Rapid developments in communications technology, transport and information bring the remotest parts of the world within easy reach (Giddens 1990: 64). The 'globalness' of the *Ummah* in this sense is constructed through mediated representations, and hence this *imagined community* (Anderson 1983) is one that is reinforced through the Islamic ideal of a united global community of believers as well as one recreated through media representations. The *Ummah* as a community of the faithful is bound by religion and this provides a framework for ethical connection and empathy in periods of strife: 'Media images can connect local communal experiences with those of the global community and thus provide powerful sources of hermeneutic interpretation to make sense of what would otherwise be disparate and apparently unconnected events and phenomena' (Urry 2000: 180). The media has an integral role to play in constructing identity and community, and thus the mediated *Ummah* is a space of cultural and religious signification. As such it provides a platform for building new forms of identity and empathy, which can mould the state of global politics.

Ahmad and Doonan (1994: 1) point out that the controversy surrounding the publication of Salman Rushdie's novel *The Satanic Verses* drove home the interconnectedness of the world through technology for 'within hours, developments in the United Kindgom – in Bradford and London – provoked responses in Islamabad and Bombay'. They assert that the scale and complexity of these contemporary information exchanges create a mediated communal consciousness among Muslims and non-Muslims such that it may sustain Huntington's (1993) hypothesis of a 'clash of civilizations' – in which Islam is a real threat in military, demographic and socio-religious terms. Geaves (2005:70) contends, in his observations of the South Asian community in Britain, that one important aspect of the Salman Rushdie affair was to transform the politics of identity from rallying around (South Asian) ethnic issues to an overt Muslim religious identity that allowed a bridge between local micro-politics and global Islamization (Geaves 2005: 70). This mediated consciousness of community and Islamization is negotiated through volatile political events and unrest.

The western vision of Islam is captured through the discourses of Orientalism which constitute a system of ideas that have allowed European society to 'manage and produce the Orient as politically, sociologically, militarily and imaginatively' inferior to its own (Said 1978: 2). Through time there has been a discursive tendency to associate the same derogatory themes and topics with Islam (Poole 2002: 43). The application of this dominant western framework creates a binary opposition between Islam and the West in the press and the wider media. In discussing the discourses of Muslim representation either through the trajectory of Orientalism (Said 1978) or through recent debates on the anti-Islamic iconography manifested through Osama Bin Laden and 9/11, there is an acknowledgement that there is a globalization of terror which implicates the Muslim community as entrapped in a hermeneutic seal of fundamentalism. Hence, words such as 'fatwa', 'Jihad' and 'Ayatollah' are common in the West (Ahmad and Doonan 1994: 2). In *Covering Islam*, Said (1981; cf. Poole 2002) identifies the 1979 revolution in Iran as the starting point of the association of Islam with militancy, danger and anti-western sentiment. Here the media becomes the site for the cultural production of knowledge, interpretation and dissemination to the wider world. It casts the global *Ummah* as a monolithic entity which is resistant to change and modernity. This has implications for the politics of identity construction for the Muslim diaspora both at local and global levels.

Satellite broadcasting and new media
One of the distinct features of satellite broadcasting is its capability to transcend geographic boundaries and to carry its signals to widely dispersed areas which may not conform to the

territorial space of a nation state. Hence, legal impositions by a state can be overcome by broadcasting by satellite from another territory. The Internet also provides global connectivity and is not sensitive to borders enforced in the real world. These ICTs allow for both broadcasting and narrowcasting, as witnessed by the proliferation of ethnic and linguistic satellite channels catering for diverse communities and niche interests, and have become platforms for the global reach of niche communities and interests.

According to Bunt (2000) there has been an increasing use of the Internet for disseminating Islamic knowledge as well as for articulating Islamic and Muslim discourses in different parts of the *Ummah* worldwide (not only, for example, in Afghanistan and Kashmir, but also in both western and eastern Europe). Both Mandalville (2001) and Bunt (2000) agree that online platforms are being increasingly appropriated to explore the *Ummah*'s questions and concerns about being a Muslim in the postmodern world. Baktiari (2000), in assessing Muslim websites, concludes that new media technologies reduce if not obliterate geographical limitations, as well as challenging traditional methods of learning and accelerating pluralism in Islamic political activity. Anderson (1997) suggests that the Internet allows existing discussions to migrate online and to highlight political and religious concerns of diasporic communities in their home environments, thus enabling Muslims to create spaces for articulation, debate and communion.

The increasing fervour to re-contextualize Islam and Islamic practices in foreign lands according to the contemporary political and social environment is evident in satellite channels such as the Islam Channel, where more than 40 per cent of the programming focuses on Islamic knowledge in formats designed to get the audience to call in with their concerns about the interpretation of the *Quran*, and Islamic practices and rituals. Channel Islam, a digital radio station based in South Africa and which is available in the African continent and Europe, also devotes large proportions of its air time to exploring Islamic issues which concern Muslim communities the world over. Like the Islam Channel, audiences are encouraged to call in with questions. New media such as the Internet are enabling literate populations to seek knowledge and communion through technology but more significantly the search for meaning is not through the authority figures of *ulemas* (Muslim scholars) who preside over the tone and agenda of the discussions, but through that of the common man struggling with the conflicts of religion and modernity. Hence the Islam that comes to the Internet is 'not the world of the *ulema* nor that of the popular Islam of non-literate masses but a middlebrow Islam associated with a more middling population ranging from fundamentalist to liberal' (Anderson 1997). According to James Piscatori and Dale Eickelman (1996) this quest for meaning takes the form of re-intellectualizations of Islam which are driven by the need to relate interpretations of Islam to current conditions of existence. The online environment provides spaces for the discussion of Islam and allows a sense of pluralism to permeate discussions which may have been previously limited to Muslim scholars and elites alone.

The Internet, besides becoming a tool and medium for a discursive re-intellectualization of Islam, also provides spaces for dissidence and militant activism. Militant organizations are increasingly using the Internet to make demands and to display atrocities such as the beheading of hostages.

This presents a moral and ethical dilemma in which ICTs, while enabling global connectivity and access, provide an international platform for publishing and showcasing violent crimes against humanity and in the process implicating the whole entity of the *Ummah*.

The Al Jazeera phenomenon

The member countries of the League of Arab States launched their first satellite in 1985 with the aim of integrating social and cultural activities of member countries and allowing public and private channels from Arab countries to broadcast their programmes through a space that went beyond the nation state to reach all Arabic-speaking countries, thus creating a pan-national broadcasting sphere.

The need to counter the western-dominated media environment has led to a growing recognition in the Muslim world that the media and information and communications technologies constitute a potentially powerful space for ideological contestation between the West and the East. The disillusionment among British Muslims with the reporting of Islam and Muslims in the British mainstream media has been a primary reason for many of them opting for Muslim media (Ahmed 2005). The Al Jazeera phenomenon to a large degree can be attributed to the rise of satellite broadcasting which can transcend the geographical, ideological and broadcasting restrictions of nation states. The emergence of pan-Arabic satellite TV stations, such as Al Arabiya and Al Jazeera, has superseded more traditional western coverage of war and conflicts in the Middle East. Al Jazeera, for example, has captured the transnational Arabic audience and reflects the role of new technologies in altering mainstream communication patterns and political agendas. In the process they create new public spheres of engagement for dialogues and discourses which may be absent in western-centric media. The broadcasting sphere thus becomes an arena for ideological battles and this is evident in the U.S. Congress approving $60 million of taxpayers' money to establish Al-Hurrah TV, an Arabic-language station to broadcast throughout the Middle East. Besides Al-Hurrah, the Bush administration has also launched Radio Sawa which, according to Dalacoura (2005), targets younger audiences with a view to initiating them into American culture and winning them over to American values.

The emergence of broadcasting stations such as Al Jazeera and the Islam Channel in London signifies a need to restructure the global mediascape to counter the representations of a western-centric media and to portray the problems of the Middle East and the Muslim community in a different light. This embedding of counter-discourses within the tapestry of existing western-oriented representations posits the former as both material and symbolic forms of cultural resistance which can provide a sense of identification for the dispersed *Ummah* or diasporic Muslim communities: in Britain, throughout Europe, and indeed globally. The need for re-mediation is often sparked by watershed events. Al Jazeera entered mainstream media consciousness after the September 11 attacks when it broadcast exclusive reports from Afghanistan, including a series of monologues by Osama Bin Laden. Its breaking of news stories associated with the 'War on Terror' meant that it became one of the most widely quoted sources on the subject.

The Ummah in a constant state of crisis

Various world events including the Gulf War, 9/11, the Moro crisis, the Kashmir problem, the ongoing Palestinian-Israeli tensions, the invasion of Afghanistan, the Bali bombings, the conflicts in Algeria, Bosnia, Chechnya and Kosovo, and the invasion of Iraq, have inevitably created an image of an *Ummah* which is in a constant state of crisis. This ongoing narrative of the *Ummah* entangled in a perpetual mode of conflict can lead to a degree of reductionism in assessing the different issues which can face the Muslim community throughout Europe and in different parts of the world. Classifying the myriad of complex problems under the banner of a 'Muslim' issue polarizes the political landscape. This polarization is complicated further by subsuming the global discourses of terror under its overarching framework.

World events and their mediated representations have consequences for Muslims at a local level. They often lead to a 'culture of blame' in which individuals and communities have to defend themselves by not condemning acts of violence in various parts of the world. This 'politics of blame' then implies that Muslim morals, ethics and notions of humanity are starkly different from those of the western world. While the politics of discontent, war, strife and natural disasters in Muslim communities can create feelings of empathy among the Muslim *Ummah* in European and other diasporic communities, they also implicate the whole of the Muslim community when an individual commits an act of violence. The politics of blame are often sustained through everyday media discourses. Thus media representations and constructions of Muslim issues consumed in one's private realm are often embedded in the wider politics and dynamics of a society. Hence the mediated *Ummah* is a dialogical space for the Muslim audience, one which envelops both the reality constructed through the media as well as the real world which lies beyond its doorstep. These shared experiences portrayed in the media reinforce a collective identity, as fellow Muslims in a community may be tackling similar issues and challenges in their everyday lives (Ahmed 2005). The frameworks within which the Muslim community has been constructed means that diasporic Muslim communities in Europe and beyond have to negotiate prejudices in real society, and the need for re-mediation is born from this need to refute negative perceptions. The globalization of the discourse of terror is partly viewed as a consequence of the Muslim inability to engage in constructive dialogue, and hence the Muslim media are seen as a necessary platform by which to bridge the gap between Muslims and non-Muslims and also to renegotiate Islam and Islamic practices on foreign soil – from London, to Paris, Berlin, Tirana, Priština, Astana and beyond.

The media as a space to re-think Islam

The need to liberate the *Ummah* from its enslaved image as an 'outcast of modernity' through traditional and new forms of media is driven by both the global context and factors within the Muslim community. The need for a new image of the *Ummah* is largely fired by the global political landscape and thus there is a renewed fervour among Muslims to convince the world that Muslims are eager for constructive dialogue and not just acts of violence or armed struggle to put their points across. Muslims themselves are also feeling the need to re-examine their own plight and to rethink Islam's position in the modern world. Islamic scholars such as Ziauddin Sardar (2002) point out that there is a need for the Muslim community to engage in *Itjihad* or 'reasoned struggle' to rethink and reformulate Islam for the present context. Sardar (2002) points out that the 'context of the *Quran* and the examples of the Prophet Muhammad which are the Muslim community's absolute frame of reference are frozen in time', and that, in order to negotiate the contemporary world, 'one needs to have an interpretive relationship with a text'. He points out that if 'the interpretive context of the text is never our context, nor our time, then its interpretation can hardly have any real meaning or significance for us as we are now'. The 'freezing of interpretation' (Sardar 2002) has denied agency to believers and the community of the faithful or the *Ummah*. In this sense, Muslim media through ICTs provide new ways of re-opening the 'gates of *itjihad*' (Sardar 2002) and the possibility to re-contextualize Islam according to contemporary needs, needs of often diasporic and westernized or Europeanized populations. This urge to review Islam finds in the Muslim media a more amenable space for civic participation and engagement than western-dominated media spaces, spaces which may be perceived as intrusions into the community's religion and culture.

Community and identity

The mediated representations of the media have repercussions for the construction of identity for the diasporic Muslim community. Satellite and Internet technologies have enabled diasporic communities to make connections with their homeland (Georgiou 2004; Karim 1998; Dayan 1998). In Europe, the media is perceived as a space for negotiating Muslims' identities as European citizens (Ramadan 1999), as well as the construction of a new 'Muslimness' through information and communications technologies. In this sense, the emergence of new forms of identity can be bound to the territory as well as be independent of it. The global media depictions of the *Ummah* can provide new forms of identity and fraternity especially for second-generation Muslims in European societies who may not share the same level of connections to their 'homelands' as first-generation migrants. Hassan (2002) reiterates that diasporic Muslim communities tend to have dual or multiple social identities comprised of national or ethnic and Islamic identities. This means European Muslim communities are forced to re-negotiate the ideology of secularism which may propound the incompatibility of religion and rationality within modern European nation states and their increasing institutionalizations of public and private realms. Unequivocally, these Muslim media provide spaces for Muslim communities to negotiate and perhaps reconcile the public and private realms in secular European societies. The tensions between private and public roles are no longer a merely individual concern but generate a space that can appropriate the collective identity, debates and discourses of the community.

A crucial element in discussing the notion of a mediated *Ummah* and the creation of communal identity is the fact that a sense of connection and fraternity can be constructed without necessarily embedding this sense of belonging or identity to a territorial context or geography. Here the role of information and communications technologies in materializing a mediated *Ummah* to a large extent defies the politics of space. Spaces and places have been crucial (but not singularly deterministic) for nationalistic sentiments, but the mediated global *Ummah* with its decentring from the Middle East (Hassan 2002) can constitute a consciousness and politics of empathy without necessarily binding it to a physical space.

The issue of territory, space and mediated politics has important consequences for the global discourse of terror and the meting out of justice at detention centres such as Abu Ghraib and Guatanamo Bay. To the public, these inaccessible fortresses are constructed and represented through the media. The delivery of justice in places where one's citizenship may not mediate the execution of justice and where international laws cannot be applied or contested, and its association with alleged suicide bombers or those propagating *Jihad*, leads to further polarization between the East and West. The administration of justice for terrorists (often described as 'Islamic terrorists') happens in physically and legally impermeable spaces where one may not be accorded the legal protections afforded in a nation state. Detention centres such as Guatanamo Bay and Abu Ghraib may symbolically capture the hegemony of the West for the mediated *Ummah*. In the context of the global *Ummah*, these spaces represent the injustice systems constructed by the West and these discourses continually recreate strands of empathy among the Muslim community.

Conclusion

The emergence of distinct Muslim media has provided a focal point through which Muslims, particularly young and diasporic Muslims, can find expression for their concerns and aspirations (Ahmed 2005: 124–125). The concept of a mediated *Ummah* while providing an iconic and cultural space for identification and connection also reinforces distinctions and differences between local and global Muslim communities. The challenges that lie ahead for Muslim communities include constructing and sustaining dialogues both within the Muslim community and with non-Muslim audiences in society through the media. The mediated *Ummah* is a dialectical space which captures not only the pluralism within the community but also the singular resonant thread which may reconcile Islam to the context of postmodern existence; a context which is confounded by a volatile contemporary political landscape where many of the ideological struggles are enacted publicly through the media space. The mediated *Ummah* has developed specific meanings and significance for European Muslims: and one might be tempted to point out that its uses of the most contemporary media technologies and forms to unite, maintain, develop and promote the cultural values of a diverse and diasporic community is something from which the European Union itself might usefully learn.

References

Ahmed, A. and Doonan, H., eds. (1994), *Islam, Globalization and Postmodernity*, London: Routledge.

Ahmed, T. S. (2005), Reading 'Between the Lines, Muslims and the Media', in Abbas, T., ed. (2005), *Muslim Communities Under Pressure in Britain*, London: Zed Books, pp. 109–126.

Anderson, J.W. (1997), 'Cybernauts of the Arab Diaspora: Electronic Mediation in Transnational Cultural Identities', in *Postmodern Culture*. Available at: htttp://www.bsos.umd.edu/CSS97/papers/ anderson. html Date accessed: 6/9/2005.

Baktiari, B. (2000), 'Cybermuslims and the Internet: Searching for Spiritual Harmony in a Digital World', in Bahmanpour, M. and Bashir, H. (eds.), *Muslim Identity in the 21st Century*, London: Bookextra, pp. 41–62.

Bunt, G. (2000), *Virtually Islamic. Computer-mediated Communication and Cyber Islamic Environments*, Cardiff: University of Wales Press.

Dalacoura, K. (2005), 'U.S. Democracy Promotion in the Arab Middle East since 11 September 2001: A Critique', in *International Affairs* 81:2, pp. 961–979.

Dayan D. (1998), 'Particularistic media and diasporic communications', in Liebes, T. and Curran, J. (eds.), *Media, ritual and identity*, New York: Routledge, pp. 103–113.

Eickelman, D., and Piscatori, J. (1996), *Muslim Politics*, Princeton: Princeton University Press.

Geaves, R. (2005), 'Negotiating British Citizenship and Muslim Identity', in Abbas, T. (ed.), *Muslim Communities Under Pressure in Britain*, London: Zed Books, pp. 66–77.

Georgiou, M. (2004), 'Consuming Ethnic Media, Constructing Ethnic Identities, Shaping Communities: a Case Study of Greek Cypriots in London', in Lind, R. (ed.), *Race, Gender, Media: Considering Diversity Across Audiences, Content and Resources*, Boston: Pearson/Allyn and Bacon, pp. 311–329.

Giddens, A. (1990), *The Consequences of Modernity*, Cambridge: Polity.

Hassan, R. (2002), 'Globalization and the Islamic Ummah: Challenge and Response', paper presented at Islam in Southeast Asia and China: Regional Faithlines and Faultlines in the Global Ummah, Symposium, 28 Nov to1 Dec 2000, City University of Hong Kong.

Hassan, R. (2003), *Globalization's Challenge to Islam, How to create one Islamic community in a diverse world*, Yale Global Online, April 2003. Available at: http://yaleglobal.yale.edu/display. article?id=1417 Date accessed: 15/3/2006.

Huntington, S. (1993), 'The Clash of Civilizations?', in *Foreign Affairs*, 72 :4, pp. 22–49.

Karim, H. (1998), 'From *Ethnic Media to Global Media: Transnational Communication Networks Among Diasporic Communities*', Economic and Social Research Council Working Papers, Oxford University, June 1998. Available at: http://www.transcomm.ox.ac.uk/working%20papers/karim.pdf Date accessed: 18/8/08.

MacAskill, E., Lavine, S., and Harding, L. (2006), 'Cartoon Controversy Spreads Throughout Muslim World,' in *The Guardian*, 4 February 2006

Mandalville, P. (2001), *Transational Muslim Politics: Re-imagining the Umma*, London: Routledge.

Poole, E. (2002), *Reporting Islam – Media Representations of British Muslims*, London: I.B. Tauris.

Rahman, F. (1982), *Islam and Modernity: Transformation of an Intellectual Tradition*, Chicago: University of Chicago Press.

Ramadan, T. (1999), *To be a European Muslim*, Leicester: Islamic Foundation.

Sardar, Z. (2002), 'Rethinking Islam', in *Islam for Today*, June 2002. Available at: http://www. islamfortoday.com/sardar01.htm Date accessed: 2/5/2006.

Said. E. (1979), *Orientalism*, New York: Vintage.

Silverstone, R. (2002), 'Complicity and Collusion in the Mediation of Everyday Life' *New Literary History* 33: 4, pp. 761–780.

Silverstone, R. (1999), *Why Study the Media?*, London: Sage.

Urry, J. (2000), *Sociology Beyond Societies: Mobilities for the Twenty-First Century*, London: Routledge.

Watt, W. M., (1955), 'Ideal Factors in the Origin of Islam', in *Islamic Quarterly* 2, pp. 160–167.

PART TWO: STATES OF THE UNION

Vernacular Geopolitics and Media Economies in an Enlarged Europe

Mark Hayward

On 9 November 2001, the New York correspondent for the Roman daily *Il Messaggero*, Stefano Trincia, published an article describing a meeting between Prime Minister Silvio Berlusconi and Saudi Prince Al Waleed. The main topic discussed at the meeting involved Berlusconi's plans to privatize Italy's state-owned energy company ENI (*Ente Nazionale Idrocarboni*), but the implications drawn by the article went well beyond this particular business deal. Drawing on information recently made public in *The Wall Street Journal*, the article explained that Al Waleed was under investigation by the FBI and the CIA due to his possible involvement in the financing of the recent attacks on the World Trade Center. The article also recounted the refusal by the mayor of New York City, Rudolph Giuliani, of a donation of ten million dollars to be used for recovery efforts from Al Waleed on the grounds that it might be tainted by his alleged relationship to Al Qaeda. It was in the context of these investigations and the emergent War on Terror that the article detailed the Saudi Prince's long-standing relationship with Italy – and with Berlusconi in particular – that included numerous agreements relating to Italian television – specifically the fact that it was Prince Al Waleed who had agreed to purchase Berlusconi's shares in the Mediaset television networks in order for the Prime Minister to avoid contravening conflict of interest laws.

Three days later, an article was published in the small daily newspaper *Libero* outlining the extensive ties between RAI, Italy's public broadcaster, and Dalla Al Baraka Investment Bank. At the heart of the story was the distribution deal signed between RAI and Arab Digital Distribution (a subsidiary of Arab Radio and Television, the media division of Dalla Al Baraka) for the global distribution of RAI International. Similar to the story about the Saudi Prince, the story was told against the background of ongoing investigations into the involvement of the bank in the financing of the attacks on the World Trade Center. In many ways, it was the same story since the other major investor in Arab Radio and Television was Prince Al Waleed, who owned 30 per cent of the company. At the time, there was concern in the media, and in the public more generally, about the implications of these relationships between the Italian media and Saudi capital. An inquiry to the Minister of Communication filed in parliament the following week by a member of the Green Party asked 'if the government did not feel it urgent and necessary to clarify the relationship [between RAI and Dalla Al Baraka], avoiding all suspicion, given the ongoing global campaign against terrorism led by Bin Laden'.

In 2003, these events returned to the public eye when a lawsuit was filed in New York against Al Baraka Investment and Development Bank for its alleged involvement in the financing of the September 11 attacks. The lawsuit once more gave rise to suspicions about the investment bank. In Italy, these suspicions were again linked in media coverage to the relationship between Al-Baraka and RAI. The questions were similar as well. Should the Italian government have an agreement with interests that are under suspicion of being involved in terrorist activities? Should the government not be particularly sensitive to this issue given that RAI International was a particularly important state institution, being the primary conduit between Italy and the millions of Italians living abroad? In Canada, for example, this information was circulated by the network's opponents who used it to suggest that the Italian service was politically compromised while RAI International was in the midst of negotiating direct access to the Canadian market with regulatory agencies.

In January 2006, the details of the relationship between RAI and Saudi finance made another, more elliptical appearance. In the lead up to the Italian election, Silvio Berlusconi complained to the press that he was tired of hearing accusations about a conflict of interest between his business interests and the public responsibilities of his office. There were, he explained, many on the Left who were also guilty of similar kinds of behaviour. Specifically, he noted the involvement of senior members of centre-Left parties in advocating for the bid made by Unipol, an insurance company with ties to Leftist investment cooperatives, for the *Banca Nazionale di Lavoro* over other offers from foreign investors. Berlusconi also indicated that this was only the beginning of what he knew about the Left's dirty dealings. Although the accusations never resulted in any serious investigations (whether because there was, as Berlusconi claimed, 'nothing actionable' in what he knew or because he was afraid of the trouble it would cause for both the Right and the Left in Italy), one name in particular seized the spotlight, that of French-Tunisian businessman and longtime Berlusconi associate Tarak Ben Ammar.

It was Ben Ammar who was the source for the information that implicated Leftist politicians in the banking scandal. Finding him more interesting than yet another scandal bringing to light collusion and corruption between Italy's political and financial elites, the papers were very quickly filled with profiles of this mystery man who seemed to be at the heart of the intrigue enthralling the Italian electorate that week. The articles recounted his youth in Italy as the son of a Tunisian diplomat (and nephew to former Tunisian president Habib Bourguibab) raised in Catholic schools (in spite of his Muslim heritage) and an illustrious history in film production (including, most recently, Mel Gibson's *The Passion of the Christ* [2004]). Central to the details of his career was his long-term relationship with Silvio Berlusconi. In particular, readers were reminded that it was Ben Ammar who had helped Berlusconi sell 25 per cent of his Mediaset Empire to Saudi Prince Al Waleed in order to comply with regulations governing conflict of interest. (A deal, the articles insinuated, that had aided in his recent ascendancy to the board of directors of Italy's oldest and largest investment bank, Mediobanca.) The articles also recounted Ben Ammar's central role in negotiating the distribution agreement between RAI and Al Baraka Investments for the distribution of RAI International.

There is a great deal that the relationship (and the stories about the relationship) between Italian media and Saudi capital can tell us about the role of media in an enlarged Europe. As much as these stories help us to map the institutional and political-economic relations that constitute the transnational networks within which cultural commodities circulate, they are significant for other reasons as well. The interest in Prince Al Waleed, Dalla Al Baraka Investment Bank and Tarak Ben Ammar is intimately related to the vernacular geopolitical knowledge that has defined many aspects of everyday life in Europe in the wake of the events of September 11. The media coverage (often invoking a hint of scandal) is grounded in the same discourses (and related anxieties) that frame the global 'War on Terror' and popular panics about the coming (or, perhaps, already current) 'clash of civilizations' between the North Atlantic world and the Muslim world that circulate in western Europe.

The goal of this chapter is to look at the way in which the ongoing stories of Ben Ammar and Dalla Al Baraka have walked the line between the 'official' mappings of corporate relations and the functioning of state institutions and less legitimate popular understandings of international politics in the post-9/11 world. In accounts of these events, these two kinds of knowledge have often been brought together, overlaid upon one another in the form of a single narrative. However, this chapter's primary purpose is not to disentagle these two aspects of the narrative, producing a political-economic mapping accompanied by an appropriately stern condemnation of the more 'scandalous' aspects of the story for being sensationalistic. Instead, this chapter will treat the narrative as an artefact produced by and attempting to describe the role of media in an enlarged Europe. It is by following this approach that many interesting insights into the meaning of an 'enlarged Europe' may come to light. Thinking about the way in which Europe has expanded in recent years also necessitates a consideration of the way in which parts of Europe have linked up with global financial and information networks and the way in which knowledge about these networks circulates through the media contributing to 'vernacular geopolitics'.

The development of Italian broadcasting beyond the national territory of Italy itself has a history that is almost as extensive as that of Italian broadcasting itself, stretching back to the first broadcasts to Africa and the Arabian peninsula in the 1930s by Mussolini's government. The role that media plays in the process of including the globally dispersed populations belonging to the Italian diaspora in both the cultural and institutional fabric of the nation is a subject that continues to be of importance in contemporary debates (as the centrality of the *voto all'estero* in the most recent elections has made undeniably apparent).

The more one traces the ways in which various broadcasters developed or attempted to develop their international services (from public broadcaster RAI, to Mediaset's aborted international service, to smaller players such as SitCom and RadioItalia), the clearer it becomes that it is impossible to understand the nature of the industry without acknowledging the crucial role of Dalla Al-Baraka Investments and its subsidiaries Arab Media Corporation (AMC) and Arab Digital Distribution (ADD) in the Italian broadcasting market. This Saudi-based company, which includes commercial and investment banks, insurance companies, and food production and processing interests, as well as its media holdings, has positioned itself as the primary distributor of Italian media content internationally. Through a global deal with RAI International as well as a variety of local deals with the smaller broadcasters, Al-Baraka Investments has played a greater role than any other single entity in organizing and regulating the development of Italian media globally in the past decade. This is most clearly apparent in the Americas, where licensing deals with ART (Arab Radio and Television) and its ethnic satellite division, REACH Media, have allowed RAI International and other Italian services to expand their distribution from pole to pole.

While funded by Saudi capital, ART was founded in Rome in 1994. It started broadcasting in January of that year from the Telespazio Center in Fucino, Italy. While it developed a group of its own broadcast services, ranging in nature from film channels to music and nature networks, the company quickly expanded into the distribution of other programming. It was as part of this expansion that the company signed a long-term deal with RAI International. Some would complain about the nature of the agreement because they felt that profits gained by the global distribution of RAI International would not be passed onto RAI. However, over the decade following the agreement RAI International was able to expand its distribution globally, although the exact nature of the relationship was never clarified.

There is a great deal of research that needs to be done regarding the media economy that developed over the course of the early 1990s between Rome and the Arab world. Along with ART, this would include a discussion of companies like Orbit that were primarily targeting the Arab market while being based in Rome. Tracing this relationship in detail would show the way in which the technological infrastructures of various European nations, often developed under public broadcast monopolies, have been transformed in recent decades into being part of transnational networks of distribution and production that occupy European space but are not primarily focused on Europe as potential audience.

The media coverage of the relationship between RAI International and Al Baraka Investments was about more than simply noting a series of business arrangements. It was framed by the cultural and political contexts that emerged in the aftermath of the attacks on the World Trade

Center in New York City. It is not enough to map these relationships as a set of economic or legal obligations. Or, rather, a broader frame is necessary if the significance (both economic and cultural) of Al Baraka is to be understood. In bringing attention to the place of Al Baraka Investments in popular discourse, we may throw into relief two factors that are closely related to the subject of this volume, media in an enlarged Europe. The first of these relates to the question of what it means to talk about an 'enlarged Europe'. The second relates to the significance of the media as a social and cultural institution and its relationship to broader questions of geopolitical power.

In many ways, the media's coverage of the figure of Ben Ammar may represent the embodiment of the tensions that were previously focused on the role of Al Baraka in Italian broadcasting. The nature of the business deals he has been involved in can hardly be surprising to any person who follows Italian economic and political events. What is more interesting about this story is the fact that the reporting of the events – the banking deal, but also the media agreements between Berlusconi, Kirch and Prince Waleed – all habitually involve the recounting of Ben Ammar's past and of his transnational political and cultural identity. This is most clear in the continual citation and recitation of his Muslim roots and Catholic education. If the events in the wake of September 11 gave rise to a feeling of terror that the Other was already inside, the stories around Ben Ammar replay these same tensions at the level of continual suspicion: suspicion of the insider who can never wholly be assimilated or brought into the community as a full member.

But the attention given to these events also speaks to a broader issue about the relationship between cultural identity and economic activity. This case is an example of the way in which the economic (as a symbolic space) has become increasingly significant for the determination of cultural identity. This is not to fall back upon the processes of determination of a vulgar Marxism, but to note that it has been increasingly apparent that the economy itself has become a site of signification. In the case of Al Baraka and Italy, it is the political economy of RAI's international channel (a channel that could not be seen in Italy itself) that came to signify issues of cultural identity and national unity. The economy was the site through which members of the national population identified themselves as having something in common. There was, after all, no suggestion that the relationship with Al Baraka was affecting the programming on the channel. It was simply distributing the signal.

This situation demands that we move beyond simply saying that media play an important role in our understanding of the geopolitical reorganization that is the enlargement of Europe. It is also important to think about how we understand media itself. Too often, the study of media falls into two general camps that remain separate from one another: on the one hand, the study of content and its reception; on the other hand, the study of the institutional and economic organizations (in which the nation state most often serves as the absolute guarantor) that structure the political economy of the media.

By thinking through the case of Dalla Al Baraka and its relationship with global Italian media, it is clear that these two approaches are mutually constitutive; the institutional and economic organization of broadcasting and the nature of its content and reception are not separable, but continually reflect and interweave with one another. Indeed, as is the case here, there are times when the political economy of the media becomes a part of media representation and must be treated as such.

In this regard, we might set this case alongside a wide variety of other phenomena ranging from the relationships between national pride and the fluctuations of currency on the international market, the relationships between the rise and fall of populist political movements and the flow of financial capital, or even the proliferation of business news in the past decade (Martin 2002). One might even note in the emergence of a cultural understanding of the economy, the parallel development of Islamic banking and finance practices since the 1970s (Maurer 2005). All of these demand that we recalibrate established understandings in media studies about the relationship between the economic, the institutional and the symbolic. And, to return to the case at hand, rethinking these questions in this way also demands that we rethink the way we approach questions about the role of media in an enlarged Europe.

At one level, the notion of an enlarged Europe might be understood as referring to the expansion of the European Union in recent years towards the East as well as any other possible expansions on the horizon. This understanding of enlargement is what is typically understood as 'geographical' in nature. At another level, we may take the theme of an 'enlarged Europe' to refer to the ways in which Europe operates on a global scale, which is to say that an 'enlarged Europe' is one that can no longer be said to be limited by the geographic boundaries of the continent itself. However, this is to take up themes that draw on a much longer history, a history that is almost coterminous with the history of the notion of 'Europe' itself. It is part of the legacy of colonialism, imperialism, and globalization to posit that Europe more than many other places on the planet has always been enlarged. Its 'footprint', to borrow a term from the language of satellite technology, has always been global.

The case of Al Baraka and the centrality of the Arab Media Corporation for almost every Italian-based media company looking to expand beyond the national market obliges us to consider the ways in which the borders of Europe are drawn. While hardly European in the traditional sense (and explicitly non-European to many), it is hard to deny that the marketing and distribution services carried out around the world by this Saudi-based investment and media conglomerate are central to understanding the ways in which Europe is enlarging.

Finally, the ways in which these relationships have been linked to the vernacular geopolitical knowledges that structure everyday life are crucial for understanding Europe as a political, cultural and economic space. In their elaboration of a critical geopolitics, Dalby and Ó Tuathail (1998: 2) offer a position very much in line with what this chapter has attempted to develop. They write:

Rather than accepting geopolitics as a neutral and objective practice of surveying global space – the conventional Cold War understanding of the concept – we begin from the premise that geopolitics is itself a form of geography and politics, that it has a contextuality, and that it is implicated in the ongoing social reproduction of power and political economy.

One of the problems of thinking about media in an enlarged Europe, as this discussion of investment in transnational Italian media has shown, is understanding the ways in which our mappings of the political economies of media and information are themselves a product of the power relations they seek to describe and do not exist merely outside of them. This means that the study of media in the regional context requires not just an expansion of the scale at which the media are studied (usually the local or the national) but also an interrogation of the methods used by researchers.

References

Birchall, C. (2006), *Knowledge Goes Pop: From Conspiracy Theory to Gossip*, London: Berg.

Dalby, S., and Ó Tuathail, G., eds. (1998), *Rethinking Geopolitics*, London: Routledge.

Martin, R. (2002), *The Financialization of Everyday Life*, Philadelphia: Temple University Press.

Maurer, B. (2005), *Mutual Life, Limited: Islamic Banking, Alternative Currencies, Lateral Reason*, Princeton University Press, Princeton, NJ.

Schleifer, S. A. (1998), 'Media Explosion in the Arab World: The Pan-Arab Satellite Broadcasters', in *Transnational Broadcasting Studies*. Available at: www.tbsjournal.com Date accessed: 18/8/08.

New Labour and the Reinvention of British and European History

Oliver Daddow

New Labour came to power in 1997 promising to modernize Britain politically, economically and socially. This chapter focuses upon one vital dimension of that government's performance: British European policy. New Labour recognized how every British government since World War Two had struggled to devise a satisfactory European policy. Seeing 'Europe' as both challenge and opportunity Tony Blair in particular wanted to leave a legacy of altering attitudes in a country widely seen as amongst the most sceptical in the European Union.

This ambition can be seen from New Labour's first day in office. On the steps of Downing Street on 2 May 1997 the newly elected Prime Minister was precise about the central place Europe occupied in his strategy for modernizing Britain: 'it shall be a government, too, that gives this country strength and confidence in leadership both at home and abroad, particularly in respect of Europe' (Blair 1997a). The last phrase 'particularly in respect of Europe' did not need to be included to give that sentence its meaning – any Prime Minister would presumably make some vague commitment to strengthening Britain's global status. So we can assume it was included for a reason, especially given New Labour's obsessive attention to its communications and media strategy and the presentation of its policies. Even if that assumption is wrong, and it was an off-the-cuff addition by Blair on the day, made in the flush of a landslide election victory, it would say something about the importance he attached to the European question that it was Europe he mentioned. Why not the 'special relationship', or the United Nations (UN), or a pledge to tackle global poverty?

The government's desire to make lasting and positive changes to British European policy is also set out in the first three of New Labour's election manifestos, even if the party became less and less ambitious in this area over time (Labour Party 1997, 2001 and 2005). Yet by almost any measurement the British public is still far from convinced either that the United Kingdom is a truly 'European' country or that the European Union is the appropriate forum within which European countries should pool their resources to further national interests (for a review of the public opinion literature see Daddow 2006: 309–12). Judging ambitions against achievements, it seems fair to suggest that we have here a clear case of policy failure.

In the literature which tries to explain the causes of this failure three explanations are prominent. First of all, we have the 'blown off course' interpretation put about by Robin Cook, Foreign Secretary during Blair's first term in office. After he resigned from the government in March 2003 Cook published extracts from the diary he had kept as a Cabinet minister, interspersed with his interpretation of key issues and points of policy debate that had broken out during his time in post. Throughout this work he stresses that Blair deserves credit for 'achieving more than any previous Prime Minister in promoting Britain's place in Europe, until the hurricane over his support for the war in Iraq blew him off course' (Cook 2003: 1). He is extremely sympathetic in lauding Blair's achievements during his first term in office, when 'he transformed Britain's relations with Europe' (Cook 2003: 131). For Cook, Blair's failure was not one related to the conduct of European policy *per se*, but how that policy fell off the foreign policy agenda as a result of the ill-conceived invasion of Iraq.

Secondly, we have the 'electoral considerations' interpretation. In 2005 the Director of the 'pro-European' pressure group the Federal Trust, Brendan Donnelly, argued that the best we could say of New Labour was that it was an 'anti-anti-European' party. The implication is that New Labour was more interested in stealing the electoral clothes of the Conservative and Liberal Democratic parties than in developing a distinctive policy of principled support for the European idea (Donnelly 2005: 2). The label further suggests that rather than creating a break with past practices, Blair instead prolonged a historic trend in British European policy, one ongoing since 1945, by opportunistically using the issue of 'Europe' as a tool to settle scores against opponents from within his party and against other parties (see, for example, Kaiser 1996). The conduct of New Labour's European policy, Donnelly suggests, became intimately woven into the fabric of the increasingly fraught relationship between the Prime Minister and the then Chancellor (and future Prime Minister), Gordon Brown. Their personal wrangling ossified still further a policy already partially paralysed by sceptical media and public opinion. To take the euro as one example, Donnelly judges that 'the need to preserve the internal and external political equilibrium of New Labour has clearly taken precedence in his calculations over any personal inclination [Blair] may have, or have had, to move to quick resolution of the single currency issue' (Donnelly 2005: 4).

Thirdly, we have the 'no strategy at all' interpretation, which is even less kind to New Labour than Donnelly and even more starkly at odds with Cook's opinion. This comes through in the work of Lance Price, a former BBC journalist turned 'spin doctor' working for Alastair

Campbell as deputy in the Downing Street Press Office and then the Labour Party's Director of Communications. Like Cook, Price has published some revealing diaries about his time working for Number Ten, and his portrait of British European policy is far from flattering. In June 1998 at a Policy Unit lunch on Europe he noted: 'Quite clear there is no coherent strategy' (Price 2005: 14). Things had not improved almost a year later when he asked himself: 'What are the actual objectives of our foreign policy?' (Price 2005:88). The main impression one has reading Price's diaries is one of policy 'drift' (Price 2005: 114) combined, paradoxically, with a supreme confidence on Blair's part that at a moment of his choosing he could oversee a successful referendum campaign on the euro (Price 2005: 123). That this campaign was never launched meant that 'by the end of 2005 Britain was no closer to joining the euro than it had been in 2001, and arguably further away than in 1997' (Price 2005: 366).

Price mainly lays the blame for Blair's hesitancy at the door of the Eurosceptical press. For example, in February 1999, he wrote of Blair being 'nervous about taking on the press in a big way. He knows what a huge battle it will be and doesn't seem ready to have it now, although the rest of us think he should' (Price 2005: 79). His diaries are replete with references to Blair trying to woo the owners and editors of key Eurosceptical British newspapers, notably *The Sun*, *The Times*, the *Daily Mail* and the *Telegraph*, into helping him make his case to the British people. Price is supported by commentators such as Polly Toynbee and David Walker who complain that New Labour did not make the most of its landslide election victory in May 1997 to sell the idea of Europe to the British public: 'The people were not prepared, quite the contrary. If entry [to the euro] had been Blair's clear intent, Labour surely needed to make a continuous and convincing public case. Labour would have had to set its face against the howling gales of anti-Europeanism swirling through the pages owned and written by Tories, Little Englanders and North Americans' (Toynbee and Walker 2001: 145). Some of these press outlets, notably the Murdoch-owned *Sun*, had willingly backed New Labour at the 1997 general election, making it doubly hard for the government to make early and decisive moves in the field of European policy. One manifestation of this came with the October 1997 decision to delay holding a referendum on Britain joining the European single currency until after the Treasury judged that the British economy had passed a vague set of 'Five Tests' showing long-term compatibility between the British and eurozone economies (Brown 1997a). In taking this step, Blair effectively gave Brown and the Treasury huge influence over how British European policy would develop, adding fuel to Donnelly's suggestion that European policy had not been subject to long-term planning based on principle but on the machinations of internal Labour party politics.

We can read in the softer criticisms of Cook and the harsher ones of Donnelly, Price and Toynbee and Walker several explanations for the failure of New Labour's European policy: it is the story of the usual suspects, the press, and a strange mixture of confidence about winning a referendum and apathy about launching one on Blair's part, combining to bog down New Labour's European policy in a mire of indecision. But none of this tells us what Blair and New Labour attempted when it *did* bother to challenge the press and to try to alter received public discourses on Europe. What is the picture there?

If we isolate some of the most common New Labour attempts to sell Europe, via the press, to the British people, we see a narrative which was almost doomed to fail from the start, even before we take into account the wider battles the government had to fight with the Eurosceptical press. After 1997 New Labour made precious little headway in developing and publicizing a distinctive alternative narrative about Britain's place in the world to challenge the hegemonic narrative about Britain's isolation from Europe so often rehearsed in the pages of the Eurosceptical press.

Analysis of 157 speeches by Tony Blair and Gordon Brown between 1997 and 2005 tells a story about New Labour's European policy that is somewhat at odds with that currently popular among even the government's fiercest critics. This perspective concurs with those of writers such as Anne Deighton (2002), who argues that New Labour presented its discourses on Europe as progressive, forward-thinking efforts to re-interpret British history, but that on closer inspection these discourses were as stuck in the past as were the discourses put about by the opponents of closer British involvement with the European Union. This allowed those adversaries, most notably the Eurosceptical press, to keep the country in a permanent state of war with the continent and thus preserve the frosty public attitude to things 'European'.

Challenging hegemonic Eurosceptic discourses: making Britain part of Europe

Through their speeches on British foreign policy in general and British European policy in particular, New Labour ministers after 1997 tried two strategies by which to bring about a real and substantive shift in the cognitive frameworks through which foreign policy was practised and talked about. First of all, in May 1997, Foreign Secretary Robin Cook announced that he wanted to give British foreign policy an 'ethical dimension' (Cook 1997). Whilst identifying enduring national interests (security, prosperity and quality of life) Cook said he wanted to put 'human rights at the heart of our foreign policy'. This apparent commitment to advancing traditional Labour internationalism was seen at the time, if not since, as a real break with past foreign policy priorities (effectively critiqued in Hill 2001: 332–40 and Williams 2005: 17–20). Intellectual substance was added to this foreign policy rhetoric in April 1999 when, in a speech strongly influenced by developments in and around the Kosovo conflict, the Prime Minister set out his 'doctrine of the international community' in which he spelt out the multifarious security challenges posed to individual nation states by global interdependence and the 'circumstances in which we should get actively involved in other people's conflicts' (Blair 1999a).

The second technique is the one that interests us here. After 1997, New Labour attempted to overcome the separation so evident in press and public discourses between 'Britain' on the one hand and 'Europe' on the other (Colley 2005: 6). This is not the place to dissect the dominant themes in Eurosceptical press discourses on Europe, not least because key components of the story will surely be well known to British and international readers alike. Robert Harmsen summarizes the plot as 'indeed, a familiar one, variably encompassing a sense of "misfit" as regards national political and economic models, as well as a perception of "misplacement" insofar as a deeper European engagement is seen to conflict with the maintenance of wider networks of Transatlantic or international ties' (Harmsen 2007: 6). Newspapers such as The

Sun, The Times, the *Daily Mail* and the *Telegraph* have routinely been shown to situate their reporting and commentary on EU affairs in a wider narrative of British separation from the continent, albeit using different linguistic techniques and historical-cultural reference points to appeal to their various readerships (Anderson and Weymouth 1999; Daddow 2007). If we were briefly to summarize some of the key themes in sceptical press discourses on Europe we might highlight: a lack of support either for the European Union in general and/or for specific policies or treaties, such as the proposed Constitution, devised by the European Union (commonly referred to by the derogatory epithet 'Brussels'); suspicion of the ambitions of key nation states (notably France and Germany) in the European Union; an instinctive preference for closer ties with the United States than the European Union; and a sense that the memory of the past (especially British 'victory' against all the odds in World War Two) pits Britain eternally against the continent. Some or all of these issues recur throughout press coverage of EU politics in the various organs of the sceptical press in Britain – and this is the hegemonic discourse referred to in this chapter.

Press discourses are resonant of the culture which constitutes them and which they help to constitute, and these ways of talking about Britain's place in the world appear to reside deeply within the collective British subconscious. To take an example from everyday vernacular, when British football teams participate in the various European club competitions such as the UEFA Cup and the Champions League, they are said to be playing *in* Europe, as if the English, Scottish and Welsh league matches played every weekend do not take place in Europe already. This way of framing the British relationship to Europe feeds into the way in which football commentators, journalists, players and supporters instinctively think and talk about the game of football, resulting in artificial binary oppositions being erected between a decent and fair-minded British 'us' on the one hand and a sly or underhand European 'them' on the other.

Hence, in the autobiography of the Liverpool and England footballer Steven Gerrard, ghost-written by Henry Winter of the *Telegraph*, we are treated to several asides on the qualities that distinguish 'British' (meaning English) from 'foreign' (sometimes but not always European) football culture. For instance, of Wayne Rooney's famous red card in England's quarter-final against Portugal at the World Cup in Germany 2006, Gerrard writes that before the flashpoint that led to Rooney's sending off we saw classic underhand tactics being deployed against the English: 'If Wayne had acted like most foreigners and fallen over at the slightest contact, England would have got the free-kick. But we're England. We don't cheat. We take the knocks [...] we don't complain or pull stunts like foreigners' (Gerrard 2006: 415). Such culturally constituted ways of constructing discursive barriers between Britain and the continent reside everywhere – even in the supposedly progressive world of academia. One of my own books on the subject is called *Britain and Europe* (Daddow 2004), highlighting just how deeply this perceived division runs, even shaping the very scholarship on the subject which actively tries to collapse the distinction! It is important to bear in mind the breadth and depth of sceptical attitudes to the continent when evaluating New Labour's failure to change public attitudes because such constructions of 'self' and 'other' are so ingrained in the collective British mindset, perhaps uniquely so.

New Labour used two tactics to try to erase the distinction between 'Britain' on the one hand and 'Europe' on the other. It first of all encouraged the British to see their history as part of the stream of wider European history rather than as antithetical to it, and to collapse the 'self' versus 'other' distinction so common in journalistic and public discourses about the European Union and the wider world of 'foreigners'. First of all they stressed how interdependent Britain has always been with the continent: economically, culturally, socially and politically. On some occasions this interconnectedness is illustrated bilaterally; for example, at the French National Assembly in March 1998 Blair reminded his audience that: 'More than trade and work, we exchange ideas and tastes, too. About fashion. Food. Design. Lifestyle. Culture. [...] Between the people of our countries there is a genuine contact. It is real. It is rooted. And it matters.' (Blair 1998b)

At other times, and this is notable when Blair and Brown talked to British audiences, these cultural exchanges were sketched in broader European (rather than country-by-country) terms. For example, in one of Blair's first big foreign policy speeches after coming to power he asserted that: 'For four centuries, our destiny has been to help shape Europe. Let it be so again.' (Blair 1998b) This idea that Britain has 'always' been at the centre of Europe became something of a Blairite mantra during his first term in office, appearing in speeches across the continent (Blair 2000a and 2000b), and also, tellingly, at the public re-launch of the cross-party Britain in Europe campaign in October 1999 (Blair 1999b). Brown, who consistently stressed the idea of British strength through diversity in the form of a simultaneously devolved and outward-looking multicultural identity, faithfully stuck to the message of the historian Linda Colley that British history has, seemingly always, been intimately interwoven with that of the continent and in fact the wider world (Brown 1999a and 2004).

Blair and Brown's second tactic was to reflect on the damage the nation's obsession with history has inflicted on British European policy in the past. They regularly indicted Conservative European policy in the 1980s and 1990s for its marginalization of the British in Europe – putting Britain in the 'isolation room' as the Prime Minister expressed it in his March 2002 parliamentary statement on the Barcelona European Council (Blair 2002). When not condemning Conservative policy, Blair actively used Europhile and in many cases openly federalist discourse (explored in Daddow 2004: 60–101) to describe the string of opportunities for Britain to participate and/or lead in Europe that both main parties of government missed after World War Two. This, he surmised, was because they 'failed the test [...] today's leaders became yesterday's men, clutching at irrelevant assumptions and forgotten shibboleths' (Blair 2001b). During his first term 'internationalist not isolationist' was how Blair spelt out the distinction between New Labour's foreign policy and British foreign policy in the previous two decades (Blair 1997b; Blair 1998a; Blair 1999a), while in his second term he relabelled it as a policy of 'engagement not isolationism' (Blair 2001a; Blair 2003).

More often than not it was left to the then Chancellor to add the intellectual ballast to this line of attack. Brown said in 1997, and repeated word for word in 1999, that Conservative European policy was based on a misreading of the implications of Britain's imperial history and Second

World War experiences: 'As the experience of the first half of this century showed – in two world wars – Britain did not and would not relinquish our role in Europe or abdicate responsibility for the progress of the continent. Europe, by virtue of history as well as geography, is where we are' (Brown 1997b; Brown 1999b). Rather than seeing in Britain's island geography an excuse for the 'little England' attitudes of the sort that support negative stereotypes about 'foreigners' on the part of the press and the public, and anti-European foreign policies on the part of the government, Brown stressed how, through history, the British have actively sought out and embraced foreign adventures: 'The British way is not to retreat into a narrow insularity and defensive isolationism but to be open and tolerant, confidently outward-looking' (Brown 1999a).

We might sum up the distinctive twist New Labour gave to British and European history by noting Brown's interpretation of the geographic separation of Britain from mainland Europe in the form of the English Channel. Using the words of another historian, this time David Cannadine, in 2004 Brown suggested we view the Channel 'not as a moat but as a highway' – a route to the wider world rather than a barrier against it (Brown 2004; Brown 2005). Bringing new meaning to a symbolically important component of discourses of European 'otherness', this metaphor illustrates just how far New Labour was prepared to go to revise accepted wisdoms about Britain and Europe.

Reinforcing hegemonic discourses: giving the media what it wants to hear

From the evidence presented so far it might be thought that New Labour made great strides in reinventing British history to fit comfortably into wider European and global narratives, so that the national history is not antithetical to the other two but subsumed by or into them. This judgement can only hold, however, if we ignore whole rafts of New Labour's foreign policy discourse since 1997 that worked to reinforce rather than destabilize conventional ways of conceptualizing Britain's role in the world. Anne Deighton makes just this point when she writes that New Labour's foreign policy rhetoric 'has been bolted on to, and has not replaced, received memories of Britain's imperial past and the concern for global powerdom and "leadership" through which these memories have been nurtured' (Deighton 2002: 120). The idea of 'bolting on' is important here, suggesting a half-hearted tacking on of new ideas to older ones which have been prominent in policy-making circles since 1945 and earlier, and a recipe for disaster if the ambition is to replace these foreign policy rhetorics rather than giving further credence to them.

This analysis of the Blair/Brown speeches confirms Deighton's opinion (2002: 115–19) that traditional Churchillian aspirations to global power and leadership permeated New Labour's foreign policy discourses. Blair's emphasis on 'leadership' outside Downing Street (1997a) was the first of many times that variants of 'lead', 'leading' and 'leadership' featured in New Labour's European discourses; they went hand in hand with the belief that, through being this 'leading partner', Britain could be able to change ('reform') the European Union from within. There was a clear danger in playing the national card when talking about Britain's relations with Europe because it created tensions with New Labour's broader 'Third Way' discourses of global interdependence and the powerlessness of individual states in the era of 'globalization' (for details, see Fairclough 2001: 21–50). There is a logical incompatibility, it seems, between the views that on the one hand globalization has radically reduced the power and importance of the nation state in the global political economy, and that on the other a country the size of Britain can exert any sort of leadership role, either globally or even in regional supranational organizations such as the European Union. By definition, such groupings work to advance national interests by collective rather than national action. Trumpeting 'leadership' in the age of interdependence was surely a sop to the British press and public – but did New Labour not see that giving them what they wanted to hear might damage efforts to publicize the European Union as a cooperative endeavour which might achieve collectively what nation states could not achieve independently?

Aside from the 'leadership' angle, we can highlight the 'global player' theme in New Labour discourse to make the same point. In speeches right through his first two terms (sometimes the very same speeches in which his pro-Europeanism glares through) Blair espoused the virtues of Britain as a 'bridge' between the Europeans and Americans. At the Lord Mayor's Banquet in 1997 it was a bare statement of fact: 'We are the bridge between the U.S. and Europe' (1997b). After nearly two and a half years in power, at the relaunch of the Britain in Europe campaign, Britain was still being portrayed as 'a bridge between the two' (1999b). Two years further on, at the European Research Institute in Birmingham, when Blair was really pushing the federalist 'missed opportunities' interpretation of British European policy, he still could not bring himself to break decisively with received discourses: 'the UK has a powerful role to play between [the] USA and Europe' (2001b).

Brown echoed Blair in saying that Britain could continue to act as a transatlantic interlocutor. Even more than that, he said, Americans *want* the British to play that role. As he told the Confederation of British Industry in 1999: 'Far from Americans seeing Britain better off detached from Europe, they themselves take the view that the more influence we have in Berlin and Paris, the more influence we have in Washington' (Brown 1999c). Ignoring the obvious retort that what the Europeans want is never mentioned, as if their views somehow matter less than America's, all this goes to support Deighton's argument that New Labour tried to have its cake and eat it, when Britain's economic and strategic position at the end of the twenty-first century called for a more thoroughgoing overhaul of foreign policy discourses. To put it simply, the elements of continuity more than outweighed the novel elements in New Labour's foreign policy discourses, and this hardly gives us cause to believe that this was a realistic effort to refashion British identity for the twenty-first century.

Conclusion

This chapter has examined the key tactics used by New Labour to reorient British foreign policy discourses after 1997. That government's ambition was to help the British press and people rethink their traditionally hostile attitude to seemingly all things European through a reinvention of British and European history. Blair and Brown told the press and the public that Eurosceptical attitudes were based on a misreading of history and that those who spun stories of British insularity and separateness from the continent lacked confidence in their and their country's multicultural, multiethnic identity. No Prime Minister after 1945 was spared the wrath of New Labour – Margaret Thatcher's resurrection of jingoistic English nationalism in the 1980s coming in for particularly vitriolic treatment.

Much of the current literature suggests that the government failed in its mission because it came up against an immovable object in the form of the sceptical press. There is much to credit this view. Lance Price's frequent references to Blair either courting or tip-toeing around the owners of newspapers such as *The Sun* and the *Daily Mail* testify to the time and energy New Labour expended on trying to manage its communications strategy on Europe. But take away the press dimension and what do we find? Is the blame for this failure to be laid entirely at the door of the press?

This chapter has argued that, yes, there were several structural constraints facing the development of a 'modern' European policy for Britain, but that to focus only or mainly on those external barriers is to disregard the failings of the New Labour project itself. There is significant evidence to support such writers as Anne Deighton, analysts who perceive huge tensions within New Labour's own discourses – discourses which tried to be all things to all audiences. In trying to keep former Conservative voters of the Centre Right on side by dredging up discourses of Britain's past military glories and its global leadership role, New Labour undermined its simultaneous efforts to bury those images through a process of discursive modernization. Giving the press and the public what they wanted to hear worked fine as an electoral strategy for the New Labour machine; but it only added fuel to the criticisms, increasingly heard even from government supporters, that the New Labour project represented the triumph of spin over substance.

References

Anderson, P. J., and Weymouth, A. (1999), *Insulting the Public?: The British Press and the European Union*, Harlow and New York: Addison Wesley Longman.

Blair, T. (1997a), speech outside Downing Street, 2 May. Available at: http://www.number10.gov.uk/output/Page8073.asp Date accessed 1/9/05.

Blair, T. (1997b), speech at the Lord Mayor's Banquet, 10 November. Available at: http://www.number10.gov.uk/output/Page1070.asp Date accessed: 1/9/05.

Blair, T. (1998a), speech at the US State Department, 6 February. Available at: http://www.number10.gov.uk/output/Page1155.asp Date accessed: 2/9/05.

Blair, T. (1998b), speech to the French National Assembly, 24 March. Available at: http://www.number10.gov.uk/output/Page1160.asp Date accessed: 2/9/05.

Blair, T. (1999a), speech at the Economic Club, Chicago, 23 April. Available at: http://www.number10.gov.uk/output/-Page1297.asp Date accessed: 6/9/05.

Blair, T., (1999b), speech about Britain in Europe, 14 October. Available at: http://www.number10.gov.uk/output/Page1461.asp Date accessed: 7/9/05.

Blair, T. (2000a), speech at Ghent City Hall, 23 February. Available at: http://www.number10.gov.uk/output/Page1510.asp Date accessed: 7/9/05.

Blair, T. (2000b), speech to the Polish Stock Exchange, 6 October. Available at: http://www.number10. gov.uk/output/Page3384.asp Date accessed: 7/9/05.

Blair, T. (2001a), speech at the Lord Mayor's Banquet, 12 November. Available at: http://www. number10.gov.uk/output/Page1661.asp Date accessed: 9/9/05.

Blair, T. (2001b), speech to the European Research Institute, Birmingham, 23 November. Available at: http://www.number10.gov.uk/output/Page1673.asp Date accessed: 9/9/05.

Blair, T. (2002), statement on the Barcelona European Council, 18 March. Available at: http://www. number10.gov.uk/output/Page1705.asp Date accessed: 15/9/05.

Blair, T. (2003), speech at the Lord Mayor's Banquet, 10 November. Available at: http://www.number10. gov.uk/output/Page4803.asp Date accessed: 15/9/05.

Brown, G. (1997a), speech on EMU, 27 October. Available at: http://www.hm-treasury.gov.uk/newsroom_ and_speeches/speeches/chancellorexchequer/speech_chex_271097.cfm Date accessed: 4/7/06.

Brown, G. (1997b), speech at the CBI, 17 July. Available at: http://www.hm-treasury.gov.uk/newsroom_ and_speeches/speeches/chancellorexchequer/speech_chex_170797.cfm Date accessed: 4/7/06.

Brown, G. (1999a), speech at the Smith Institute, 15 April. Available at: http://www.hmtreasury.gov.uk/ newsroom_and_speeches/speeches/chancellorexchequer/speech_chex_19990415.cfm   Date accessed: 4/7/06.

Brown, G. (1999b), speech at the TUC Conference on EMU, 13 May. Available at: http://www. hmtreasury.gov.uk/newsroom_and_speeches/speeches/chancellorexchequer/speech_chex_ 130599.cfm Date accessed: 4/7/06.

Brown, G. (1999c), speech at the CBI Annual Conference, 1 November. Available at: http://www. hmtreasury.gov.uk/newsroom_and_speeches/speeches/chancellorexchequer/speech_ chex_011199.cfm Date accessed: 4/7/06.

Brown, G. (2004), British Council Annual Lecture, 7 July. Available at: http://www.hm-treasury.gov.uk/ newsroom-_and_speeches/press/2004/press_63_04.cfm Date accessed: 4/7/06.

Brown, G. (2005), speech at the Academy of Social Science, Beijing, 21 February. Available at: http:// www.hmtreasury.gov.uk/newsroom_and_speeches/press/2005/pre ss_20_05.cfm Date accessed: 4/7/06.

Colley, L. (2005), *Britons: Forging the Nation 1707–1837*, London and New Haven: Yale University Press.

Cook, R. (1997), speech at Foreign and Commonwealth Office, 12 May.

Cook, R. (2003), *The Point of Departure*, London: Simon and Schuster.

Curtice, J. (2001), 'What We Think We Know', in Rosenbaum, M. (ed.), *Britain and Europe: The Choices We Face*, Oxford: Oxford University Press, pp. 15–20.

Daddow, O. J. (2004), *Britain and Europe since 1945: Historiographical Perspectives on Integration*, Manchester: Manchester University Press.

Daddow, O. J. (2006), 'Euroscepticism and the Culture of the Discipline of History', in *Review of International Studies* 32:2, pp. 309–28.

Deighton, A. (2002), 'The Past in the Present: British Imperial Memories and the European Question', in Müller, J.-W. (ed.), *Memory and Power in Post-War Europe: Studies in the Presence of the Past*, Cambridge: Cambridge University Press, pp. 100–120.

Donnelly, B. (2005), 'The Euro and British Politics', Federal Trust European Policy Brief, 15, September 2005. Available at: http://www.fedtrust.co.uk/admin/uploads/PolicyBrief15.pdf Date accessed: 3/4/07.

Fairclough, N. (2001), *New Labour, New Language?*, London and New York: Routledge.

Gerrard, S. (2006), *Gerrard: My Autobiography*, London, Toronto, Sydney, Auckland and Johannesburg: Bantam Press.

Harmsen, R. (2007), 'Is British Euroscepticism Still Unique?: National Exceptionalism in Comparative Perspective', in Coman, R., and Lacroix, J. (eds.), *Les Résistances à l'Europe: Cultures Nationales, Idéologie et Stratégies d'acteurs*, Brussels: Editions de l'Université de Bruxelles, pp. 69–92.

Hill, C. (2001), 'Foreign Policy', in Seldon, A. (ed.), *The Blair Effect: The Blair Government 1997–2001*, London: Little, Brown and Company, pp. 331–53.

Kaiser, W. (1996), *Using Europe, Abusing the Europeans: Britain and European Integration 1945–63*, Basingstoke: Macmillan.

Labour Party (1997), 'Because Britain Deserves Better', election manifesto.

Labour Party (2001), 'Ambitions for Britain', election manifesto.

Labour Party (2005), 'The Future for Britain', election manifesto.

Price, L. (2005), *The Spin Doctor's Diary: Inside Number Ten with New Labour*, London: Hodder and Stoughton.

Toynbee, P., and Walker, D. (2001), *Did Things Get Better? An Audit of Labour's Successes and Failures*, London and New York: Penguin.

Williams, P. D. (2005), *British Foreign Policy under New Labour, 1997–2005*, Basingstoke: Palgrave Macmillan.

Influences on the Editorial Opinions of the British Press Towards the European Union

Julie Firmstone

This chapter gives an overview of the findings of a study into the editorial opinions of the British press towards European integration. The main aim of the study was to present a sociological investigation of the extent to which newspaper editorial coverage of Europe is shaped by a range of internal and external factors. A dual method approach was taken to achieve this. First, the practice of opinion-leading on European issues at ten British national newspapers was examined through interviews with journalists. Second, the construction of editorial opinion on European issues in editorial articles was assessed in a content and framing analysis. The findings from interviews with journalists and a content analysis of editorials were comparatively analysed in order to evaluate the relationship between potential influencing factors and content, and to address the research question: what factors influence newspapers' editorial opinions on European integration?

The British press: communicating the European Union in exceptional circumstances
The role of the British press in communicating Europe is complicated by the historical and contemporary nature of Britain's contentious relationship with Europe. In comparison to other Member States, Britain has a higher level of scepticism towards the EU within political and public opinion, and its position outside the Eurozone means that it is less integrated with the European Union. Further, three conditions create an exceptional set of circumstances within which British national newspapers mediate between the political system and the public on issues

relating to European integration. First, whereas newspapers traditionally base their editorial positions regarding political issues on their partisan stances, questions arising from Britain's membership of the European Union do not fall neatly into the traditional partisan divisions of Left and Right. While this is also true of other Member States such as Germany (Voltmer and Eilders 2003: 11), the division of opinion in Britain has sustained a contentious debate among political parties that makes this cleavage less straightforward. Second, the circumstances in which newspapers have the potential to influence public opinion towards the European Union differ from those in most other Member States. Where the public is not well informed or cognitively active on matters of social or political interest, framing can heavily influence their responses to media coverage of issues in such cases (Iyengar 1991; Kahneman and Tversky 1984; Zaller 1992). Given that few citizens of the European Union have direct personal experience of EU institutions it is argued that the public rely on the media to guide their opinion about the European Union (Gavin 2000). Indeed, in Eurobarometer surveys, the British public regularly report that they depend on the mass media as their main source of political information about the European Union, and have a relatively low level of knowledge about the European Union. Eurobarometer surveys also show that British citizens are less knowledgeable about the European Union in comparison to other EU citizens. For example, in a survey across the 25 Member States, the overall average of citizens who had heard about the draft European Constitution was 67 per cent, whereas only 50 per cent of UK respondents had heard of the Treaty (Eurobarometer 2005b). Further, when asked how often they discussed European affairs with friends or relatives, 48 per cent of British citizens said they never talked about EU issues, whereas the average for all EU citizens was 40 per cent (Eurobarometer 2006). Therefore, British citizens' relatively low levels of knowledge and experience of EU politics provide an opportunity for newspapers to shape public opinions towards Europe. The third specific circumstance relates to the potential influence of newspapers' opinions on the political agenda when it is considered that the media also play a role as opinion-leaders for politicians and political elites, and are used by politicians as an indicator of public opinion (Cohen 1983; Linsky 1986).

Within this context, the British media, and more commonly the press, have been consistently criticized for their coverage of the European Union. Having taken a largely supportive position at the outset of Britain's membership of the European Union in the 1970s, some newspapers adopted a sceptical stance in the early 1980s (Wilkes and Wring 1998). Since then, the government, politicians, the European Commission and pro-European sections of the press have regularly denounced newspapers' contributions to the debate over Europe, and alleged that British newspaper coverage is exceptional in its anti-European characteristics. For example, Peter Mandelson, when Secretary of State for Northern Ireland, stated that although he did 'not deny the right of the press to take positions on Europe [...] the British people and the democratic debate are starting to lose out from the nature of the coverage' (Greenslade 2000). This image of the British press is also emphasized by a body of research which raises concerns over the performance of the press in communicating Europe to the British public. Studies suggest that the public has only limited access to information about the European Union and that this information is negative and nationally focused (Anderson 2004; Anderson and Weymouth

1999; Cole 2001; Morgan 2004). More seriously, some research claims to have found examples of xenophobia, especially in coverage of BSE where 'xenophobia and paranoia were clearly visible' (Morgan 2004: 45) and newspapers contained 'spectacular images of jingoism and xenophobia' (Brookes 1999: 247). Furthermore, cross-nationally comparative studies have concluded that these characteristics are a more dominant feature of the press in Britain than elsewhere in Europe, and indicate that further research is needed to provide a better understanding of this 'exceptional' situation (Kevin 2003; Law, Middleton and Palmer 2000; Trenz 2004, 2007).

A common explanation for the exceptional treatment of Europe by the British press is that responsibility lies with newspaper proprietors who are seen as the main drivers of negativity towards the European Union (Anderson 2004; Anderson and Weymouth 1999). In some cases, newspapers' attitudes towards European issues have been criticized as being disingenuous and undermining their contribution to democratic debate (Anderson 2004). For example, Anderson claims that certain proprietors do not believe in the nationalist editorial line that they promote, and that 'when this hypocrisy is considered in tandem with the extent to which the papers involved have chosen to omit or distort basic facts about the European Union in their pursuit of an agenda that is at root driven primarily by proprietorial economic motives, it can only be concluded that an attempt is being made to doubly deceive their readers' (Anderson, 2004: 169). However, the claims of these and other studies regarding factors influencing European coverage in British newspapers are often based only on the analysis of newspaper content and lack other evidence (Anderson 2004; Anderson and Weymouth 1999; Werder 2002). Of those studies that have taken a sociological approach, a relatively small body of research points to several factors that are important in the production of news coverage of Europe. These include resources for news gathering, the influence of editorial policies towards the European Union on news, and the communication strategies of the European Union as a news source (Baisnée 2002; Meyer 1999; Morgan 1995; Statham 2006; Tumber 1995). The research presented in this chapter aimed to address the gap in the understanding of influences on editorial coverage of Europe.

Several concepts motivated the focus of the research on editorial opinions as distinct from the informational format of news. First, in light of the criticisms of the British press, the analysis of editorial opinion builds a more accurate picture of the attitudes and positions of the British press to Europe than approaches that do not distinguish between editorials and news content. Second, it is important to gain an understanding of editorial opinions because several studies demonstrate that this organizational viewpoint is important in shaping the coverage of Europe provided by EU correspondents (Baisnée 2002; Morgan 1995). Third, it is important to distinguish between the press's role as an information-provider and the independent contribution newspapers are able to make to the debate on Europe through critical analysis and interpretative evaluations in editorial comment. In taking this approach this research adds to an emerging area of political communications studies that treats newspapers as active participants in the political process (Eilders 2000, 2002; McCombs 1997; Page 1996), and a growing body of research into editorial opinions on Europe (Firmstone 2003, 2007; Koopmans and Pfetsch 2006; Trenz

2007; Voltmer and Eilders 2003). Considering newspapers as active and independent actors in the political process through their editorial roles further underpins the need to question influences on newspapers' opinions. Price suggests 'this activist role of the media, especially newspapers, ensures continuing concern over possible biases in news and editorial practices, owing to the political leanings of network executives, publishers, producers, or rank-and-file journalists' (Price 1992: 82). Further, despite the seriousness of the accusations levelled at the press, research into newspapers' positions on EU issues and the forces that motivate newspapers' attitudes towards the European Union remains scarce (Gavin 2001). In order to address these concerns, this study investigates how journalists, editors and proprietors influence editorial opinion and assesses the influence of these actors vis-à-vis other potentially important factors.

Research design

This study empirically investigated both *how* editorial opinion on Europe is constructed and *why* opinion is provided in such a way. The question of how opinion is constructed was addressed through a content analysis of editorials published on a range of European issues in ten national newspapers: *The Guardian, The Times, The Independent,* the *Telegraph,* the *Daily Mail, The Express, The Sun, The Mirror, The Scotsman,* and the *Financial Times* (*FT*). The analysis of editorials was approached from a political communications perspective and drew on theories of agenda-setting and framing. The strategic selection of these newspapers allowed for a comparative analysis of the different types of newspapers that characterize the British press system (tabloid, mid-market tabloid and broadsheet). Given that research into coverage of Europe outside of key events is lacking (de Vreese 2001: 283), a total of 923 editorials were selected from a sample collected every other day excluding Sundays in 2002 on seven issues. The analysis was conducted in two stages. The first stage measured the salience of issues with an EU dimension in comparison to non-EU issues. The second stage of the analysis developed an approach for analysing frames that acknowledged that editorials are a distinctive journalistic style in which newspapers make arguments, take controversial positions and express calls for action (Hynds 1990). Here Entman (1993, 2000) and Nelson, Clawson et al.'s (1997) definitions of framing were operationalized to evaluate the positions, problem definitions and consequences, causes of problems, and recommendations for solutions given in editorials. This framing analysis was made on a reduced sample of 108 editorials selected from the 923 editorials on two specific issues: the single currency and the Constitution.

The question of why opinion is provided in such a way was explored through semi-structured interviews with a group of elite journalists to establish the practices and policies newspapers have for producing editorial opinion. In order to allow the findings of the two research approaches to be compared, journalists were selected from the same ten newspapers that were analysed in the content analysis. Twenty-seven journalists involved in the leader-writing and political reporting of Europe were interviewed face-to-face in 2003 using a semi-structured schedule (Statham, Firmstone and Gray 2003). This included ten Political Editors, six EU correspondents and eleven leader-writers/editors.

The interviews gathered information on two broad topics. First, the organizational context in which editorial opinion on Europe is produced was investigated. This established the roles, resources, routines and editorial policies newspapers have for producing editorial opinion on Europe. Secondly, journalists were asked about the factors that are important in shaping the editorial opinions of newspapers. Although it is not possible to discuss these findings in detail in this chapter, the key findings from the comparative analysis of the interviews and the content analysis are summarized to provide an insight into the most important factors that shape newspapers' editorial opinions towards Europe.

Overview of factors that influence editorial opinions on Europe

Drawing on the work of Shoemaker and Reese (1996) the study developed a model of potential influences on opinion that was used as a framework to guide the research. The 'model of influences on editorial opinion' shown in Figure 1 illustrates that editorial opinion on Europe was treated as a dependent variable (shown in the centre of the model) that can be influenced by eleven factors that are shown as operating at three different levels: internal organizational, internal individual, and external extra media. Two internal levels are shown in the inner ring of

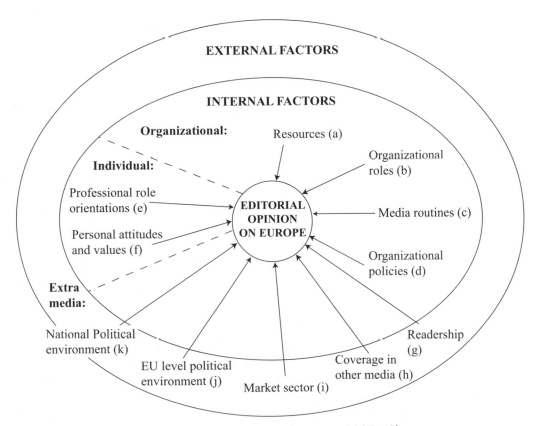

Figure 1. Model of influences on editorial opinion (Firmstone 2007: 40).

the model, the organizational and the individual levels. The external extra media level is situated in the outer ring. These three levels, the eleven factors and their main roles in influencing editorial opinions on Europe are discussed (with the letter corresponding to each factor in the model shown in brackets). In particular, the influence of the factors on the quantity, direction and framing of editorial opinion are explored.

Internal organizational factors

Variations in the resources (a) and roles (b) newspapers have for producing editorial opinions on Europe were important in influencing content. The number and type of leader-writers newspapers had for producing editorials on Europe varied from one to ten, and was differentiated on the basis of newspaper format (tabloids had fewer than broadsheets). Resources for producing comment on Europe also varied in terms of the access leader-writers had to news gathered in Brussels by EU correspondents. While none of the tabloids had EU correspondents all broadsheets had at least one (apart from the *Scotsman*). With the exception of two of the ten papers (*Sun* and *Telegraph*), newspapers with a greater number of journalists in the leader-writing team, access to more specialized knowledge on the topic, and to EU correspondents, produced a higher quantity of editorials on Europe than papers without such resources. Irrespective of roles and resources, almost all papers concentrated their EU opinion-leading scope on two out of the seven issues selected: monetary policy and European integration. Examining these two main issues in greater detail showed that better-resourced papers did tend to produce a greater range and a more in-depth style of opinion-leading than those with fewer resources. Variations in resources and roles did not bear any relationship to the position and direction of newspaper opinions on Europe. There were no notable differences in the positive or negative positions taken by newspapers with more or fewer resources or roles allocated to producing opinion on Europe.

The framing analysis measured the geographical scope of actors in order to evaluate the way in which newspapers identify either national British actors, EU level actors or non-British national actors as being responsible for causing or dealing with problems related to the single currency and the Constitution. This showed that the nature of the European issue being commented on was more important in the way an issue was framed than the level of resources a newspaper had for producing opinion on the topic. For example, there were no differences in the way newspapers with access to more or fewer resources framed the issue of the single currency. All newspapers, regardless of whether they had a specialist team or EU correspondent, framed the euro in predominantly national terms.

In investigating media routines (c) for producing editorials the study developed a model of the editorial production process. Within this routine, the research identified five key editorial values on which journalists judge the suitability of an issue for editorial comment. The two most important editorial values are the assessment of news values and the level of editorial interest of the newspaper in the issue, with less consideration given to the three other criteria: the perceived interest of readership (g) in the issue, the place of the issue in the campaigning strategy (part of d) of the paper, and the relevance of the issue to coverage of Europe in other media (h). The principle of news values suggests that newspapers' judgements about the newsworthiness of European issues are based on common criteria (Galtung and Ruge 1965; Hallin and Mancini 2004; McQuail 2000). Thus it was expected that newspapers would report similar European issues and events and, if news values play an important role in the selection of editorial topics, would select similar issues for editorial comment.

However, the analysis demonstrated significant variations in the European issues on which newspapers comment. This suggests that the selection of issues for comment was not principally motivated by news values, and/or that news values were overridden by other editorial values in the selection process. A second indication that news values are not the primary motivating factor for issue selection is the differences in patterns in the timing of coverage of each issue in editorial agendas. The analysis found very little consonance in the European issues and events covered in newspapers' editorial agendas. A key finding of the study was that the motivations of editorial values are far removed from those normally associated with news values since they are less related to assessments of what is of interest to readers, and more concerned with the interests of individual journalists and the editorial policies of a paper. While journalists' applications of news values rely on common profession-based understandings (Donsbach and Patterson 2005; Hallin and Mancini 2004; Tumber and Prentoulis 2005), editorial values for European issues were determined by newspaper-specific factors and were not simply an extension of news values.

One of the most important criteria in journalists' judgements about the editorial value and subsequent selection of an issue was the level of the newspaper's editorial interest in European affairs. Journalists described editorial interest as comprising of a variety of factors specific to their newspapers and the individuals working within them. Four key internal factors were seen to determine the level of editorial interest in Europe: (1) the interest of the paper as an organization; (2) the collective interest of the group of journalists in the leader conference; (3) the interests of individual journalists; and (4) the interest of the editor. The study demonstrated that the level of editorial interest not only plays an important role in influencing the selection of issues for comment, but also determines the wider editorial policy of the paper by feeding into the editorial importance placed on giving opinion on European issues.

The study defined organizational editorial policies (d) as representing the editorial line of a newspaper and the importance of an issue in the opinion-leading objectives of a paper. These policies provide key explanations for the opinions that newspapers produce on Europe and, in some senses, editorial policies are equivalent to the editorial opinion of a paper. For example, the line of a paper on Europe ultimately dictates the direction of opinion that is published in editorials. Editorial lines on Europe are not explicitly communicated to journalists. Instead they are learned through experience, and in this sense the findings demonstrate that editorial policies operate in a similar way to news policies (Breed 1955; Sigelman 1973; Soloski 1989). The editorial lines of articles in the content analysis accurately reflected journalists' understandings of their papers' lines on specific aspects of European integration. One of the ways in which organizational editorial policies shape editorial content is therefore by being understood and put into practice by leader-writing journalists. However, editorial policies can be less concrete and encompass judgements relating to the value and importance of pursuing a particular policy that are often based on the opinions of individuals involved in the process (as discussed below).

Some papers have editorial policies to run campaigns which influence journalists' judgements of the editorial importance of an issue during the selection process, and represent a motivating criterion of editorial values (*The Independent*, *Mirror*, *Daily Mail* and *The Sun*). It would be logical to expect that the four papers that pursued a campaigning policy would publish a greater quantity of editorials on European issues than those papers that did not pursue such policies. However, the content analysis did not show a relationship of this kind. Whilst a campaigning policy did not influence the quantity of European editorials, it was apparent in the range of issues that were selected for comment. For example, the *Mirror* campaigned in favour of the euro and published the highest level of commentary on the subject of all the papers. *The Independent* ran a more general campaign calling for Britain to become closer to the European Union and also published a relatively large quantity of editorials on European integration.

Internal individual factors

The personal attitudes and values (f) of key individual journalists at the majority of papers had an impact on the editorial policy of the paper and, as a consequence, shaped the content of opinion-leading in the following three ways. First, the consensus and strength of personal opinions at the *Mirror*, *Daily Mail*, *Telegraph* and *The Sun* resulted in the pursuit of particular editorial policies on Europe that explained the content of their editorial agendas. For example, the fervently pro-euro views of the *Mirror*'s Chief Leader Writer and his personal decision that the *Mirror* should pursue a pro-euro campaign were reflected in the dominance of the single currency in the paper's editorial agenda. On the opposite side of the debate, the vigorous and personal opposition of key journalists at the *Daily Mail*, *The Sun* and the *Telegraph* resulted in a high level of editorial interest, and subsequently high editorial importance, in commenting on European integration.

Second, whilst a consensus in the attitudes of journalists at these papers resulted in consistent editorial policies on Europe, at other papers disagreements between key leader-writers and political journalists had the opposite effect. The level of discord between key journalists at *The Guardian* and the *FT* and the resultant unresolved editorial lines were evident in both papers' framing of the single currency debate, which is best described as taking a position of 'constructive criticism' rather than a specific side. Thus, the composition of individual journalists involved in leader-writing teams had an important effect on the way in which editorial policies were maintained and implemented.

Third, the personal attitudes of editors shaped editorial opinion as a result either of changes in editorship or of the continuing influence of long-serving editors who maintained the paper's policy on Europe. The study analysed the factors that induced change and/or stability in editorial lines towards Europe and identified editors and, ultimately, proprietors as the primary influence on the direction of editorial policy and the most likely catalysts for changes in the direction of editorial lines. These findings indicate that rather than being influenced by constraints from levels above them – as is suggested by Shoemaker and Reese's (1996) hierarchical model of influences on content – individuals were seen to contribute to levels above them such as the organizational level of editorial policy.

Journalists also influence the content of opinion-leading on Europe by pursuing the commonly perceived professional role-orientation of a leader-writer (e). Leader-writers at the vast majority of newspapers considered editorials to fulfil an additional role to that of information provision. This was evident in the framing analysis which showed that editorials are often written in such a way as to attempt to influence politics either indirectly (through reaching public opinion) or directly (by targeting opinions directly at politicians). The following evaluation of a journalist's strategic use of editorial comment is representative of the perceptions of many of the leader-writers interviewed. The journalist explained that although he writes editorials for the readers, he also sees them as a medium through which he can address his newspaper's opinions directly to political actors. In particular, it is his intention that his messages in editorials on Europe be noticed by key government figures such as the Prime Minister and the Chancellor of the Exchequer: 'Overwhelmingly I'm writing in the vain hope that Tony Blair will read it the next morning – amongst other people. [On the single currency] you're writing obviously for the readers, but because of the nature of this event, and the issue, you are addressing the PM and the Chancellor amongst other people (they're the top of the tree). You're not solely addressing them, it's not like the reader is invited to be a spectator. My conversation is with the readers, but it's done by addressing the government and if necessary addressing particular ministers' (Chief Leader Writer, *The Guardian*).

This role perception corresponds with that of American leader-writing journalists who have been found to 'see themselves as influencing public officials and other citizens in their reaction to social and moral issues' (Hynds and Archibald 1996: 19).

External extra media factors
Although readership is shown as an external factor, readerships influence editorial opinion from both within and outside newspapers. Judgements of readership interest operate as an internal influence as one of the criteria used to judge the editorial value of an issue during the selection process, and as an external factor in shaping the nature of editorial content (g). A lower level of coverage would be expected at papers where readers were perceived to have little or no interest in the European Union (tabloids or 'red-tops'). Similarly, where readers were judged to have a relatively high level of interest in the European Union it would be expected that a higher quantity of European issues would be selected for comment (mainly broadsheets or 'upmarket' titles). A comparison of journalists' assessments of their readership's interest in EU politics with the levels of commentary on EU issues at their papers established that this relationship exists at the majority of the papers (with four notable exceptions: *The Sun*, *The Guardian*, *Telegraph* and *Independent*). For example, the relatively high salience of EU issues in the *FT* and *Times* corresponded to a high perceived level of interest among their readers. Similarly, a low salience

of EU issues in the agendas of the *Mirror* and *Express* is consistent with the perceived low levels of interest among their readers. In contrast, despite journalists' perceptions that their readers were either not at all or only a little interested in European politics, *The Sun* and *The Guardian* selected a high quantity of European issues for comment in comparison to other papers. An internal factor – a high level of editorial importance – overrides this external factor at these papers. Readership demand for opinion was only a factor which influenced the specific direction of opinion-giving at a few newspapers. For example, appealing to the above-average interest of *FT* and *The Independent* readers in EU issues was one of the motivations for these papers' lines in support of Europe.

In addition to readership, four other factors external to news organizations played limited roles in determining opinion on Europe: coverage in other media (h), the market sector (i), the EU-level political environment (j) and the national political environment (k). Unlike many of the internal factors discussed, the interviews showed the role of these external factors to be limited. They are only of importance at a minority of newspapers and are therefore relatively weak influencing factors. With the exception of the readership factor, it was difficult to detect the influence of these external factors in the content and framing of opinion.

It should also be noted that, unlike in the production of news, external sources are not a direct factor in influencing the production of editorials. News sources are relevant influences in determining which European issues reach the news agenda, and are then available for selection by leader-writing teams. They therefore have an indirect role in shaping editorial agendas. Editorial opinion is less influenced by external sources than news reporting, and more influenced by journalists as individuals.

Discussion and implications

The greater potential for individual journalists to contribute to all aspects of editorial opinion (compared to the role of individuals in shaping news content) is a key finding of this study. Journalists working on editorial opinion occupy a position of influence within newspaper organizations that gives them with the opportunity to make a significant contribution to the opinion of their newspapers towards European integration. This concurs with Shoemaker and Reese's observation that 'it is possible that when communicators have more power over their messages and work under fewer constraints, their personal attitudes, values and beliefs have more opportunity to influence content' (Shoemaker and Reese 1996: 91). Although individual journalists are unlikely to effect a complete change in the direction of opinion towards Europe (this change only happened at one newspaper in the study, and in that case as a result of a change in ownership), individual journalists influence opinion-leading on Europe in two significant ways.

First, leader-writing journalists, and in some cases Brussels- and Westminster-based journalists, help to shape the level and qualitative nature of editorial content by providing resources for producing editorials, fulfilling specialist leader-writing roles, shaping editorials through their personal attitudes towards Europe, and pursuing professional role-orientations. Leader-writing journalists shape the visibility (quantity and range) of EU issues by taking key decisions about the issues that are commented on through their participation in leader conferences (mainly in the 'upmarket' press) or consultations with the editor (in the tabloids). Particularly in the case of the 'upmarket' titles, some journalists are considered 'experts' on European issues. Their views on, and experiences of, European issues make a major contribution to the opinions published in the names of their newspapers.

Second, individual journalists play dominant roles in determining one of the most important criteria of the 'editorial values' by which European issues are judged for selection: the level of editorial interest in the leader-writing team.

On the basis of these findings it seems possible that key journalists at some newspapers may have an equal or greater influence on editorial opinions than proprietors. Certainly, in the day-to-day production of opinion, individual journalists have greater opportunities to directly shape newspapers' opinions than is attributed to them by many studies of news production. News production studies tend to see individuals as 'replaceable cogs in the wheel' and suggest that 'news changes very little when the individuals who make it are changed' (Golding and Elliot 1979: 209). These findings suggest that the opposite is true in the field of opinion-leading, and that a newspaper's style of opinion-leading on Europe may change if key individuals involved in its production, such as leader-writers, change. Such changes have the potential to impact opinion in several ways, such as by altering the balance of agreements within leader-writing teams, changing the level of editorial interest in opinion-leading, and altering the focus of editorial campaigns on Europe. In the specialist role of leader-writing, individual personalities are important and may have the power to promote and push certain ideological viewpoints towards the European Union.

References

Adam, S., Berkel, B., Firmstone, J., Gray, E., Koopmans, R., Pfetsch, B., et al. (2002), *Codebook for Content Coding of Commentaries/Editorials*, Berlin: WZB.

Anderson, P. (2004), 'European Studies', in Harmsen, R., and Spiering, M. (eds.), *Euroscepticism: Party Politics, National Identity and European Integration* Vol. 20, Amsterdam: Rodopi, pp. 151–170.

Anderson, P., and Weymouth, A. (1999), *Insulting the Public? The British Press and the European Union*, Harlow: Longman.

Baisnée, O. (2002), 'Can political journalism exist at the EU level?', in Kuhn, R., and Neveu, E. (eds.), *Political Journalism: New challenges, New practices*, London: Routledge, pp. 108–127.

Breed, W. (1955), 'Social control in the newsroom: A Functional Analysis', in *Social Forces* 33, pp. 326–335.

Brookes, R. (1999), 'Newspapers and national identity: the BSE/CJD crisis and the British press', in *Media, Culture & Society* 21, pp. 247–263.

Cohen, B. (1983), *The Public's Impact on Foreign Policy*, Lanham, MD: University Press of America.

Cole, P. (2001), 'What chance serious debate in the modern media?', in *Aslib Proceedings* 53:4, pp. 124–130.

de Vreese, C. (2001), '"Europe" in the News. A Cross-National Comparative Study of the News Coverage of Key EU Events', in *European Union Politics* 2:3, pp. 283–307.

Donsbach, W., and Patterson, T. (2005), 'Political News Journalists: Partisanship, Professionalism, and Political Roles in Five Countries', in Esser, F., and Pfetsch, B. (eds.), *Comparing Political Communication: Theories, Cases and Challenges*, Cambridge: CUP, pp. 251–270.

Eilders, C. (2000), 'Media as Political Actors? Issue Focussing and Selective Emphasis in the German Quality Press', in *German Politics* 9:3, pp. 181–206.

Eilders, C. (2002), 'Conflict and Consonance in Media Opinions: Political Positions of Five German Quality Newspapers', in *European Journal of Communication* 17:1, pp. 25–63.

Eurobarometer (2005a), *Eurobarometer 64*, Brussels: European Commission DG Communication.

Eurobarometer (2005b), *The Future Constitutional Treaty (Special EB 214/Wave 62.1)*, Brussels: European Commission DG Communication.

Eurobarometer (2006), *The Future of Europe (Special EB 251/Wave 65.1)*, Brussels: European Commission DG Communication.

Firmstone, J. (2003), *'Britain in the Euro?' British Newspaper Editorial Coverage of the Introduction of the Euro* (Working Paper 5/03), EurPolCom, Leeds: University of Leeds.

Firmstone, J. (2007), *The Editorial Opinions of the British Press on European Integration*, Leeds: University of Leeds (Ph.D. dissertation).

Firmstone, J. (2008), 'The editorial production process and editorial values as influences on the opinions of the British press towards Europe', in *Journalism Practice* 2:2, pp. 212–229.

Galtung, J., and Ruge, M. (1965), 'The Structure of Foreign News', in *Journal of International Peace Research* 1, pp. 64–90.

Gavin, N. (2000), 'Imagining Europe: Political Identity and British Television Coverage of the European Economy' in *British Journal of Politics and International Relations* 2:3, pp. 352–373.

Gavin, N. (2001), 'British journalists in the spotlight: Europe and media research', in *Journalism* 2:3, 299–314.

Golding, P., and Elliot, P. (1979), *Making the News*, London: Longman.

Greenslade, R. (2000), 'The Euro's not for spinning', in *The Guardian*, 10 July 2000.

Hallin, D., and Mancini, P., eds. (2004), *Comparing media systems: three modes of media and politics*, Cambridge: CUP.

Hynds, E. (1990), 'Changes in Editorials: A Study of Three Newspapers, 1955–1985', *Journalism Quarterly* 68, pp. 302–312.

Hynds, E., and Archibald, E. (1996), 'Improved editorial pages can help papers' communities', *Newspaper Research Journal*, 17:1–2, pp. 14–24.

Iyengar, S. (1991), *Is Anyone Responsible? How Television Frames Political Issues*, Chicago: University of Chicago Press.

Kahneman, D., and Tversky, A. (1984), 'Choice, values and frames', in *American Psychologist* 29, pp. 341–350.

Kevin, D. (2003), *Europe and the Media*, London: Lawrence Erlbaum.

Koopmans, R., and Pfetsch, B. (2006), 'Obstacles or motors of Europeanization? German media and the transnationalization of public debate', in *Communications* 31, pp. 115–138.

Law, M., Middleton, D., and Palmer, J. (2000), 'The Press Reporting of European Economic and Monetary Union in four European countries: A comparative analysis', in Baerns, B., and Raupp, J. (eds.), *Transnational Communication in Europe*, Berlin: Vistas, pp. 88–100.

Linsky, M. (1986), *How the Press Affects Federal Policy Making*, New York: Norton.

McCombs, M. E. (1997), 'Building Consensus: The News Media's Agenda-Setting Roles', in *Political Communication* 14, pp. 433–443.

McQuail, D. (2000), *McQuail's Mass Communication Theory*, London: Sage.

Meyer, C. (1999), 'Political Legitimacy and the Invisibility of Politics: Exploring the European Union's Communication Deficit', in *Journal of Common Market Studies*, 37:4, pp. 617–639.

Morgan, D. (1995), 'British Media and European Union News: The Brussels Beat and its Problems', in *European Journal of Communication* 10:3, pp. 321–343.

Morgan, D. (2004), 'Media Coverage of the European Union', in Bond, M. (ed.), *Europe, Parliament and the Media*, London: The Federal Trust, pp. 35–54.

Page, B. (1996), 'The Mass Media as Political Actors', in *Political Science and Politics* 29:1, pp. 20–24.

Price, V. (1992), *Public Opinion*, Newbury Park: Sage.

Shoemaker, P.J., and Reese, S. D. (1996), *Mediating the Message*, White Plains, NY: Longman.

Sigelman, L. (1973), 'Reporting the news: An Organizational Analysis', in *American Journal of Sociology* 79:1, pp. 132–151.

Soloski, J. (1989), 'News Reporting and Professionalism: Some Constraints on the Reporting of News', in *Media, Culture & Society* 11:2, pp. 207–228.

Statham, P., Firmstone, J., and Gray, E. (2003), *Interview Questionnaire for Interviews with Journalists: Editor/Political Editor/Political Lead Writer*. Available at: http://europub.wz-berlin.de/codebooks. en.htm Date accessed: 18/8/08.

Trenz, H. (2004), 'Media Coverage on European Governance', in *European Journal of Communication* 19:3, pp. 291–319.

Trenz, H. (2007), 'Quo vadis Europe? Quality Newspapers Struggling for European Unity', in Fossum, J. E., and Schlesinger, P. (eds.), *The European Union and the Public Sphere: A Communicative Space in the Making?*, London: Routledge, pp. 89–109.

Tumber, H. (1995), 'Marketing Maastricht: The EU and News Management', in *Media, Culture & Society* 17:3, pp. 511–519.

Tumber, H., and Prentoulis, M. (2005), 'Journalism and the making of a profession', in de Burgh, H. (ed.), *Making Journalists*, London: Routledge, pp. 58–75.

Voltmer, K., and Eilders, C. (2003), 'The Media Agenda: The Marginalization and Domestication of Europe', in Dyson, K., and Goetz, K. (eds.), *Germany, Europe and the Politics of Constraint*, Oxford: Oxford University Press, pp. 173–197.

Werder, O. (2002), 'Debating the Euro: Media Agenda-Setting in a Cross-National Environment', in *Gazette: The International Journal for Communication Studies* 64:3, pp. 219–233.

Wilkes, G., and Wring, D. (1998), 'The British Press and Integration', in Baker, D., and Seawright, D. (eds.), *Britain For and Against Europe: British Politics and the Question of European Integration*, Oxford: Clarendon Press, pp. 185–205.

Zaller, J. (1992), *The Nature and Origins of Mass Opinion*, New York: CUP.

News from Brussels, in Brussels: EU Reporting as Part of a 'Glocalized' and Market-driven Journalism: A Case Study of the Belgian Newspaper De Morgen

Kristel Vandenbrande and Davy Geens

This chapter approaches EU reporting as a pertinent case through which to study the interaction between different social dynamics and changing journalistic praxis, culture and contexts. This case study analyses EU reporting as an integral part of today's newspaper journalism, analogous with, for example, the work of Garcia and Le Torrec (2003).

This approach differs clearly from the one dominant within the tradition of political communication, where the central research topic could roughly be summarized as 'the extent to which the media contributes to and reflects the process of European integration' (Kevin 2003: xvii; see also Semetko et al. 2001; Meyer 2005; Trenz 2004).

Within a normative and functionalist perspective on democracy and media, this might certainly be a relevant question. From a critical and culturalist perspective, however, it is all too narrow a question, neglecting the singularity of journalism as a cultural artefact that comes about within a specific context in interaction with diverse dynamics.

Europeanization, or more generally the globalization of political structures and levels of decision-making, might undoubtedly be one of those dynamics. But it is certainly not the only, and probably not the most important, one. Research in media history, political economy and media sociology has convincingly demonstrated that the dynamic processes that have profoundly reshaped newspaper journalism over the last two decades in western regions are caused not so much by changing political structures as by expanding market logic.

Particularly during the last decade, almost all of western Europe witnessed declining newspaper readerships, which led to a more reader-driven journalism. In several countries, including Belgium, this tendency was accompanied by a so-called 'depillarization' or depoliticization of the daily press. The resultant growing competition obliged newspapers to redefine their profiles by choosing clear positioning strategies for their 'products' on the national or regional newspaper markets. This repositioning was accompanied by the financial demands of new owners: private media companies require newspapers to be cost-effective (see Biltereyst and Van Gompel 1997 for an extended overview of the Belgian Dutch-language case).

These commercializing tendencies are well known. Nevertheless, it is important to recall them. Even though several studies of EU reporting point out the importance of a contextualized approach, they rarely elaborate a research design that pays attention to these external dynamics (Slaatta 2005 and De Bens et al. 2005 are exceptions). We believe it is essential to be mindful of this larger context, in order to make sense of EU reporting and to avoid a narrow and Eurocentric scope. This chapter endeavours to do so by keeping the insights of political economy and media sociology in mind as an orienting theoretical frame.

The case study
This case study focuses on the Belgian Dutch-language newspaper *De Morgen*. *De Morgen* is what we may call, for lack of a more suitable word, a 'quality newspaper'. It originated as a left-wing newspaper financed by the Socialist Party. In the 1980s, it came close to closure, but its fortunes slowly revived in the 1990s after it had been bought, depoliticized and repositioned by what is today one of the largest Flemish media companies, De Persgroep. Currently it addresses a rather well-educated readership and has a circulation of about 54,000 copies (against a total population of six million Dutch-speaking Belgians).

The focus on one particular newspaper seemed relevant as such a specific approach enabled us to avoid the pitfalls of such artificial universal constructs as 'EU reporting', constructs which ignore the diversity of newspapers, journalistic styles and cultures.

Unlike most existing research on the production of EU reporting, our focus was not to be on the so-called Brussels newsbeat (see Slaatta 1999; Baisnée 2002; Statham 2004), but on the praxis, position and perception of EU reporting within the national newsroom.

The first reason for this choice is the specificity of the Belgian case. The 'triadic structure of the European newsroom' (de Vreese 2003: 162) – with a central headquarters coordinating coverage in cooperation with the politics units and the Brussels desk – is almost non-existent for Belgian newspapers. As most editorial offices are situated in Brussels only a few minutes away from the EU's headquarters, it is less necessary to have permanent EU correspondents. Only two Flemish newspapers have chosen to do so: *De Standaard*, the immediate competitor of *De Morgen*, and *De Tijd*, a business paper.

A second reason to focus on the national newsroom goes beyond the specificity of the Belgian context. Specialist EU correspondents represent only a small part of the editorial staff involved in covering EU issues. Other journalists write a large proportion of the articles on the European Union. By focusing on this important but often neglected part of journalistic praxis, this study aims to avoid a narrow and institutional definition of EU reporting.

We conducted a series of semi-structured in-depth interviews with the editorial staff of *De Morgen*. These interviews not only dealt with EU reporting, but also focused on the general journalistic culture and praxis of the newspaper. Journalists of different sections and at different levels were interviewed in order to achieve a better understanding of the diverse perceptions and dynamics at work. We interviewed the Editor-in-Chief, the Deputy Editor-in-Chief, two Copy Editors, the Financial Editor, the Foreign Affairs Editor, two journalists writing for the politics section and one journalist writing for the foreign affairs section.

As *De Morgen* is a small newspaper with a relatively limited staff, all of them write articles on a daily basis, except for the Editor-in-Chief whose contribution mainly consists of editorials and some articles in the weekly magazine of the newspaper.

This chapter highlights some findings from these interviews, findings which suggest a broad theoretical and methodological relevance, as they point to the value of this kind of idiosyncratic, contextualized and non-Eurocentric approach to EU reporting.

Adapting to a global editorial project

Throughout the interviews it became clear that the position and nature of EU reporting could only be fully understood in relation to, and as an integral part of, the broader editorial project of the newspaper.

Discussing the status of EU coverage in their paper, the editors all considered it important to focus on EU matters. But they immediately qualified this by pointing out that they did not have any political 'mission' in relation to the European Union. They did not want to report on the EU 'for the sake of the EU', but rather said they did so because they consider the European Union to be one of the relevant political forces in today's global (or 'glocal') society. The editorial board repeatedly emphasized the fact that – as a defender of the idea of globalization – the paper played an important role in pointing out the interconnectedness of different international perspectives and levels of decision-making. This broader editorial project also affected the way EU issues were covered. Within such a perspective there was only a limited interest in the EU institutions as such. Or as the Deputy Editor-in-Chief said: 'At the paper we think there are more doors to Europe than the big one over there at the European Parliament.'

This non-institutional and issue-driven approach to EU matters results in a form of coverage in which the European dimension is most often integrated in other glocalized stories, stories which have more global, national or local outlooks. This means that EU coverage is not always as visible – and discernible by traditional modes of content analysis – as it is in more institutional approaches.

Adapting to market logic

During the interviews, it also became clear that the specificity and perceived quality of EU reporting could only be understood within the logic of a market-driven journalism defined by dynamics of positioning and distinction, perceived audience preferences and cost-efficiency strategies.

Firstly, the specificity of *De Morgen*'s EU reporting can only make sense in relation to the positions of other newspapers on the national newspaper market. The editorial board described EU reporting above all as an essential dimension of their positioning strategy as a 'quality' newspaper. In the same way as international, foreign and cultural news, EU news was described as being an important characteristic, or, as one of the Deputy Editors called it, the 'symbolic capital', of upmarket titles: 'Leaving out this kind of news would alter our label as a "quality paper".'

But the paper's EU coverage is also a matter of positioning in the national market of 'quality papers', of generating sufficient differentiation from its direct competitor, *De Standaard*. It was striking that all respondents – both editorial board members and journalists – spontaneously used these discourses of distinction and positioning as they described what they believed good EU reporting was about. All defined it as a reporting that is less institutional, specialized and 'inner-circle' than that of *De Standaard*.

Secondly, EU reporting can only be understood as part of the general audience-driven project of the newspaper. The editorial board and other senior writers emphasized that the paper, which almost had to close in the 1980s, only managed to survive by adopting an audience-driven journalism. This point was repeatedly made during the interviews. The readers were not only described as the principal source of income for the paper but also as 'the clients to be served' and the 'ultimate judges' of the newspaper's quality.

Within this line of reasoning, good EU journalism was depicted as journalism that:

- Is in line with the perceived preferences, interests and attitudes of the readers, offering a form of reporting that operates as a kind of 'agenda-setting', keeping the readers in touch with the main trends and challenges in a Europeanized and glocalized late modern society and encouraging them to reflect upon these issues.

■ Is written from a bottom-up perspective, incorporating the European dimension in broader related stories about what it means to live in an Europeanized and glocalized world

■ Is especially sensitive to the aspects of EU politics that the readers are thought to be particularly concerned about

It is notable in this context that, whereas the editorial board members were referring to (what they clearly considered to be) the undeniable facts of market research, the other journalists alluded more to some kind of working definition, a vaguer and more general image, of their readers. The latter made such comments as 'I suppose our readers expect this.'

It was also interesting to see how the journalists constructed these imaginary readers by repeatedly comparing them to another imagined audience, that of their direct competitor *De Standaard*. They described their proper readership as one that is less interested in institutional perspectives and does not want to be 'annoyed' by a form of reporting that covers every single step in decision-making processes, or that focuses on the partisan politics of the European Union. In this way their reflections on their readers' preferences clearly intersected with their discourses on distinction and positioning.

Good EU journalism was defined as achievable, economically realistic and cost-efficient. It was described as making choices, opting for high productivity and using the limited available resources to produce copy that is rewarding and provides an added value to the newspaper in general. During the interviews, good EU journalism was also talked about as 'principally doing what one is good at and renowned for', as putting to best use the newspaper's limited resources to focus on the styles and genres for which the paper is well-known (i.e. interviews, issue-driven journalism, background pieces and human interest articles), and making extensive use of other available sources (institutional press releases, press agency releases) for other routine coverage.

Adapting to an editorial organization
It is within this combination of editorial and economic logic that we need to make sense of some of the paper's organizational choices.

Since the European Union is considered to be an integral part of today's global society, *De Morgen* has chosen not to establish a separate Europe section. Neither does the paper have a European issues specialist to deal with all EU stories. All journalists working in different areas are expected to have a certain European (as well as a more general international) awareness: from the specialist in environmental issues to the journalist writing on education.

The editorial management also emphasized that having such an EU specialist would not be cost-effective for a small newspaper with a limited number of staff and a non-institutional, bottom-up approach to EU coverage. The Editor-in-Chief mentioned that if they had chosen a more institutional approach, as their competitor *De Standaard* has, having a permanent correspondent would be something to consider, even despite the paper's limited resources. He added that in the context of the paper's actual editorial line a permanent correspondent would not be a high priority – even if the resources were available – since such a correspondent would probably soon succumb to an institutional and 'insider' perspective – a kind of journalism the paper would not want to foster. This view was echoed by the rest of the editorial staff, which suggests a general commitment to a particular journalistic culture, well illustrated by the words of one political editor: 'Of course as journalists we somehow envy permanent correspondents for the kind of inside information they obtain, but certainly not for the kind of institutional reports they have to write.'

The more senior of our respondents also reminded us that there is a pragmatic historical reason for not employing specific EU editors. Years ago the paper did have such specialists. When they resigned, De Morgen was left with a huge knowledge gap to be filled. Since this situation affected various sections, the management decided that it was better to reorganize the newsroom, making the newspaper less vulnerable in an era of depoliticization and increasing competition – in which journalists need to be more flexible and switch more easily from one job to another.

In general, these kinds of findings remind us that a newspaper's use of EU correspondents cannot be interpreted as a direct indication of its view of the importance of European affairs. The employment of specialist EU correspondents can at most be seen as an indication of a specific approach to EU matters.

The fact that the newsroom of De Morgen is based in Brussels only three metro stops away from the EU's central institutions also needs to be taken into account. The newspaper's physical presence in Brussels has several advantages. It allows the paper to take last-minute editorial decisions, allowing cost-effective coverage when journalists are sent to the EU's headquarters to report on 'really big news'. International news media, press agencies and institutional press releases are used as an 'early warning system' to this end. In that sense De Morgen has an advantage over other small 'quality papers' elsewhere in Europe.

Only at times of key events would De Morgen send reporters to the EU's headquarters. It was interesting to see how this strategy was justified according not only to the political importance of these events – journalists who attended such events also stressed their rather formal and ceremonial character. This editorial strategy was justified within the framework of a market-driven journalism. Such key events were described as situations in which readers expected their paper to offer a more than usually institutional level of coverage. They were also seen as very productive events, where the return on investment was guaranteed.

These insights permit us to put findings from content analyses – often showing significant differences in the attention given to frequently occurring key events (such as European summits), unique events (such as enlargement, the introduction of the euro) and routine news periods (de Vreese 2003: 115) – into perspective. This journalistic logic might help to explain, to some extent, why such 'prescheduled battles [...] propel the European Union into relatively large and concentrated amounts of news coverage' (de Vreese 2003: 114).

Finally, it is important to add that their reflections on the need for economic efficiency were not perceived as a constraint by the journalists interviewed. Rather, economic efficiency was described as an essential dimension of their own definition of quality journalism. This economic logic appeared to be an integral part of their journalistic culture.

EU reporting in small newspapers: matters of scale

The example of *De Morgen* and *De Standaard* demonstrates how two smaller-scale competing newspapers can – and as competitors within a small market probably will – adopt different approaches to EU journalism. Their size in no way directly determines their editorial strategy. However, this does not mean that these newspapers are entirely free to choose any kind of editorial strategy. Scale does matter. EU reporting by a large 'quality paper', in a substantial newspaper market and language zone, of course allows for different possibilities than the coverage produced by a small 'quality paper' in a relatively restricted market and language zone. It is important to keep this in mind when one is comparing EU reporting from an international perspective or when one is debating the role of national newspapers within the European public sphere. The following section elaborates on how size matters in the case of *De Morgen*.

First of all, resources are limited and a central issue is how best to allocate them. For example, only six full-time journalists cover the politics section. The foreign news section boasts five journalists, the economic and financial news section three.

In its pursuit of financial stability, the paper has entered into a series of bilateral copyright agreements with four foreign and international newspapers – *Le Monde* (France), *De Volkskrant* (Netherlands), *The Independent* (UK) and *The New York Times* (USA) – as an alternative to a prohibitively expensive network of international correspondents. These agreements not only afford financial benefits; they also offer an added value to the whole paper, giving it a certain international character and confirming its image as a 'quality paper'.

However, the editorial board members pointed out the limitations of these bilateral agreements when it comes to EU reporting. First, articles from these copyright partners are only seldom used in the context of EU reporting, as these articles are often written from a domestic perspective and the paper is not allowed to rewrite them. Second, the notion of a real European or international exchange of articles and viewpoints seems to be somewhat idealistic. The exchange remains rather a one-way system. As a small paper, *De Morgen* is happy to be able to reproduce articles from the other papers, but its own articles are hardly ever reproduced by the other – much larger – newspapers. This may lead us to question optimistic analyses that seem to present such copyright agreements as a step towards a European journalistic network (see de Beus and Mak 2004: 8).

One could therefore imagine the advantages of different modes of collaboration with *small* foreign newspapers. Such collaborations have not been implemented, and probably will not be implemented in the near future. The editorial board members commented that the very idea of such collaborations was not very realistic in the short term, not even with Dutch newspapers (which use the same language). Their line of reasoning on this issue was the same as one advanced in various academic studies: namely that news remains something highly defined by and performed within the lines of historically constructed national borders, in a 'persistent national media order' (Slaatta 2005: 7–8). Although Flanders and the Netherlands share the same language, they have clearly distinct news markets and their own journalistic and political cultures.

However, even without such formal collaborations, foreign and international newspapers play an important role in the day-to-day practices of EU reporting and other international coverage. Every morning a large selection of these newspapers arrives at the newsroom. This selection includes American, British, Dutch, French, German, Italian and Spanish titles. These papers (and their websites) are used extensively. Journalists said that they used them as an 'early warning system' to keep them in touch with the latest trends and debates, and as a 'barometer' to indicate when an issue becomes a really 'hot topic' that should be covered in their own paper. They also noted that these papers provided them with background information essential to their own reporting. These papers were clearly crucial to the daily production of international and glocalized news stories.

Scale is not only a question of resources but also of prestige. Journalists familiar with the practices of the Brussels newsbeat observed, for example, that even if a paper as small as *De Morgen* had extra resources and a permanent EU correspondent at its disposal, this journalist would still be limited by the paper's relative lack of prestige: whistleblowers, for instance, would prefer to take their stories to the big international newspapers.

Concluding remarks

This paper demonstrates the relevance of an idiosyncratic, non-Eurocentric approach to EU reporting, analyzing it as a narration amongst other narrations: as an integral part of today's journalism and a newspaper's broader editorial project. From this perspective we may observe that *De Morgen*'s EU reporting can only fully be understood within the context of the diversity of dynamic processes that shape and reshape today's journalism.

The 'Europeanization' and globalization of society might certainly be included in these processes, but the logic of market-driven journalism also needs to be taken into consideration. EU news is often all too easily described as 'non-commercial' news, which is not particularly saleable. However, this study suggests that it would be wrong to think of EU reporting – and by extension any other form of international or political journalism – as something separated from market logic. This study illustrates that one can only make sense of the production, the position and journalists' perceptions of EU reporting in *De Morgen* within the larger context of Belgium's contemporary market-driven journalism. High-quality EU journalism may therefore be defined as something that always needs to be put into the perspective of a paper's positioning, profiling and differentiation within a national news market.

References

Baisnée, O. (2002), 'Can political journalism exist at EU level?', in Kuhn, R., and Neveu, E. (eds.), *Political Journalism. New Challenges, new practices*, London: Routledge, pp. 108–28.

Biltereyst, D., and Van Gompel, R. (1997), 'Crisis and Renewal of the Fourth Estate. On the Post-War Development of the Flemish Newspaper press', in *Communications* 22:3, pp. 275–300.

De Bens, E., et al. (2005), 'Adequate Information Management in Europe. The case of Belgium', report by AIM project. Available at: http://www.aim-project.net/uploads/media/Belgium.pdf Date accessed: 26/4/06.

De Beus, J., and Mak, J. (2004), 'Final case report of on communication strategies of the media. Case report The Netherlands', report by Europub.com. Available at: http://europub.wz-berlin.de/Data/reports/WP6/WP6%20CR/D6-2%20WP6%20CR%20NL.doc Date accessed: 26/4/06.

De Vreese, C.H. (2003), *Framing Europe. Television news and European integration*, Amsterdam: Aksant.

Garcia, G., and Le Torrec, V. (2003), 'Introduction: l'information de masse comme révélateur des logiques médiatiques. Enjeux et perspectives d'analyse' in Garcia, G., and Le Torrec, V. (eds.), *L'Union Européenne et les médias. Regards croisés sur l'information européenne*, Paris: L'Harmattan, pp. 9–17.

Kevin, D. (2003), *Europe in the Media. A Comparison of Reporting, Representation, and Rhetoric in National Media Systems in Europe*, London: Lawrence Erlbaum Associates.

Machill, M., et al. (2005), 'Europe-Topics in Europe's Media. The Debate about the European Public Sphere: A Meta-Analysis of Media Content Analyses', in *European Journal of Communication* 21:1, pp. 57–88.

Meyer, C.O. (2005), 'The Europeanization of Media Discourse: A Study of Quality Press Coverage of Economic Policy Coordination since Amsterdam', in *Journal of Common Market Studies* 43:1, pp. 121–48.

Semetko, H.A., et al. (2001), 'Europeanised Politics – Europeanised Media? European Integration and Political Communication', in *West European Politics* 23:4, pp. 121–41.

Slaatta, T. (1999), *Europeanization and the Norwegian News Media. Political Discourse and News Production in the Transnational Field*, report 36, University of Oslo: Department of Media and Communication (Ph.D. dissertation).

Slaatta, T. (2005), 'Europeanisation and the news media: issues and research imperatives', paper presented at the *First European Communication Conference*, Amsterdam, 24–26 November 2005.

Statham, P. (2004), 'Pressing Europe?: Journalists and the "Europeanisation" of the Public Sphere', report by Europub.com. Available at: http://europub.wz-berlin.de/Data/reports/WP6/D6-2%20WP6%20Integrated%20Report.pdf Date accessed: 26/4/06.

Trenz, H.-J. (2004), 'Media Coverage on European Governance. Exploring the European Public Sphere in National Quality Newspapers', in *European Journal of Communication* 19:3, pp. 291–319.

Challenges of Media Concentration: The Case of Regional Press Ownership in the Czech Republic

Monika Metyková and Lenka Waschková Císařová

Developments in regional press ownership in the Czech Republic illustrate key issues connected with the transformation of a Communist media system to free-market pluralism. The Communist era in Czechoslovakia came to an end in late 1989; in early 1993 the country split into two separate states: the Czech Republic and Slovakia. In May 2004 the Czech Republic (along with Slovakia) became a member of the European Union. The country has a population of 10 million people.

Media ownership, and in particular the concentration of such ownership, has been subject to much academic scrutiny and discussion. In addition to the possible effects of media ownership concentration on democratic processes and the distribution of symbolic resources in society, its economic effects have also been discussed.

A discussion of Czech regional media ownership would be inadequate should it not take into account the normative framework that has been set up to regulate it. There is no Czech legislation dealing explicitly with ownership of the press; thus this ownership is subject to competition policy, and decisions regarding cases of media concentration fall within the jurisdiction of the Office for the Protection of Competition (the anti-monopoly office).

In the following section we will offer a brief overview of literature published in the English language on the media transition in post-Communist countries, concentrating in particular on media ownership; we will then move on to a discussion of media ownership concentration and the concerns it raises for academics as well as policy-makers. These sections provide a framework for our case study which we will present in the final part of the chapter.

Changing media systems in East Central Europe

Over the last fifteen years a limited number of studies dealing with media transformation in East Central Europe (ECE) and aspects of ownership change have been published in the English language. A review of these studies confirms Coman's findings in 2000 when he conducted a similar exercise involving studies of eastern European media transformations published in English between 1990 and 1999. He identified two prevalent frameworks: 'the *public space* or *public sphere* (ideas, debates and free speech are democracy's base) and *roles and the social effects of the press* (mass media have an influence on society and individuals congruent or divergent referring to a certain assumed mission)' (2000: 50).

Some of the studies published in the English language deal with general systemic changes in post-Communist countries and their impact on media systems (for example, Sparks 1998; O'Neil 1997; Downing 1996) and the possibility of implementing western European media models. Sparks (2000) and de Smaele (1999) both conclude that western media models are not easily transposed to East Central European countries. Sparks further argues that the implication of the ECE transformations for the larger framework of the democratization of the media lies in the realization that media can be democratized only if the power of the elites that control them is reduced.

Several studies published in English deal with developments characteristic of particular media – for example, Gulyas (2003) examines changes in print media in the Czech Republic, Hungary and Poland (in particular the processes of the democratization, marketization and commercialization of the press). She argues that the most important general differences between Communist and post-Communist print media in those countries involve the aims of print media production, motivating forces, the roles and involvement of the state, the functions and behaviours of companies, and media control (2003: 82).

The latest and most comprehensive overview of the ownership of print and broadcast media in post-Communist East Central European countries can be found in a volume edited by Petković (2004) which includes eighteen country reports, a regional summary and a discussion of the relationship of ownership to media independence and diversity. Other studies provide insight into country-specific media ownership or particular investors, such as Sparks's (1999) discussion of Central European Media Enterprises, one of the major players in television broadcasting in the ECE region.

The transformation of ECE media systems has been characterized by the changing role of the state in relation to the media. Following the fall of Communism, new regulatory frameworks have been developed; however, there are only a handful of studies available in the English language that deal with changes in media regulation in east central Europe. Sparks (1998) explores some aspects of broadcasting regulation in specific ECE countries; the autumn 1999 special issue of the *Media Studies Journal* provides an overview of regulatory developments in East Central European countries; Goldberg (1997) offers a study of media and broadcasting regulation in Hungary; Pavlik and Shields (1999) discuss aspects of the Czech television broadcasting regulation; and Metykova (2004) outlines developments in public service broadcasting legislation in the Czech Republic and Slovakia.

Our literature review suggests that media ownership concentration in particular ECE print media markets and its possible and actual impacts are under-researched. Similarly, the regulation of print media (and in particular its ownership or any policies related to it) in post-Communist countries has not yet been adequately scrutinized.

The Czech print media market and its regulation

Since 1989 the Czechoslovak and later Czech print media market has undergone major changes in a number of respects.

There are six major national daily newspapers available in the Czech Republic, four of them 'quality papers' (*Mladá fronta DNES, Lidové noviny, Právo* and *Hospodářské noviny*) and two of them tabloids (*Blesk* and *Šíp*). Ownership of these dailies is for the most part in the hands of foreign investors; only one, *Právo*, has a Czech owner.

It is difficult to assess the total number of print media titles that have been published in the country in the last seventeen years as there is no reliable database available. The Czech Press Act delegates the responsibility for registering print media titles to the Ministry of Culture; the

Table 1. Major Czech national dailies in 2005. Source: Šmíd (2004) and Audit Bureau of Circulation CR.

Title	Publisher	Owner	Average Circulation (year 2005)
Blesk	Ringier ČR a. s.	Ringier Nederland	524 595
MF DNES	MAFRA a. s.	RBD	
		MAF a. s.	299 889
Právo	Borgis a. s.	Zdeněk Porybný	
		Small shareholders	170 583
Šíp	Vltava-Labe-Press a.s.	Passauer Neue Presse	70 400
Lidové noviny	Lidové noviny a. s.	Pressinvest a. s. (owned by the RBD)	
		Small shareholders	69 884
Hospodářské noviny	Economia a. s.	HB-DJ investments ČTK	
		Small shareholders	63 476

registration process, however, is inefficient as it does not distinguish publications according to their types. Furthermore, the registry of print media is not updated on a regular basis.

Today there are 8,000 print media titles registered with the Czech Ministry of Culture. Of these about 2,500 are regional periodicals. Yet, according to other sources (telephone directories and publishers), there are only 146 regional newspapers in the Czech Republic. Eighty-four of these are owned by the Passauer Neue Presse group.

The most important aspect of the legislative framework that relates to print media is the Press Act. The Act does not specifically distinguish between the local and regional press; rather, it sees them as part of the print media system in general. The Act does not deal with issues of ownership concentration or the entry of foreign owners into the Czech print media market. The only law that limits media ownership in the Czech Republic is Act no. 231/2001 Coll. on Radio and Television Broadcasting, which, however, only deals with plurality of content in radio and television broadcasting in terms of cross-ownership regulation.

The Czech regional press and its development since 1989

Regional press markets tend to be under-researched, yet – as Doyle points out – 'in most large European countries other than the United Kingdom (for example, France, Germany) and in the USA, regional dailies play a much more important role than national titles. Modernization and urbanization have created more demand for local communication and the structure of the press has evolved as a collection of small regional or city-based markets, providing mainly "responsible" product' (2002: 125). Local and regional media are committed to a local news agenda and coverage of local public affairs, which is too trivial a task for the national media, but also provide practical information and space for various announcements (deaths, weddings etc.) that are relevant to readers' everyday lives.

Prior to 1989 the Czechoslovak regional press consisted of newspapers published by county councils and committees of the Communist Party. The fall of Communism in November 1989 was followed by the privatization of old titles and the establishment of new privately owned print media. Foreign owners entered the regional press market, and in some cases the management and journalists of regional print media outlets established private companies which took over newspaper titles as well as their newsrooms, equipment and subscribers.

It was for the most part German investors who entered the Czech print media market. Before 2001 there were four major German publishers on the scene: Passauer Neue Presse, Rheinisch-Bergische Druckerei and Verlagsgesellschaft, Mittelrhein Verlag Koblenz and Frankenpost Verlag. However, after 2001 only two major players – Rheinisch-Bergische Druckerei (RBD) and Passauer Neue Presse (PNP) – remained to divide the Czech market between themselves. RBD owned two major national dailies (*Mladá Fronta Dnes* and *Lidové noviny*), and the regional press market fell under the ownership of PNP through its Czech subsidiary Vltava Labe Press (VLP) – Deníky Bohemia, Deníky Moravia.

It has been argued (see, for example, Čelovský 2001; Šmíd 2004) that a cartel agreement is involved; however the Czech Office for the Protection of Competition has never ruled on this issue. One of the Office's more controversial decisions involved the sale and acquisition of titles by VLP and another German publisher Rheinisch-Bergische Druckerei in 2001. The Office argued that it was not authorized to scrutinize the merger as the merged company would not have more than a 30 per cent share in the market (a threshold defined in then valid legislation that determined whether a merger had to be approved by the Office).

Regional press ownership in the Czech Republic and its possible impacts
The topic of media ownership has been widely discussed in media and communication studies. Opinions on the significance of media concentration vary greatly, from the notion that the dangers of concentration have been exaggerated as the media industry remains essentially fragmented, to the view that powerful media moguls have taken over global markets.

According to James Curran (2002) there are four sources of concern related to the question of concentration: (1) concentration of symbolic power possibly distorts the democratic process; (2) the power concentrated in the hands of media moguls can be used in a one-sided way; (3) concentration distorts competition; and

> to this can be added perhaps a fourth concern. The dominant position that emerged in this debate [the exchange on www.opendemocracy.com] – that media concentration undoubtedly exists but matters relatively little – fairly accurately reflects the balance of opinion, both in the relevant academic literature and in wider political debate. This is giving rise to a one-sided protection of our freedoms: a state of constant alert against the abuse of state power over the media, reflected in the development of numerous safeguards, not matched by an equivalent vigilance and set of safeguards directed against the abuse of shareholder power over the media.

Concentration in media markets has been of concern to policy-makers and the usual tool used to prevent such concentration within the European Union and its Member States is competition policy. Doyle argues that 'competition policy has traditionally worked on the assumption that the efficiency of markets depends directly on their competitive structure and, especially, on the extent of seller concentration' (2002: 168). Structural interventions such as limits on media ownership are often therefore introduced in order to promote market structures which are less concentrated. However, as we have already pointed out, Czech regional press ownership is regulated solely by competition policy and is supervised by the Office for the Protection of Competition.

Although the Czech antimonopoly office never ruled that VLP has a dominant position in the print media market – mainly due to the fact that it views the national print media market in its entirety and not in terms of any of its individual segments (i.e. regional and local markets) – both horizontal and vertical concentration are evident in the Czech Republic's regional press market. Horizontal concentration is represented by VLP's ownership of more than half the titles of the Czech regional press and the fact that these are published in every district of the Czech Republic. The VLP group publishes 84 regional newspapers, 73 dailies and 11 weeklies. In addition, the company publishes a new national daily tabloid called *Šíp*. We can also identify vertical ownership concentration in the Czech Republic – VLP owns, for example, the agency that sells advertising space in VLP newspapers, four print production companies and a distribution company.

Evidence of the influence of the concentration of regional press ownership in the Czech Republic is scarce and anecdotal. Here we offer three examples of such evidence. The first relates to the distortion of competition, the case of *Jihlavské listy*. The paper's Czech owners refused to sell it to VLP, which then attempted to prevent the daily from being printed or distributed. Petr Klukan, the Editor-in-Chief of *Jihlavské listy*, has revealed that VLP's print production company (which printed *Jihlavské listy*) threatened not to print the paper (Klukan and Pilařová 2002). Subsequently, *Jihlavské listy* changed its print production company and they now print their newspapers under less favourable conditions (their current print facility is significantly further away from their centre of operations than the original facility).

Further anecdotal evidence on the convergence of regional press content was presented in a television documentary entitled *Are These Newspapers We Can Trust?* (Czech Television 1, 18/12/01). It pointed out that in the whole of the Czech Republic the content of regional newspapers is largely identical. The programme-makers pointed out that all the VLP newspapers are prepared in the company's central newsroom and different regional supplements are then

Table 2. Regional daily newspapers published by Vltava-Labe-Press (VLP).

Dailies	Average Circulation (2005)
Dailies South Bohemia	42 430
Dailies North Bohemia	46 379
Dailies Central Bohemia	58 001
Dailies East Bohemia	53 526
Dailies West Bohemia	56 538
Dailies Bohemia Total	**256 874**
Dailies South Moravia	42 515
Dailies North Moravia	50 137
Dailies Central and East Moravia	37 325
Daily Vysočina	16 778
Dailies Moravia Total	**146 755**
Total VLP	**403 629**

Source: Audit Bureau of Circulation CR.

added. They compared issues of all these regional dailies, and showed that almost their entire front pages and their first few pages of national and foreign news were identical.

Evidence of the influences of ownership on the production process or content is hard to find, although such influences provoke serious and long-term effects, including issues of self-censorship. In the Czech case several former employees of publishing houses have given accounts of such influences: for example, the former Editor-in-Chief of the regional daily *Svoboda*, Ivo Šebestík, recalls an attempt by the German publisher (Rheinisch-Bergische Druckerei) to influence press content (Čelovský 2001, 2002). Other Czech journalists have recalled such pressures when interviewed by one of this chapter's authors for an EU-funded project.

The scope of this chapter has allowed us to provide only a brief overview of the current state of the Czech regional press market, a situation which is characterized by the dominant position of a single publisher. Concentration in the regional press market has potentially severe consequences which are, however, not acknowledged in Czech legislation. Although examples of such consequences are as yet largely anecdotal, this remains an issue whose significance cannot in the long term continue to be ignored.

References

Bagdikian, B. (1997), *The Media Monopoly*, Boston: Beacon Press.

Čelovský, B. (2001), *Konec Českého Tisku?* [*Is This the End of the Czech Press?*], Šenov u Ostravy: Tilia.

Čelovský, B. (2002), *Konec Českého Tisku* [*The End of the Czech Press*], Šenov u Ostravy: Tilia.

Coman, M. (2000), 'Developments in Journalism Theory About Media "Transition" in Central and Eastern Europe 1990–99', in *Journalism Studies* 1:1, pp. 35–56.

Compaine, B. (1982), *Who Owns the Media?: Concentration of Ownership in the Mass Communications Industry*, White Plains, N.Y.: Knowledge Industry Publications.

Cooper, M. (2003), *Media Ownership and Democracy in the Digital Information Age*, Stanford: Centre for Internet and Society, Stanford Law School.

Curran, J. (2002), 'Global Media Concentration: Shifting the Argument'. Available at: www.opendemocracy.com Date accessed: 23/5/02.

Czech Television (2001), 'Noviny, Kterým Se Dá Věřit? [Newspapers We Can Trust?]', in *Klekánice*, 18 December 2001.

de Smaele, H. (1999), 'The Applicability of Western Media Models on the Russian Media System', in *European Journal of Communication*, 14: 2, pp. 173–189.

Downing, J. (1996), *Internationalizing Media Theory : Transition, Power, Culture : Reflections on Media in Russia, Poland and Hungary, 1980–95*, London: Sage.

Doyle, G. (2002), *Understanding Media Economics*, London: Sage.

European Federation of Journalists (2003), *Eastern Empires: Foreign Ownership in Central and Eastern European Media: Ownership, Policy Issues and Strategies*, Brussels: European Federation of Journalists.

Goldberg, D., Prosser, T., and Verhulst, S., eds. (1997), *Regulating the Changing Media: A Comparative Study*, Oxford: Clarendon Press.

Gulyas, A. (1998), 'Tabloid Newspapers in Post-Communist Hungary', in *Javnost-The Public* 5:3, pp. 65–77.

Gulyas, A. (2003), 'Print Media in Post-Communist East Central Europe', in *European Journal of Communication* 18:1, pp. 81–106.

Hallin, D. (1994), *We Keep America on Top of the World : Television Journalism and the Public Sphere*, London: Routledge.

Hallin, D. (1996), *The 'Uncensored War': The Media and Vietnam*, New York: Oxford University Press.

Klukan, P., and Pilařová, D. (2002), 'Přežijí Alespoň Některé Poslední Nezávislé Regionální České Listy? [Will at Least Some of the Last Independent Czech Regional Papers Survive?]', in *Britské listy*, April 2002.

McChesney, R., and Herman, E. (1997), *The Global Media: The New Missionaries of Corporate Capitalism*, Washington, D.C.: Cassell.

Meier, W. A. and Trappel, J. (1998), 'Media Concentration and the Public Interest', in McQuail, D., and Siune, K. (eds.) *Media Policy: Convergence, Concentration and Commerce*, London: Sage, pp. 38–59.

Metyková, M. (2004), 'Establishing Public Service Broadcasting in the Slovak Republic (1993–2004): From State Control to the European Single Market', in *Trends in Communication* 12:4, pp. 223–232.

O'Neil, P., ed. (1997), *Post-Communism and the Media in Eastern Europe*, London: Frank Cass and Co.

Pavlik, P., and Shields, P. (1999), 'Toward an Explanation of Television Broadcast Restructuring in the Czech Republic', in *European Journal of Communication* 14:4, pp. 487–524.

Petković, B., ed. (2004), *Media Ownership and Its Impact on Media Independence and Pluralism*, Ljubljana: Peace Institute.

Šmíd, Milan (2004), 'Czech Republic', in Petković, B. (ed.), *Media Ownership and its Impact on Media Independence and Pluralism*, Ljubljana: Peace Institute, pp. 141–164.

Sparks, C. (1998), *Communism, Capitalism and the Mass Media*, London: Sage.

Sparks, C. (1999), 'CME and Broadcasting in the Former Communist Countries', in *Javnost-The Public* 6:2, pp. 25–44.

Sparks, C. (2000), 'Media Theory After the Fall of European Communism: Why the Old Models from East and West Won't Do Any More', in Curran, J., and Park, M. (eds.), *De-Westernizing Media Studies*, London: Routledge, pp. 35–49.

PUBLIC INTEREST SPEECH AND INVESTIGATIVE JOURNALISM: LATVIA, THE *DIENA* CASE AND THE EUROPEAN COURT OF HUMAN RIGHTS

Richard Caddell

Media law is considered to be very much in its infancy in the countries of the former Soviet Union and the Warsaw Pact, as the Communist system stifled free speech on the part of its citizens. Given the lack of a truly free media during much of the latter part of the twentieth century, it is of little surprise that the rules on defamation that are so deeply embedded in most western liberal democracies have remained somewhat stunted in a number of countries of the 'new' Europe. As new media opportunities have developed at an exponential rate in many parts of central and eastern Europe, legislators – faced with the already immense task of reforming their domestic legal systems – have been somewhat slow in elaborating norms to guarantee freedom of expression beyond general anti-censorship provisions, and in enshrining new rights and defences to protect journalistic endeavour. Accordingly, in a number of these countries it may be considered that key sectors of media law have yet to be fully developed in line with the freedoms enshrined under the European Convention on Human Rights that their governments have undertaken to guarantee in domestic law.

In Latvia, the lack of an effective defence for journalists to criticize the conduct of public officials, and the continued existence of legal provisions that seemingly permit authority figures to stifle debate about their activities with the threat of defamation writs, have recently come to a head, culminating in a major action brought in the European Court of Human Rights by the country's leading newspaper – which successfully argued that the current position constitutes a violation of free speech rights guaranteed under the European Convention. This chapter therefore seeks to offer an examination of the current law of libel regulating the acceptable boundaries of criticism of public officials, with an appraisal of the litigation brought both domestically and in the European Court of Human Rights which may potentially usher in a new dawn of press freedom in Latvia.

Public interest speech and its importance

One of the principal aims of investigative journalism is to uncover public misfeasance and to expose duplicity, corruption and misconduct. It may be considered especially important that such iniquity is revealed where the culprit is a public official, elected to serve the interests of the public as opposed to pursuing their own agenda. With this in mind, free speech laws have often sought to provide a degree of protection for the whistle-blowing journalist in the form of a distinct defence that shields the news-gatherer from the so-called 'chilling effect' of a libel action and allows her/his work to continue, relatively free from harassment by those seeking to conceal their wrongdoing (Barendt 2005: 154–197).

The most famous articulation of the protection of investigative journalism through the defence of public interest privilege is that established by the U.S. Supreme Court, acting under the First Amendment to the Constitution, in the celebrated case of *Sullivan v. Times Newspapers* (1964). Here it was held that a public official is precluded from bringing an action of defamation in relation to unfavourable reports of their conduct, unless the statement has been made with 'actual malice' on the part of the defendant. In this manner, the Supreme Court enshrined the journalist's right to undertake 'vehement, caustic, and sometimes unpleasantly sharp attacks on government and public officials' and promoted a culture of investigative reporting with broad protection for the reports ultimately produced. This was subsequently extended further in the United States to any 'public figure' (*Gertz v. Welch* 1974) and includes assertions of both fact and satire (*Hustler Magazine and Flynt v. Falwell* 1988). While very few jurisdictions have imported undiluted the strident First Amendment protection guaranteed in the United States, it is nonetheless clear that in virtually all liberal democracies there is a strong emphasis on the protection of this type of reporting.

Public interest privilege has also been enshrined by the European Court of Human Rights in its voluminous case-law related to freedom of expression. Freedom of expression is guaranteed under Article 10 of the European Convention on Human Rights, which states:

1. Everyone has the right to freedom of expression. This right shall include freedom to hold opinions and to receive and impart information and ideas without interference by public authority and regardless of frontiers. This article shall not prevent States from requiring the licensing of broadcasting, television or cinema enterprises.
2. The exercise of these freedoms, since it carries with it duties and responsibilities, may be subject to such formalities, conditions, restrictions or penalties as are prescribed by law and are necessary in a democratic society, in the interests of national security, territorial integrity or public safety, for the prevention of disorder or crime, for the protection of health

or morals, for the protection of the reputation or rights of others, for preventing the disclosure of information received in confidence, or for maintaining the authority and impartiality of the judiciary.

The protection afforded to news-gatherers under this provision has been elaborated further in a series of key cases. The leading judgement on political commentary is considered to be *Lingens v. Austria* (1986), an action that arose where an Austrian newspaper claimed that the then Chancellor of the country had protected a series of former Nazis from prosecution. Here the Court established categorically that a politician 'inevitably and knowingly lays himself open to close scrutiny of his [sic] every word and deed by both journalists and the public at large, and he [sic] must consequently display a greater degree of tolerance'. While this does not prescribe *carte blanche* to subject any politician to the most unfair invective, the protection of personal reputation, according to the Strasbourg judiciary, must be 'weighed in relation to the interests of the open discussion of political issues'. This position was elaborated further in another Austrian case, *Oberschlick v. Austria* (1997), where a politician was described as an 'idiot'; here the Court ruled that even insulting or scathing personal criticism may fall within the ambit of speech protected under Article 10. Furthermore, particular value is given to reporting that raises issues of substantial public interest (see *Jersild v. Denmark* 1994), and a journalist is permitted to make a series of value judgements in his/her articles – provided that they are not presented as assertions of fact (*Schwabe v. Austria* 1992). These principles have been entrenched in a large number of subsequent cases and the importance of freedom of expression has long been emphasized by the Court in its Article 10 jurisprudence (Nicol, Millar and Sharland 2001: 1–27).

Public interest privilege and libel law in Latvia

Freedom of expression in Latvia is primarily guaranteed under Article 100 of the Constitution, while the legal basis for libel actions is established under both the Civil Law and the Criminal Law of Latvia. Civil liability for defamation is established under Article 2352a of the Civil Law, which empowers the injured party to bring a court action to have the offending statement formally retracted. According to Article 2352a, the only defence available to the person disseminating the statement is that of truth. If the defendant fails to prove the veracity of the offending statement, then the injured party may seek to have the allegations retracted in the press and must be paid compensation, the amount of which is to be determined at the discretion of the court. Accordingly, damages and fines imposed by the Latvian courts are something of a lottery and are largely dependent on the individual circumstances of the case. However, as a general rule, the courts usually award significantly less than the claimant requests, and damages are higher in the civil courts than under criminal law.

Like most states party to the European Convention on Human Rights, Latvia also provides for criminal sanctions for libel, detailed in Articles 156 to 158 of the Criminal Law, under which it is an offence intentionally to insult another person's honour in writing, by deed or verbally in public. An amendment to these sections in June 2003 established the penalty for conviction as being a maximum fine of up to fifty times the monthly minimum wage, or community service. For intentionally distributing false information, either in print or verbally in public, the courts may impose community service or a fine of up to sixty times the monthly minimum wage.

Rather more controversially, in addition to the general criminal sanctions that apply in relation to libel, the Criminal Law also contains a very specific provision concerning the position of public officials. As part of a section entitled 'Offences against State Order', Article 271 of the Criminal Law protects the honour and reputation of state officials by establishing liability for defamation or slander against such a person while they are discharging their duties. The sanctions available upon conviction are severe: up to two years' imprisonment, community service or a fine of up to sixty times the monthly minimum wage. Although rarely invoked (Caddell and Aile 2004: 144), this provision of the Criminal Law has proved to be highly controversial, not least because it appears to be incompatible with the tenor of the various pronouncements of the European Court of Human Rights on press freedom, and since 2002 there have been concerted efforts within Parliament to remove or at least amend this section (Caddell and Aile 2004: 144).

Despite the relative disuse of this provision of Latvian libel law, it retains an intimidating presence in cases where public figures have been criticized, ridiculed or lampooned in the national press, and it may therefore give rise to what is referred to in legal parlance as the 'chilling effect' on journalistic endeavour. The 'chilling effect' is the term applied by free speech lawyers to a cause of action which, although it may not ultimately be invoked by the offended party, may nonetheless provide a sufficient threat to deter further news-gathering on the issue. Indeed, the 'chilling effect' of an ultimately unpursued libel action has long constituted an effective tactic by celebrities and other public figures in the United Kingdom, although, as two leading practitioners note, '[t]hreats by angry complainants and their solicitors to stop the presses with eleventh hour libel injunctions are largely bluff' (Robertson and Nicol 2002: 105).

Leading Latvian government officials have often felt justified in threatening the pursuit of legal action against sections of the media that have reported their (mis)deeds in a less than flattering light. One particularly notorious example occurred in 2004, when Minister of Defence Atis Slakteris was heavily criticized for his unusual behaviour while bestowing medals on Latvian soldiers returning from service in Iraq. Threatening litigation against *Latvijas Avize* over reports that he had been under the influence of alcohol at the time, Slakteris angrily demanded to know 'which reporter has been crazy enough to do something like this and who should be called to responsibility for damaging the immaculate image of the Defence Minister' (Caddell 2005: 216). While the threat of action appears to have subsequently vanished into the ether, it is not difficult to see how publishers and individual journalists may be vulnerable to pressure in this manner. It is indeed this very position, and the fact that investigative journalism – or even basic reporting – could be so easily threatened by the lack of an effective public interest defence that formed a central tenet of the complaint ultimately advanced by *Diena* in the European Court of Human Rights.

The *Diena* litigation

The *Diena* litigation arose as a result of a series of extraordinary events surrounding a relatively obscure privatization scheme for a petroleum export company based in Ventspils, a small port town near the Latvian capital Riga. Ventspils Nafta was identified as a candidate for privatization in the mid-1990s, and, in February 1998, questions arose within the Latvian Privatization Agency (LPA) over a proposed payment scheme for petroleum assets belonging to the state. Here, Latvijas Naftas Tranzits, a private fuel export company that was involved in the purchase of part of Ventspils Nafta, sought to use privatization certificates as a means of payment in lieu of hard currency. The LPA referred the matter to the Latvian Ministry of Finance, which, after a series of deliberations, rejected the proposal due to its projected effects upon the state budget.

On 5 May 1998 the LPA agreed a draft regulation governing financial arrangements within the privatization process, which established a series of strict conditions in relation to the use of privatization certificates as a means of payment. By a striking coincidence, on the same day the claimant in the eventual libel action, Laimonis Strujevičs, was appointed Minister for the Economy, and as part of this office was also automatically appointed Chairman of the LPA Council and Authorised LPA State Representative. Strujevičs quickly became involved in the Ventspils Nafta privatization saga when, on 15 May 1998, the LPA Council established a three-member sub-group to examine the proposals for amendments to the privatization payment system, headed by the Minister himself. A draft regulation was duly produced which altered the rules on payment, permitting an entity to purchase previously nationalized property using the very privatization certificates that the Ministry of Finance had categorically rejected as detrimental to public finances.

It is not difficult to understand the Ministry's objections. While the actual economic machinations of the scheme are highly complex, the end result is extremely simple: a company wishing to fund privatization in this manner would be able to secure enormous financial rewards with only a nominal investment, thereby depriving the government of significant income from the sale of its industrial assets and diverting this profit into private pockets. The implications were particularly significant in the case of Strujevičs; prior to his promotion to the government he had been an executive director of a company by the name of Ventamonjaks, an independent entity yet part of a wider economic group that included Latvijas Naftas Tranzits, the very company that stood to gain substantial commercial advantages if the proposed use of privatization certificates were to be formally sanctioned by the Minister. The implications were clear: at best, Strujevičs could be considered as facing a substantial conflict of interest through his personal efforts to reform the privatization process in this manner; at worst, this was an act of flagrant economic corruption of the type that has blighted many post-Communist societies in eastern Europe.

Aivars Ozolins firmly drew the latter conclusion. Ozolins, a journalist, worked for the first defendant, the leading Latvian daily newspaper *Diena*, as a political correspondent. In an article published on 13 July 1998 under the highly prejudicial headline, 'How to steal millions', Ozolins calculated that if Latvijas Naftas Tranzits were to be permitted to purchase state assets in this manner it would have gained in excess of eight million lats (some 12 million euros) in exchange for a nominal outlay. Ozolins's strongly worded article accused the consortium of 'pillaging the public Treasury', identifying Strujevičs as the primary facilitator of this arrangement, and called for the scheme to be formally vetoed by the government.

If Ozolins was hoping to ignite political pyrotechnics, he succeeded admirably. The *Diena* article caused a storm of outrage within Latvia's corridors of power. Even during the process of drafting this particular regulation, the question of alternative payment had been controversial, with Roberts Zile, then Minister of Finance, formally registering his concerns with both Strujevičs and the LPA. Despite the controversy, however, Strujevičs was able to approve the new regulations in his capacity as Minister and state representative. In response, Ozolins published a further two articles in *Diena* on 17 and 22 July 1998 accusing Strujevičs of 'coming to devastate Latvia' and dubbing the Minister the 'Ali Baba of Ventspils'. On 23 July the Prime Minister himself was forced publicly to express his disapproval of the proposed scheme. As the pressure intensified on Strujevičs, the Minister eventually conceded defeat over the proposed regulation and formally suspended the measure on 28 July, declaring to the press corps that his decision had been made 'under pressure', naming *Diena* as the main source of this pressure. Three days later, the Prosecutor-General announced that Strujevičs' proposed legislation was incompatible with the law, a decision which drew a defiant response from the Minister himself, declaring that he had not changed his mind on the issue. Nonetheless, the Latvian cabinet changed it for him: on 4 August the Council of Ministers collectively called upon Strujevičs to repeal the offending legislation and it was promptly withdrawn the next day.

Throughout this process Ozolins heaped ever more invective upon Strujevičs in a series of articles written during July and August 1998, calling for the Minister to be dismissed and for the privatization legislation to be annulled, and likening Strujevičs to a member of the Communist *nomenklatura* that had enjoyed special privileges of rank throughout the Soviet era. As Ozolins's articles expanded into attacks on the wider government for permitting Strujevičs to remain in power, the Latvian parliament debated the scandal, with several deputies subjecting the embattled Minister to a series of personal insults based on his links with industry. This appeared to be the final straw for Strujevičs, who initiated defamation proceedings shortly afterwards against both the newspaper and its journalist.

In October 1999, Strujevičs successfully sued both defendants in the Zemgale District Court, obtaining a court order for the retraction of part of the previously published articles and compensation of seven thousand lats. This judgement was appealed by both parties – Strujevičs had actually sued for moral damages of ten thousand lats and had also sought a formal apology from the defendants, which was not forthcoming from his unrepentant opponents, nor was it ordered by the court. The Riga District Court upheld the majority of the claimant's petition, but reduced the damages payable to four thousand lats. The case was promptly appealed to the Latvian Supreme Court, which ordered the case to be reheard on the basis that the Riga District Court had failed to take into consideration relevant case-law of the European Court of Human Rights in arriving at its decision, notably the requirement to consider the importance of free speech in a democratic society derived from the judgements in *Lingens v. Austria* and *Jersild v. Denmark.* Nonetheless, the Riga District Court penalized the defendants still further, ordering a retraction of many of the key allegations listed in Ozolins's first articles and increasing the compensation payable to Strujevičs to six thousand lats. A further appeal to the Supreme Court, on the basis that the District Court had failed to heed the advice of the Supreme Court in substance, was dismissed by a unanimous vote.

In rejecting the final appeal, the Supreme Court stated categorically that the defendants had overstepped the boundaries of press criticism and that Strujevičs was entitled to protection from, and restitution for, these vitriolic insinuations (*Strujevičs v. A/V Diena and Aivars Ozolins* 2002). In particular, the Supreme Court considered that the allegations arising from Ozolins's investigative journalism might have jeopardized the presumption of innocence incumbent upon the Minister were he to have been formally accused of having broken the law, as indeed the statement from the Prosecutor-General appeared to suggest. Furthermore, while the Supreme Court recognized that the case-law of the European Court of Human Rights permits – and, indeed, does not discourage – the publication of strong views as to the conduct of public officials, it was considered by the panel of judges that the language used by Ozolins had been 'outrageous' and had exceeded the permissible limits of fair comment upon the Minister in both his personal and professional capacities. Having exhausted all other avenues of appeal, the defendants then petitioned the European Court of Human Rights, claiming that the various decisions of the Latvian courts had infringed their rights to freedom of expression as guaranteed under Article 10 of the European Convention on Human Rights.

Latvia and the European Court of Human Rights
The appeal by *Diena* and Ozolins was eventually decided by the European Court of Human Rights in July 2007 (*A/S Diena and Ozolins v. Latvia*), amid a growing sense of unease among domestic civil libertarians that Latvian defamation law afforded rather more protection to the interests of public officials than to the needs of investigative journalism, and a feeling that substantial reform was required to mitigate the chilling effect that could arise from the application of provisions such as Article 271 of the Criminal Law. Indeed, as Caddell and Aile observe, 'it has been argued that a number of norms originating from the immediate post-Soviet period of the early 1990s no longer correspond to the legal and democratic principles of Latvia; as yet, however, the politicians have failed to agree on an acceptable modification of this provision' (Caddell and Aile 2004: 143).

Given this unsatisfactory situation, it is perhaps inevitable that some form of challenge to the current legal position would be forthcoming, particularly since the Strujevičs affair was hugely controversial in Latvia and the defendants felt that the law of libel had been unfairly weighted against their efforts to expose corrupt practices. Indeed, the protection afforded to public officials had already run the gauntlet of the European Court of Human Rights in a case decided some three years previously, one which had constituted the first finding of a breach of Article 10 against any of the Baltic States. In *Vides Aizsardzibas Klubs v. Latvia*, an environmental pressure group based in Riga had fallen foul of the law relating to public officials and underwent a process of protracted litigation similar to *Diena's*. In November 1997, at their tenth General Assembly, VAK had adopted a resolution condemning the Minister for the Protection of the Environment and Regional Development, as well as other local officials, for failing to take action to address environmental problems in the Mersrags sand-dunes in the district of Talsi, on the Gulf of Riga. This resolution was subsequently reprinted in the local newspaper *Talsi Vestis* and, in response, in February 1998 the local authority brought an action under Article 2352 of the Civil Law contesting the veracity of VAK's allegations, claiming some 500 lats in compensation and demanding that the offending article be formally retracted by the newspaper in question.

The District Court of Talsi found in favour of the municipal authority in a judgement delivered on 23 August 1999, awarding them 220 lats in compensation and ordering VAK to publish a retraction and an apology. An appeal to the regional court in Kurzeme failed in November 1999. This led to a further appeal to the Supreme Court in February 2000, arguing that Articles 13 and 47 of the Law Concerning the Protection of the Environment had been violated (respectively, failure to protect the environment and failure to adequately protect natural resources). This appeal was also unsuccessful, which resulted in VAK petitioning the European Court of Human Rights, alleging that it had suffered a violation of its rights under Article 10. In upholding the applicant's claim, the Court ruled that there had indeed been a breach of Article 10, noting that NGOs had a role in society that is analogous to that of the press, namely bringing matters of public importance to the attention of society. Furthermore, it was held that Latvia had failed to demonstrate that the interference with VAK's freedom of expression had been necessary in a democratic society and that the libel award was considered disproportionate to the legitimate aim pursued.

The *Diena* appeal involved a broadly similar set of legal arguments and a similar outcome to the VAK case. The applicants contended that, as is well established in Strasbourg jurisprudence, the press is required to play the role of both a watchdog and a bloodhound, to detect instances of public misfeasance and to vociferously disseminate such findings when they occur. Accordingly, Article 10 places a high value on this type of activity, and a corresponding degree of legal protection is afforded to journalistic endeavour to promote vigilance of this nature. Furthermore, the language that had been used by Ozolins, although strong, was compatible with his right as a public commentator to advance phrases that may be impassioned and even offensive – especially since the offending articles had been located in the newspaper's commentary section. Accordingly, the applicants argued, the state and the domestic courts had placed an excessively high importance on the protection of the Minister's reputation and had failed to take into sufficient consideration the role and responsibility of the press in imparting such information.

In response, the government countered that the actions of the authorities both had been proportionate and had pursued a legitimate aim. Moreover, the language used by Ozolins in his reports had been utterly unacceptable and had used a variety of terms associated with criminality, whereas in actual fact the Minister himself had never been formally accused, investigated or convicted of any such illegal conduct. As a result, the phraseology deployed by the applicants had strayed from the confines of a value judgement and instead constituted assertions of fact masquerading as fair comment. This latter argument was highly significant, especially since this is primarily the reason as to why a previous action alleging a violation of Article 10 rights concerning the defamation of a public figure in the Baltic States – this time in Estonia – had been struck down by the Court. In *Tammer v. Estonia* (2001), the applicant had been fined the modest sum of 220 Estonian kroons (approximately 14 euros) for having described the wife of a former Estonian Prime Minister in the national press as an *abielulõhkuja* and a *rongaema*. (An *abielulõhkuja* is a homewrecker, while a *rongaema* is an unfit mother.) The Court considered the use of such terms to have been excessive on the part of the applicant and unworthy of Article 10 protection since they 'amounted to value judgements couched in offensive language, recourse to which was not necessary in order to express a "negative" opinion', especially since in the view of the court, the applicant 'could have formulated his criticism of Ms Laanaru's actions without resorting to such insulting expressions'. Although, rather oddly, the Latvian government ultimately chose not to cite *Tammer* in support of its arguments, the parallels were nonetheless clear.

Despite this, the Court ruled against the government and observed that the publications in question referred to a matter of genuine public interest and that in bringing the issue to the wider public consciousness both applicants had been fulfilling their allotted role as a press watchdog. Moreover, Strujevičs was not only the serving Minister for Economics but also the head of one of the most important national political parties and, accordingly, the acceptable limits of public criticism were broader in his case than for an ordinary private individual. Likewise, the Court noted that the articles produced by Ozolins were part of some 53 articles about the affair published in *Diena* and that the facts repeated in these pieces afforded some basis for Ozolins to arrive at his conclusions; therefore, they could be considered to be genuine opinion pieces as opposed to sets of assertions laundered as editorial content, for which no protection accrues under Article 10. While refusing to pronounce upon the factual merits of the offending articles, it was felt that the words adequately described the wider debate over the issue in Latvia, where Strujevičs had been criticized stridently by his own colleagues – including a senior Minister and the Prime Minister himself. As such, the use of strongly critical words could be justified, and, although the Court expressed no wish to comment upon the quality of Ozolins's work, given the circumstances of the case it was reasonable to permit the journalist to state what were clearly labelled as his own views on a matter that was already well-debated within Latvian society.

Accordingly, the Court held that contrary to the view of the Latvian courts, the applicants had not overstepped the limits of press freedom and that the government had failed to establish a pressing social need for such a draconian approach to the articles in question and had in fact placed the protection of the Minister's reputation over and beyond the right of applicants freely to address urgent issues of public importance. Consequently, the interference with the applicants' freedom of expression could not be considered to have been necessary in a democratic society and *Diena* was awarded nearly 14,000 euros in compensation for the breach of its Article 10 rights.

Concluding remarks
The *Diena* litigation may ultimately constitute a milestone in the story of the development of modern press freedom in Latvia, with the European Court of Human Rights having categorically

ruled against the government on a second separate occasion on the issue of its protection of public officials from popular criticism. While the country's legislators have presided over the impressive feat of returning Latvia to a vibrant democracy after fifty years of Soviet domination, it may be considered that the story of free speech may be entering a new phase, and that many of the norms introduced in the immediate post-Soviet period to enshrine civil and political freedoms are now themselves insufficient in the light of Latvia's international commitments. Indeed, it must be strongly questioned as to whether a provision such as Article 271 of the Criminal Law is truly compatible with the requirements of Article 10 of the European Convention on Human Rights and, in the light of the *Diena* case, whether its continued presence in the statute books is ultimately tenable.

Political commentators and investigative journalists play a key role in the safeguarding of democratic values and this principle has long been recognized by the European Court of Human Rights. Where domestic laws are framed in a manner that confers broad powers upon public officials freely to pursue legal action against those who would seek to expose wrongdoing in the public interest, it is clear that the role envisaged for the press by Strasbourg – that of a vigilant watchdog – is gravely undermined. Accordingly, it is to be hoped that the Latvian parliament swiftly learns the lessons of the *Diena* judgement and moves expeditiously to reform Latvian libel law, so as to promote a far stronger measure of protection for statements made fairly and in the public interest, and correspondingly to dilute the ability of those who have elected to place themselves in positions of enhanced public scrutiny to avoid searching investigations into their conduct in office.

Unless and until the law is brought closer into line with the spirit of the *Lingens* principle, Latvia will continue to run the gauntlet of Article 10. Indeed, it must be considered a serious indictment of the current system that the courts at every level have displayed a distinct lack of empathy with the Strasbourg line in the context of political criticism. In this respect, and despite the exceptional progress that has been made in the country since the transition to democracy, it is clear that the story of Latvian press freedom still has some distance left to run.

References

Barendt, E. (2005), *Freedom of Speech*, Oxford: Oxford University Press.

Barendt, E., Lustgarten, L., Norrie, K., and Stephenson, H. (1998), *Libel and the Media: The Chilling Effect*, Oxford: Oxford University Press.

Caddell, R., and Aile, S. (2004), 'Defamation of Public Officials: Latvia and the European Court of Human Rights', in *Communications Law* 9:4, pp. 142–144.

Caddell, R. (2005), 'Media Law and the Transition to Democracy in the Baltic States', in *Communications Law* 10:6, pp. 213–218.

Fenwick, H., and Phillipson ,G. (2006), *Media Freedom under the Human Rights Act*, Oxford: Oxford University Press.

McConchie, R., and Potts, D. (2004), *Canadian Libel and Slander Actions*, Toronto: Irwin Law.

Nicol, A., Millar, G., and Sharland, A. (2001), *Media Law and Human Rights*, London: Blackstone Press.

Robertson, G., and Nicol, A. (2002), *Media Law*, London: Penguin Books.

Challenges for Romanian Investigative Journalism

Valentina Marinescu

Since 1990, the development of Romania's press industry has been determined by different legal-economic stipulations. The 'media brands market' rooted the industry in specific economic rules relating to privatization, share-holding, strikes, reorganizations, bankruptcy, mergers, and divisions. Between 1947 and 1990 the major media-holder was the state (Petcu 2000: 70). After 1990 a significant part of the press became private property.

In contrast with the press, Romania's audio-visual sector is strictly governed by the Constitution as well as by specific regulations. The two fundamental Romanian audio-visual laws are the Audio-visual Law, passed in 1992 and revised in 2003, and the Law Concerning the Organization and the Operating of the Romanian Radio Society and the Romanian Television Society, passed in 1994.

Sociological data suggest that Romanians have atypical 'social behaviour' in terms of their attitudes toward the country's integration in the European Union. In 2004 and 2005, Eurobarometer data showed that Romania boasted the highest scores for confidence in the European Union (74 per cent in 2004 and 68 per cent one year later) among the 29 countries included in the survey (Eurobarometer 2005b: 8).

The same data indicate major differences between the Romanian people and the citizens of other EU countries in terms of their confidence in other institutions. Citizens of other Member

States had most confidence in their armed forces (69 per cent), NGOs (68 per cent) and institutions of justice (68 per cent), while Romanians favoured the Church (82 per cent), the European Union (74 per cent) and the armed forces (74 per cent). One possible reason for this is Romanians' lack of knowledge concerning the way the public sector works (Eurobarometer 2005a: 40).

Analyses of professional journalism in Romania during this period have not represented a 'sociology of journalism'. Most of the studies have focused upon the history of the profession and Romanian journalism's growth into maturity, as well as its inherent difficulties in building up a specific identity.

In 1995 Coman (1995: 43) wrote that 'the greatest enigma in the Romanian press is [...] the journalists'. The reason for this was a lack of 'adequate training'. The huge 'heterogeneity' that characterized this group (Coman 1995: 43–44) was expressed in their inability to form a real 'professional body'. By 2002, the professional problems, far from being solved, had become more acute: 'The people working in the press are in deep ambivalence: they benefit from a prestigious status but, at the same time, suffer an often negative social image; they have and proclaim their autonomy, but they are subjected to political and economic pressure; they are visible and even famous, but they are not secure in their profession, being possible victims of budget cuts; they promote a discourse centred round the idea of "exceptionalism", but the experience of daily work confronts them with adversity and humiliation' (Coman 2002: 13–14).

After 1990, journalists as a 'professional body' faced the need to develop their own ideology, their own identity. The years of post-Communist transition have resulted in a confused and complex situation: 'journalists are subjected to various chaotic pressures and that is why they can hardly define their social role and a coherent mission; the fluidity of this system could generate a crisis of professional identity, thanks to the uncertain, uneven role journalism has played in Romanian society since December 1989' (Coman 2002: 14).

Investigative journalism

The research for this chapter involved a set of 44 interviews with Romanian investigative journalists and a content analysis of 277 articles in three newspapers in 2002 (116 articles) and 2006 (161 articles).

Our samples show that investigative journalism made up only 8 per cent of total editorial content in 2002, but that by 2006 this figure had risen to 11 per cent. There was also a shift in the focus of investigative journalism over this period. In 2002 the investigative articles concentrated on the current and past misdeeds of political figures, while in 2006 the majority of the pieces explored cases of economic, social, personal and political corruption. In 2002, 36 out of 116 investigative articles focused on public institutions (in general, the police, the law courts and local government), and in 2006 these issues were the subject of 58 out of a total of 161 investigative articles.

During these four years there was a significant change not only at the level of the journalistic aims but also at the level of the political characters – the subjects of the articles. In 2002 the journalists' investigations concentrated on corruption cases involving members of the Romanian Parliament; in 2006 their investigations were divided into clearly defined fields and concerned matters of more general interest: economic, social and political issues. It is also notable that by 2006 stories focusing on corruption were no longer spread throughout the general content of newspapers, but were confined to clearly delineated sections.

In 2002, 62 per cent of investigative stories included the journalists' own opinions; by 2006, this figure had decreased to 45 per cent. It can also be seen that between 2002 and 2006 the tone of these pieces became less 'accusing' and more morally neutral.

The interviews conducted with 44 investigative journalists for this chapter demonstrated only the absence of any standard body of opinion on (and within) Romanian journalism. Indeed, opinions on various questions were split more or less down the middle: 29 out of 44 referred to problems in Romania's media-related legal framework; 25 out of 44 were concerned by media ownership issues; 32 out of 44 by financing, production and distribution issues; 23 out of 44 were unhappy with the structure of the media market. However, one can see certain common themes emerging, specifically in terms of the deficiencies of press distribution networks. The interviews also suggested a general body of opinion on the subject of the factors influencing the integration of the Romanian media system into EU norms.

A number of these factors – such as market development and freedoms of expression and of information – were viewed as positive influences by the interviewees. However, other factors – including issues of political pressure and decreasing living standards (and their knock-on effects on media markets) – were viewed as detrimental. Overall, the journalists did not see themselves as bearing any responsibility for the development of the country's media system: they viewed the integration of this system within EU norms as entirely a matter of governmental responsibility.

These 44 interviews produced only five references to professional organizations, and none of the journalists interviewed made reference at any point to the potential improvements that EU integration may bring to their professional status.

Overall, the interviews indicated that Romanian journalists believe that the integration of the Romanian mass media within the structures and standards of the European Union will be possible through the following strategies:

- Strengthening the independence of mass media from political power – which would, in their opinion, require the adoption of new regulations.
- Redefining the financing structures of the state audio-visual sector – in fact, redefining the role and social functions of public radio and television services.
- The appearance of international media corporations on the Romanian market – more precisely, the inflow of foreign capital into the Romanian mass media system.

The opinions of these Romanian journalists reveal certain discrepancies within the country's generally positive image of the European Union; indeed, they suggest that (paradoxically) the nation's opinion-formers may be at odds with the perspectives of their nation. The content analysis suggests minor (though perhaps significant) shifts in the attitudes and practices of Romanian journalists towards western European professional values and norms; yet the interviews suggest an ambivalence – even a wilful ignorance – on issues of European Union integration and how that integration will continue to influence the development of their own profession and industry. The relatively low socio-political status of journalists in Romania – and their lack of any respected, active or influential professional bodies – suggests that, despite minor changes in their working practices, Romanian journalists may for some time yet avoid adopting the rights and responsibilities of their western European counterparts.

References

Coman, M. (1995), 'Romanian Journalism in a Transition Period', in *The Global Network* 3:1, pp. 28–48.

Coman, M. (2002), 'Controlul câmpului profesional', in *Jurnalism şi Comunicare*, 1:1, pp. 5–16.

Eurobarometer (2005a), Bucharest: Delegaţia Comisiei europene la Bucureşti.

Eurobarometer (2005b), Bucharest: Delegaţia Comisiei europene la Bucureşti.

Petcu M. (2000), *Tipologia presei româneşti*, Iaşi: Editura Institutul European.

Media Development in Moldova and European Integration

Liliana Vitu

Recent opinion polls confirm that the media in Moldova continue to enjoy a relatively high degree of public trust, with 60 per cent of citizens ranking the media ahead of all other institutions apart from the Church in terms of trustworthiness. However, since the Communist Party – the Party of Communists of the Republic of Moldova (PCRM) – came to power in 2001, international media watchdogs have noted a decline in media freedoms in Moldova.

Compared with the first post-independence decade – when newly emerging private media outlets played a notable role in shaping public discourse – Moldova has in recent years seen relative media pluralism give way to a more restricted media landscape, a landscape now characterized by attacks on investigative journalists, the closure of inconvenient media outlets and outright bias on the part of government-controlled media organizations. Even though the Moldovan authorities agreed to strengthen media freedoms in the EU–Moldova Action Plan signed in 2005, they are still far from tackling this issue with any degree of seriousness.

Weakened by years of political and economic pressure, the media in Moldova are therefore not in a position to serve the public interest by pushing for democratic reforms or better government policies. Until this happens, Moldova will struggle to strengthen its ties with the European Union and to ensure the sort of political and economic changes needed for a significant and sustainable increase in living standards.

From high goals to low scores

The PCRM's victory in both parliamentary and presidential elections in 2001 brought about a rapid worsening of the journalistic working environment in Moldova. Two years into the PCRM's tenure a report by Freedom House criticized an increase in self-censorship and a rise in lawsuits being brought against journalists, as well as the lack of editorial independence on the part of the public broadcaster, Teleradio-Moldova (TRM). One year later, Freedom House (2004) downgraded the Moldovan media from 'partly free' to 'not free' as a result of tightening government control over TRM and increasing pressure on independent newspapers. The 2005 report by Freedom House was similarly negative, criticizing the pro-government bias of the public broadcaster, an attack on an investigative journalist, attempts to close down two independent broadcasters, and the failure to fix a ceiling on the libel fines applicable to media organizations.

During the PCRM's first term in office other international groups also began to raise the alarm. The Media Sustainability Index, which is produced by the International Research and Exchanges Board (IREX), revealed in 2004 that most private media suffered from financing problems that left them highly susceptible to editorial interference by domestic political forces. IREX noted other factors also hindering the development of the Moldovan media, including a lack of experienced managers and a lingering Soviet-style perception of the press as a propaganda tool. Another well-known press organization, Reporters without Borders, reported in 2006 that Moldova had fallen eleven places from the previous year to 85th worldwide in terms of media freedoms, or almost 30 places behind neighbouring Romania.

Moldovan non-governmental organizations have echoed these international criticisms. In recent years frequent calls have been heard for more solidarity among journalists and for the authorities to ensure respect for the freedom of expression, access to information and the transparency of public institutions. Through public statements, protest marches and memoranda, Moldovan media NGOs have tried to persuade the government to refrain from the sort of practices that had become all too common and that had ensured a high degree of censorship within both the public and private media: denying accreditation for inconvenient media outlets, issuing specific orders to journalists on what events to cover, arbitrary sackings, and using news content as a tool to pursue party-political gains.

Public broadcasting – the government's mouthpiece

Both Moldovan and international observers agree that the government's failure to transform Teleradio-Moldova from a propaganda instrument into a genuinely independent public broadcaster is by far the most pressing issue in the country's media landscape. TRM is the most widely watched news-provider and the only station with nationwide reach, which gives it huge importance: almost three-quarters of respondents in a May poll listed television as their primary news source (IPP 2007), while over half of respondents in the same poll named TRM as their most trusted media source. The government's failure to open up the organization to opposition parties and other alternative viewpoints is therefore of critical concern.

Pressure to reform TRM had first begun to intensify in early 2002, when 500 employees launched a work-to-rule protest over censorship and bias at the company. The first declaration issued by the Anti-Censorship Committee set up by the protesting journalists stated that 'despite its proclaimed public status, the company continues to promote news coverage that defies all ethical standards. There is no delimitation between news and opinion, while public debates and political talk-shows are discouraged' (February 2002). The protesters also said that they were outraged by management attempts to make employees join pro-PCRM trade unions, and that ongoing harassment had 'killed' freedom of expression and the will of journalists to report in a professional manner. Several news reporters, editors and producers taking part in the action were dismissed.

The protest by TRM employees increased the international spotlight on Moldova's media problems. In April 2002 the Parliamentary Assembly of the Council of Europe (PACE) issued a statement calling on the Moldovan leadership 'to embark without delay on work to transform Teleradio-Moldova into an independent public corporation', in order to end censorship and ensure that representatives of opposition parties were able to take part in televised debates. PACE's demands met with a hostile reception from the Moldovan authorities. The country's President and PCRM Leader, Vladimir Voronin, stated that he would not allow state television and radio to be transformed into public institutions, and suggested that those who wanted a public broadcaster 'should launch a new one'. Mr Voronin claimed that 'as a citizen' he had reservations about the Council of Europe's recommendations, while Communist MPs said the recommendations ignored 'Moldovan realities' (IJC 2002).

Although combined international and domestic pressure forced the Parliament to adopt a law on reforming TRM in the summer of 2004, concrete improvements at the broadcaster have been minimal. Independent media monitoring has shown no significant improvements in terms of editorial independence or an end to pro-government bias. The authorities continue to ensure that their own stories concerning Parliament, the Presidency and other government institutions are regularly inserted into news programmes, and the company's overall editorial policy remains subject to a large degree of political pressure. The Moldovan authorities seem unrepentant about the lack of reform at TRM. The Prime Minister, Vasile Tarlev, has suggested that it would be unfair for the public to be 'less and less informed about the great achievements of the central authorities', and has claimed that an agreement was reached with TRM's president to establish exactly what should be broadcast about the government (Info Prim Neo 2007).

International representatives have stressed, at least in private discussions, that Mr Tarlev's statements go against European standards and the media reform commitments undertaken by Moldova in its Action Plan agreed with the European Union. More publicly, the international community has continued to voice deep reservations about the state of media freedoms in Moldova. For example, the OSCE Mission to Moldova has expressed concern about the pace of reforms at Teleradio-Moldova, which 'has made almost no progress towards becoming a truly independent public service broadcaster since its formal transformation in August 2004', and has urged the newly elected Supervisory Board to 'lose no more time in initiating fundamental and visible changes in the way the broadcaster reflects public and political life in the country' (OSCE 2007). At the time of both the 2005 parliamentary election and the 2007 local elections, the international community similarly echoed the concerns of domestic NGOs that the national broadcaster was being used to promote the ruling party and weaken its political opponents.

Formal access to information and weak opinion pluralism

Moldova's implementation of the Law on Access to Information also remains problematic. The law had been widely lauded when passed in May 2000. Moldova had been the first country in the Commonwealth of Independent States to pass such a law, and it was hoped that this would encourage more investigative journalism and thereby increase the transparency of official decision-making processes. However, the government has been reluctant to allocate the funds or appoint the personnel needed for the law to work. In a 2006 survey entitled *The Mirage of Transparency*, the Centre for the Promotion of Freedom of Expression and Access to Information concluded that public officials still did not know the content of the law, or else were simply ignoring the law in an attempt to conceal their professional inactivity. Although officials were no longer merely refusing to release information, as they had in the first years following the passage of the law, they were now relying on a set of formal answers to requests for information, which effectively ensured the same result.

In recent years the Moldovan authorities have frequently used various forms of economic pressure to restrict media pluralism. Independent media outlets have seen their finances limited through lost advertising revenue – which the government redirects towards more docile media – and have been obliged to pay discriminatory fees to the state publishing house and the monopoly press distributor, the Post of Moldova. They have also suffered from arbitrary licence-annulments and hefty fines for alleged defamation. These tactics have resulted in the closure of many media outlets and an increase in self-censorship – even to the extent that three TV channels and four radio stations declined to cover the 2005 general elections or broadcast any form of election advertising.

A number of high-profile attempts to limit media pluralism have sparked both domestic and international criticism in recent years. The most recent of these came at the end of 2006, when Moldovan media NGOs severely criticized the application of the country's Audio-Visual Code to two public stations with anti-Communist editorial policies, Antena-C and Euro-TV. The authorities had controversially closed the two stations in December 2006, before proceeding with their un-transparent sale to new owners, who went on to cut staff levels sharply despite calls from diplomatic missions to ensure 'the continued functioning of both broadcasters, drawing on their experienced staffs'. The OSCE Mission noted at the time that 'the immediate reduction in news and information programming at Antena-C and the change in its broadcasting schedule following privatization [...] show a disregard for these recommendations' (OSCE 2007). Media NGOs said the decision was politically dictated and bore no relation to professional media development.

The controversy surrounding Antena-C and Euro-TV came in the wake of other disturbing attempts by the authorities to limit the media landscape. In June 2005, the government cited a 'lack of financial resources' in its decision to close a public news agency Info-Prim, which had been based in Chisinau town hall and was seen as sympathetic to the capital's opposition mayor, Serafim Urechean. The treatment of Info-Prim contrasted with that of two relatively more loyal state newspapers, *Moldova Suverna* and *Nezavisimaia Moldova*, a few months earlier. Under pressure from international and national media organizations, the government had agreed to relinquish its control of these newspapers. However, it then continued to permit them to remain in their existing offices, and appears to have done little to ensure an independent editorial stance on the part of either publication. The two still publish eulogies upon the President, the Parliamentary Speaker and the Prime Minister, along with editorials praising official policies.

The government has further ensured media loyalty by allowing local authorities to re-establish 25 Soviet-style subsidized newspapers in recent years. By November 2005 this had triggered calls from the Association of Independent Press to guarantee equal opportunities for private publications. After its members were repeatedly denied access to local government events, the AIP also urged the country's leadership to ensure free access to information for all media (AIP 2006).

Excessive fines for defamation are another feature of Moldova's media scene. A high-profile incident came in July 2005, when the courts ordered *Moldavskie Vedomosti*, a Russian-language opposition newspaper, to pay two thousand dollars (more than 50 times the minimum monthly salary) for defaming the director of the government-owned Moldovan railroad company. The newspaper had disclosed irregularities and abuses alleged to have occurred during the renovation of the company's headquarters. *Moldavskie Vedomosti* appealed the decision to the European Court of Human Rights, and the U.S. State Department 2006 Country Report described the incident as a serious violation of the freedom of the press.

Attacks on independent media – challenges to the freedom of speech

The independent media in Moldova have faced not only economic and legal pressures, but also more direct attacks on journalists themselves. This issue surfaced most recently in advance of the June 2007 local elections. Two months before the vote, the police detained two television crews filming an opposition protest march. A reporter from Pro TV was taken to a police station 'for identification', even though he had already presented all the necessary documents, while a cameraman for DTV was ordered to surrender his video-taped footage. The main NGO coalition monitoring the election campaign, the Civic Coalition for Free and Fair Elections, subsequently condemned the incident as leaving 'no room for doubt over regrettable accidents'; on the contrary, it suggested that these actions were not random: 'We are qualifying all these actions as [...] attempts to intimidate citizens who share different views from the official ones, and as an attempt to curtail freedom of expression.'

A few months earlier, two independent Romanian-language newspapers, *Jurnal de Chisinau* and *Ziarul de Garda*, had also come under direct pressure. In October 2006 a break-in at the *Jurnal de Chisinau* resulted in the loss of a computer used by a political reporter who had published investigative pieces on public figures collaborating with the security services. That same month, *Ziarul de Garda* reported threats issued by state officials, as well as other, unidentified individuals, to encourage it to abandon certain of its investigations. The newspaper also reported attempts to corrupt its journalists and intimidate sources. At around the same time, hackers entered the website of the Centre for Journalistic Investigations and destroyed an archive of more than a hundred investigations.

The most serious attack on media freedoms came in June 2004, when an investigative reporter at the opposition newspaper *Timpul*, Alina Anghel, was attacked outside her home by two assailants armed with a metal bar. Ms Anghel was hospitalized with a concussion and broken arm. According to local and international organizations, the attack was directly linked to her professional activities. Ms Anghel had written a series of investigative pieces on corruption among public servants. *Timpul* eventually lost a civil libel suit related to one of her investigations, and was forced into bankruptcy after being ordered to pay $120,000 for 'moral damages'. The OSCE Representative for Freedom of the Media, Miklos Haraszti, has noted that large civil defamation penalties are often misused by public officials, and has recommended the setting of a 'reasonable ceiling' (OSCE, 2006).

European integration
One of the priorities of the EU–Moldova Action Plan is to ensure respect for the freedom of the media and for freedom of expression. Under the terms of this plan, the Moldovan authorities agreed to 'ensure a transparent relationship between the authorities and media institutions in line with Council of Europe recommendations, and that state financial assistance for media would abide by strict and objective criteria equally applicable to all media outlets; and to put in place and implement an appropriate legal framework guaranteeing freedom of expression and of the media, in line with European standards and on the basis of the recommendations of the Council of Europe'.

However, insufficient levels of media freedom and independence have been cited as key shortcomings in the implementation of the Action Plan, both by the European Commission and by the Moldovan organizations that monitor the government's performance. This issue has frequently been raised by the diplomatic community in Chisinau. On one occasion, in May 2005, western diplomats published a joint statement calling on the country's leadership to develop a more vibrant and independent media: 'We attach great importance to freedom of expression and plurality of the media. A free, plural and independent media is essential to underpin the democratic process. We call on Moldova to adhere fully to its obligations to OSCE, the European Union and the Council of Europe, as well as other international commitments.' One year later, they again urged the government to 'move from words to deeds' and respect 'the spirit of common European values' when implementing broadcasting reforms. They also pointed to a lack of progress in the field of media reform as well as obstacles to the independent press.

The political and economic pressures faced by the Moldovan media place the country outside of European norms. Despite professing to want to move closer to the European Union and eventually to join the club, Moldova's leaders still seem to want to be judged relative to other members of the Commonwealth of Independent States, rather than in comparison with the former Communist countries now in the European Union. Moldova would do well to learn from the example set by neighbouring Romania, an EU member with which it shares a common history, culture and language. The Romanian path could serve as a model for media development and provide valuable lessons concerning the need for critical media scrutiny, the importance of enshrining rights to the access to and dissemination of information, and the rights of journalists to practise their profession freely and safely. Regrettably, the PCRM, which will remain in power until at least the spring of 2009, continues to fall short of embracing these democratic principles.

References

Anti-Censorship Committee (2002), *Public Statement*, 23 February 2002.

Civic Coalition for Free and Fair Elections (2007), *Statement on the abuses of the police forces*. Available at: http://www.alegeri.md/en/2007/coalition2007/ Date accessed: 18/8/08.

Council of Europe Parliamentary Assembly (2003), *Freedom of Expression in the Media in Europe*. Available at: http://assembly.coe.int/Documents/AdoptedText/ta03/EREC1589.htm Date accessed: 18/8/08.

EU-Moldova Action Plan (2005). Available at: http://ec.europa.eu/world/enp/pdf/action_plans/moldova_enp_ap_final_en.pdf Date accessed: 18/8/08.

Freedom House (2004), *Freedom of the Press 2004: A Global Survey of Media Independence*, Washington: Freedom House.

Independent Journalism Centre (2002), *Moldovan Media News*. Available at: http://www.ijc.md Date accessed: 18/8/08.

Info Prim Neo news-agency (2007), *News report*, 3 August 2007.

Institute for Public Policy (2007), *Barometer of Public Opinion*. Available at: http://www.ipp. md Date accessed: 18/8/08.

International Research and Exchanges Board (2004), *Media Sustainability Index*. Available at: http://www.irex.org/msi Date accessed: 18/8/08.

Reporters Sans Frontieres (2006), *Worldwide Index of Press Freedom*. Available at: http://www.rsf.org Date accessed: 18/8/08.

Transitions Online (2006), *Our Take: In This Crowd, 79th Ain't Bad*. Available at: http://www.tol.cz/ Date accessed: 18/8/08.

U.S. Department of State (2007), *Country Reports on Human Rights Practices in Moldova – 2006*. Available at: http://www.state.gov/g/drl/rls/hrrpt/2006/78828.htm Date accessed: 18/8/08.

Maintaining Old Traditions of Media Diversity in Europe: The Non-Muslim Minority Media in Turkey

Eylem Yanardagoglu

The European Union enlargement strategy, which was agreed at the 1993 Copenhagen Summit, adopted stability as its major component because of the turbulent events in the 1990s – particularly in eastern Europe – fuelled by the resurgence of ethnic, religious and regional identities. Protection of minorities became a significant concern for European governments, one which eventually prompted them to recognize the cultural heritage and diversity of Europe (de Vries 2002). A diverse media structure that could enable expressions of cultural diversity was considered part and parcel of the recognition and maintenance of diversity, a phenomenon which now is numbered amongst the most fundamental human rights and freedoms by European institutions and statutes.

When Turkey was accepted as a candidate country at the Helsinki Summit in December 1999, it was considered to have 'the basic features of a democratic system' but still had serious shortcomings in the areas of the protection of minorities and human rights (Commission of the European Communities 2004: 165). In order to overcome these shortcomings, and to comply with the Copenhagen political criteria which have become the conditions for negotiations with candidate states, Turkey underwent one of the most comprehensive democratization reforms in its history. These colossal structural reforms were especially crucial in such areas as freedom of expression, human rights and the protection of minorities (Baç Müftüler 2005; Özbudun and Yazici 2004).

Although Turkey has not yet signed the two essential documents related to minority protection and media diversity, it has taken preliminary steps to ensure minority language media provisions. This process began with allowing Kurdish language broadcasting on public television and radio in 2004 and on local commercial channels in 2006. Previously unthinkable, Kurdish language broadcasts not only contributed to the visibility of cultural diversity in the Turkish media scene, but also signalled a shift in the way cultural identities are perceived in the public domain (Yanardagoglu 2007).

The specific multicultural situation of Turkey is mainly due to the presence of national minorities rather than economic migrants, but the acknowledgement of cultural diversity in Turkey has always been a thorny issue. This is due to historical tensions that can be traced back to the collapse of the multi-religious, multi-ethnic Ottoman Empire and the emergence of the putative mono-cultural nation state in the 1920s. In order fully to grasp the complexities of the Turkish case and to locate its media diversity in context, it is essential to consider the 'old' minority media provisions in Turkey that formed one of the oldest minority media systems in Europe.

This chapter focuses on one aspect of the minority media structure in Turkey that mediates the presence of non-Muslim 'official minorities' – the small non-Muslim Armenian, Rum (Greek) and Jewish communities. The aim is to provide a background for their existence, reveal their unique characteristics and situate them within the broader studies and burgeoning literature on ethnic minority and diasporic media in a European context.

Through interviews conducted with key media personnel, this chapter will offer an overview of perspectives upon cultural diversity and the situation of non-Muslim minority media practices in Turkey.

Turkey's minorities and its cultural diversity

One of the key texts in this area suggests that any analysis of minority media must consider the social and political environment of society as a whole, the international context in which minority demands or needs are perceived, and the socio-economic conditions of the ethnic minority community itself. In addition, the 'prevailing ideology of the state' in terms of its ability to tolerate diversity within its own political structure is considered as a crucial factor influencing the emergence and survival of minority media (Riggins 1992: 16).

It is essential in the Turkish context to consider the historical background that bears upon the nation's perception of minorities and citizenship, and its recognition of diversity. Turkey emerged as a Republic after the collapse of the multi-religious and multi-cultural Ottoman Empire. The diverse nature of the Ottoman system was seen as the primary cause of its dissolution. People living under Ottoman rule were not national citizens but subjects of the Sultan. The population was composed of different ethno-religious communities, and the main differentiation in society was between Muslims and non-Muslims. The majority of Muslims were members of Turkish, Kurdish and Arabic communities. Each ethnic community, organized under the *millet* system had its own language and educational institutions. When the Republic was established, the position of the non-Muslim minorities was framed by the constitutive Lausanne Treaty of 1923. The Kurds, being Muslim subjects of the Ottoman Empire, were not recognized as a 'minority' in this process because the Treaty only accepted 'religion' as a legitimate basis for difference (Soner 2005).

The non-Muslim population's demographic make-up had been changing since the end of the First World War. Before the war Christians comprised 20 per cent of the population of Anatolia. This number dropped to one in 40 after the Republic was established in 1923 (Keyder 2005).

The infamous loss of most of the Armenian population took place in 1915–17; while another major event that led to the further homogenization of the population was the exchange of peoples between Greece and Turkey that took place in 1923. The Lausanne Treaty provided that, except for the Rum of Istanbul and the Turks in Western Thrace, almost 900,000 of the Greek Orthodox population of Anatolia were exchanged for about 400,000 of the Muslim population of Greece.

In the initial years of nation-building and in the wake of the Second World War, cultural and economic *Turkification* policies targeted non-Muslim minorities, leading to their gradual decline and to the further demographic homogenization of Turkey. These policies strained relations between the state and minorities, and caused their eventual and continuous emigration. The emigration of non-Muslims which started in the late 1940s had a direct impact on the survival and existence of these communities and their media.

Until the 1990s, non-Muslim minority issues continued to be a somewhat taboo subject. However, due to internal and external dynamics, such as the growing presence of identity politics in the public domain and the effects of globalization and increasing integration with the European Union, it has been possible to observe an 'opening up' in the acknowledgment of issues that are pertinent to ethnic diversity in Turkey. It can be argued that, within Turkey, each minority community faces different problems with bureaucracy or prejudices in the public sphere, and that these all have an impact on the way their media operate.

The official minority media structure in context

Today's non-Muslim minority media represent a legacy of the imperial *millet* system in which each community had the right to produce their own publications and newsletters. The first newspapers in the Ottoman Empire emerged during the modernization period of the mid-nineteenth century. The first official gazette of the Empire was published in languages spoken by the country's various communities, including Greek, Arabic and Armenian. The Lausanne Treaty, which stipulated non-Muslims' rights and liberties, also provided that these communities could have publications and broadcasts in their own languages. In this way it was possible for the diverse Ottoman print media scene to be transferred to the Republican milieu.

Today the non-Muslim minority media operate mainly as a result of voluntary efforts and their main aim is to preserve the languages and cultures of their communities. They also have an immanent relationship to diasporic cultures in that they cater to the needs of their communities by informing them not only of local minority issues but also of their diasporic connections.

They display characteristics common to 'community' media – locally oriented and produced content catering to small geographic regions and geographically dispersed groups (Jankowski 2002). However, 'minority media' is a more appropriate term in that it refers to alternative, ethnic and religious media outside the mainstream – media which may demonstrate diverse approaches to the situations of minority communities. Furthermore, it is necessary to distinguish non-Muslim minority media in Turkey from such religiously oriented community media as the Muslim media in France and Britain, because their religious affiliations are not the only determinants of their content.

The Armenian press

The first Armenian newspaper was a version of the first official gazette which emerged in 1831, but subsequent publications progressed into such forms as children's magazines, medical journals and a pioneer feminist magazine – some of which continued into the Republican period (Karakaşli 2001). Today, the Armenian community has only three newspapers catering for a population estimated at 60,000 people. These are *Jamanak*, *Marmara* and *Agos*. All are delivered to the neighbourhoods where Armenians reside in Istanbul and are mailed to subscribers around the world.

Jamanak was established in 1908. It is the oldest continuing publication in Turkey and the oldest Armenian newspaper in the world with an uninterrupted publication. It has a daily circulation of 1,500 copies and mainly focuses on diplomacy and Turkish foreign policy. According to its general director (interviewed for this study), *Jamanak* has an implicit and natural relationship with the diaspora media as both benefit from pooling resources and news stories.

Marmara was established in 1940 as a daily newspaper and it has a circulation of 1,500 copies a day. In 2000, with the launch of its Internet site, it became the first Armenian newspaper online. The extended family members of Istanbul Armenians circulate copies of the newspaper among other members of the diaspora but it is difficult to estimate how many readers it actually reaches. Although its mission is to preserve the Armenian language and encourage its proper use, it has been publishing a supplement in Turkish every week since 2000 in order to reach those who can speak but cannot read Armenian.

Agos is the youngest of the community newspapers and was established in 1996 with a mission to become a 'bridge' between the Armenian community and society at large. It is a bilingual weekly that displays a more adversarial character than the other community newspapers. In its news selection *Agos* privileges items related to the democratization process in Turkey. Its Editor-in-Chief Hrant Dink (interviewed for this study in 2004 and 2005) distinguished *Agos* from other community newspapers – which in his view prioritized the preservation of culture and language but lacked a wider concern for minority rights. For him, the emergence of *Agos* symbolized an 'uprising' against both the state and community bureaucracy: '*Agos* has struggled with state bureaucracy by bringing problems to public attention, and combating negativity in public opinion. *Agos* completely opened its community to the wider society and also struggled with the community bureaucracy that still wants to see this community only as a religious community.'

Despite trying to fight prejudices and problems inherent both in minority and majority bureaucracies and public opinion, *Agos* and Hrant Dink became targets of the very xenophobia they were trying to eliminate. Hrant Dink was shot dead in Istanbul in January 2007, in broad daylight in front of his newspaper offices, by a 17-year-old boy – apparently because he insulted 'Turkishness' in one of his pieces for the paper. Perhaps unsurprisingly, this event raised international concerns about 'a resurgence of xenophobic nationalism' in Turkey (The Economist 2007: 39–40).

From the perspective of media freedom and diversity, *Agos* is unique in Turkey and bears comparison with other European minority media outlets which emerged in reaction to the 'invisibility and/or vilification of the minority community in the majority ethnic media' (Husband 2005: 467). This does not hold true for all the minority publications in Turkey in that many newspapers hark back to the Ottoman tradition in which every community was either catered for in the official gazette's minority language editions, or minority communities and religious organizations already exploited their right to publish their own newsletters and magazines (Topuz 2003).

The Jewish press

The first Jewish newspapers in Turkey can be traced back to the nineteenth century but today the community has only one newspaper, *Şalom*, which was established in 1948 in the Judaeo-Spanish language Ladino. It has been bilingual since 1984, but it remains the only Ladino print publication in the world. *Şalom* publishes four thousand copies weekly, a quarter of which are mailed abroad for the readers in the diaspora who are either emigrant Turkish Jews or academics who are interested in Ladino.

The paper relies heavily on foreign newspapers and the Internet as news sources and dedicates more space to events that take place in the diaspora than would interest the home community. *Şalom* has grown from four to twenty pages in the last decade and now employs a staff of 40 people, though more than half of these are volunteers. The preservation of a readership among younger generations is one of the biggest challenges faced by minority community media, and this remains a central concern for *Şalom*. According to its editor (interviewed for this study): 'Our most important mission is to make the younger generations read the newspaper and to include them in the future administrative cadres of the newspaper. Therefore, we have been trying to keep a balance in the issues covered in the newspaper so that it is interesting for our youth. We have pages that teach of traditions and religious festivities. But we also have arts and sport pages in order to attract young people.'

The newspaper strives to create wider social awareness and to combat prejudices in society through such activities as book fairs and cultural festivals. *Şalom* aims to serve the community, and through recent efforts it has also strived to establish links with the mainstream media, thereby contributing to the continuity between minority and majority media outlets.

The Rum (Greek) press

The Rum press similarly flourished during the reformation period of the nineteenth century, but, following the exchange of populations between Greece and Turkey, it had to adjust itself to the change and loss of its readership (Türker 2003). During the early Republican years, the Greek community in Istanbul had around thirty newspapers, but currently there are only two – *Apoyevmatini* and *Iho*.

Apoyevmatini was established in 1925 and is one of the two oldest newspapers in the history of the Republic (along with the Turkish daily *Cumhuriyet*). The history of *Apoyevmatini* parallels the history of Istanbul's Rum community, whose population declined from 100,000 to 2,000 over this period. International and national tensions (such as the Cyprus problem) have had a negative impact on the Rum press. Furthermore, the decline of the population has made *Apoyevmatini* dependent on the efforts of one person, its Editor-in-Chief: 'Apoyevmatini reflects what I think, because there is nobody else. Therefore the target of the newspaper is limited, and I only deal with things that I can do and will be able to do. What I can do is to publish a newspaper in Greek, and use the language properly.'

Apoyevmatini today operates as a one-man-show through the efforts of an editor who speaks of its technology as 'slightly better than that of Gutenberg'. *Apoyevmatini* publishes around 500 copies daily, and remains a pivotal node of communication for the community, while also aiming to educate younger generations in the proper use of the Greek language.

Iho was established in 1977 at a time when the Rum community was in deep decline, and its general director is the only journalist who has remained on staff since the paper's early days – the rest of his original colleagues have emigrated. It is an evening newspaper and sells about 400 copies each day. Due to financial constraints its staff comprises only five (or sometimes fewer) people who work either voluntarily or part-time. The most important element of the newspaper is its community news, but it also offers a wider coverage of world and European events. Its editor sees the transformation of the content of the newspaper in the last decade as being due to improvements in Turkey's relations with Greece and the European Union: 'We give summaries of the Turkish morning papers every day. Over the last couple of years we have also started giving summaries of the Greek morning newspapers. Greek-Turkish relations occupy a very important position, as our community has been affected by these throughout its history. News from the Balkans and the Middle East, and, in the last ten to fifteen years, European Union news, is also covered in the newspaper. Only world news of great importance makes the main headlines – otherwise it is covered in the world news section. It is community news and problems that feature first.'

Despite being the smallest minority community in Turkey, Istanbul's Rums actively maintain their language and community through these two community newspapers, both of which have strived to adapt themselves to contemporary developments.

Concluding remarks

The character of the minority media in Turkey has been transformed as a result of the continuous emigration of non-Muslim populations and the advance of new information technologies. They now bear similarities with diasporic media cultures, which, as Georgiou has suggested, 'develop in the intersection of local, national and transnational spaces' in which their audiences are addressed both 'in their particularity and also in the universality of their imagined cultural existence' (Georgiou 2005: 482–483).

These minority media share a non-profit, voluntary orientation and make similar efforts to maintain their diminishing communities by serving their communication needs. They all suffer to some extent from a lack of financial resources and human capital, and their biggest challenge is to attract the readership of younger generations. They may not seem significant in terms of the technologies they use and the sizes of their audiences, but they are the legacy of an ancient multicultural tradition in Turkey, and they are adjusting themselves to contemporary contexts. These non-Muslim minority media not only maintain the channels of communication between geographically dispersed members of each community, but also support the survival of cultures at risk of extinction – such as the Rum community in Istanbul.

Minority media are directly influenced by the conditions of the communities they serve, and the broader social and political conditions in the nation at large. Minority communities combat a variety of negative representations, and these factors inevitably impact upon the ways in which their media outlets operate.

Before the murder of Hrant Dink, it appeared that Turkey's minority media were awakening – were becoming more active in the ways they relate to their diaspora and Turkish society as a whole. This was a result of the positive effects of Europeanizing reforms in particular, and of internal dynamics in Turkey in general, which generated an openness in the discourses available within the public sphere. In light of recent events, however, the future of these minority media outlets remains uncertain.

One possible future is that the processes of cultural liberalization, as supported by the efforts of these minority media outlets, are reversed, and that these minority media will remain ghettoized. Nevertheless, the Turkish example offers new insights into the ways in which media and cultural diversity policies are implemented in the European context, and may inform valuable new approaches – particularly in relation to those other eastern European countries in which diversity is embedded in historical and political tensions between various national minorities.

References

Baç Müftüler, M. (2005), 'Turkey's Political Reforms and the Impact of the European Union', in *South European Society and Politics* 10, pp. 17–31.

Commission of the European Communities (2004), *Regular Report on Turkey's Progress Towards Accession*, SEC. de Vries, G. (2002), 'Conference Opening: The European Charter for Regional or Minority Languages -an instrument for diversity and peace in Europe', in *From Theory to Practice- The European Charter for Regional and Minority Languages*, Strasbourg: Council of Europe Publishing.

Georgiou, M. (2005), 'Diasporic Media Across Europe: Multicultural Societies and the Universalism–Particularism Continuum', in *Journal of Ethnic and Migration Studies* 31, pp. 481–498.

Husband, C. (2005), 'Minority Ethnic Media As Communities Of Practice: Professionalism and Identity Politics in Interaction', in *Journal of Ethnic and Migration Studies* 31, pp. 461–479.

Jankowski, N. (2002), 'The Conceptual Contours of Community Media', in Jankowski, N., and O.Prehn, O. (eds.), *Community Media in the Information Age: Perspectives and Prospects*, New Jersey: Hampton Press, pp. 3–17.

Karakaşlı, K. (2001), 'Gazetelerin Satıraralarında' (In between the lines of newspapers), in *Görüş Ağustos – Ermeniler Özel Sayısı*, pp. 66–69.

Keyder, Ç. (2005), 'A history and geography of Turkish nationalism', in Birtek F., and Dragonas, T. (eds.), *Citizenship and the Nation State in Greece and Turkey*, London: Routledge.

Özbudun, E., and Yazıcı, S. (2004), *Democratization Reforms in Turkey (1993–2004)*, Istanbul: TESEV Publications.

Riggins, H. (1992), *Ethnic Minority Media: An International Perspective*, London: Sage.

Soner, A. (2005), 'Citizenship and the minority question in Turkey', in Keyman, E., and İçduygu, A. (eds.), *Citizenship in a Global World: European Questions and Turkish Experiences*, London: Routledge, pp. 289–311.

The Economist (2007), 'Turkish nationalism: Waving Ataturk's Flag', March 10, pp. 39–40.

Topuz, H. (2003), *II. Mahmut'tan Holdinglere Türk Basın Tarihi* (From Mahmud II to the Holdings: Turkish Press History), Istanbul: Remzi Kitabevi.

Türker, O. (2003), 'Cumhuriyet Döneminde Istanbul'un Rum Basını' (The Istanbul Rum Press in the Republican Era), in *Tarih ve Toplum*, Temmuz, pp. 4–8.

Yanardagoglu, E. (2007), 'New Ethnic Minority Media System in Turkey: The Kurdish language broadcasting on public and local television in Europeanization Reform period (2001–2004)', paper presented at the Community Broadcasting workshop at the Central European University, Budapest, 17–18 May 2007.

New Media, New Europe: Estonia's E-mediated State

Alec Charles

This collection has examined the ways in which the media influence, and are influenced by, political, economic and ideological factors within European society. This final paper continues this theme by exploring the direct effect of new media forms upon citizenship, governance and democracy in one of the European Union's fastest developing new Member States.

Problems of e-democracy

'Will the Internet foster global democracy?' ask Bynum and Rogerson (2004: 318). 'Or will it become a tool for control and manipulation of the masses by a handful of powerful governments?'

Their questions echo the fears of a number of writers on the subject of electronic democracy. 'Whether e-government or e-service provision has much to do with participation or democracy is [...] questionable,' write Gibson et al. (2004: 8). 'Technology [add Raab and Bellamy] becomes a tool for the reinforcement of existing power structures' (2004: 21).

According to Margolis (2007: 2), the electronic gap comes to reflect the socio-economic divide: 'we have witnessed a normalisation of the politics of cyberspace, the emergence of a political and economic order that largely replicates that found in the physical world'. As 'citizens of lower educational attainment [are] less likely to be online' (Nixon and Kontrakou 2007: xxi), it appears inevitable that, as Åström (2004: 107) suggests, 'Internet voting certainly shifts the bias toward the middle and upper classes: the already politically active.'

The controversies related to the uses of electronic governance have become a crucial academic concern. 'Are we creating a bipolar society of computer-literate insiders and everyone else?' Neumann (2004: 208) asks. 'Are we disenfranchising any sectors of society, such as ordinary mortals and people who do not have computer resources?'

It appears that we may be doing precisely that. As Nicholas Pleace (2007: 69) points out, 'poor Internet access remains strongly associated with households with low incomes, the very people with whom e-government needs to engage. [...] The implications for electronic voting are obvious. The poorer parts of the population are less likely to vote.'

The uneven distribution of access to the Internet's intellectual and cultural capital is a problem not only for an electronic society as a whole; it is also a specifically critical issue for the practices of online government. This is witnessed by the United Nations's World Public Sector Report, which in 2003 warned that broad sections of national populations were not necessarily reaping the benefits of state investments in e-government.

The Baltic Tiger

Perched on the north-eastern edge of Europe, and wedged in between Finland, Russia and Latvia, the Baltic republic of Estonia achieved independence from the Soviet Union in 1992, and joined the European Union on 1 May 2004.

It has a population of about 1.3 million people, of whom 125,799 are stateless (OSCE 2007: 10). Most of these non-citizens are ethnic Russians. This disenfranchised minority represents the most extreme example of the massive disparity between Estonia's socially, economically, educationally and politically privileged and disadvantaged classes.

In 2004, Estonia was ranked fourth in the Heritage Foundation's list of nations which foster economic freedoms. It should be stressed that the Heritage Foundation tends to define its notion of economic freedom in terms of the freedoms of owners and employers, rather than those of employees or citizens – or, indeed, of the unemployed or the stateless.

The laissez-faire economic policies adopted by successive governments elected since Estonia regained its independence (policies such as the rejection of corporate taxation and progressive income tax) have enriched particular geographical, social and industrial sectors. The capital city Tallinn (with a population of 430,000 people) has developed a booming middle class and IT sector. However, Estonia's wealth remains concentrated in the area of Tallinn, in the north-west of the country. Questions remain as to how – and whether – this new-found prosperity can be harnessed to improve the lives of the general population. Indeed, Mikecz (2005: 153–154) writes that: 'north-western Estonia, which is home to 38 per cent of the country's population and 44 per cent of its labour force [...] has attracted over 88 per cent of foreign capital. [...]

Estonia has the highest levels of income inequality in the EU. [...] 18 percent of the population has a disposable income less than 60 per cent of the national median income'.

Estonia is therefore a key case in the debate as to whether new media are likely to improve the lives and rights of entire populations, rather than merely of their more privileged sections – not only because of the country's current uneven distribution of economic opportunities and social and intellectual resources, but also because of the fact that Estonia has, for the last decade, attempted to position itself as a society at the cutting edge of contemporary information technologies: 'E-stonia' – as it has liked to fashion itself.

In 1997, Estonia launched the 'Tiger Leap Initiative', an ambitious and remarkably successful economic, technological and educational programme designed to establish Estonia as a modern and competitive e-state. Even before this initiative, Estonia's financial industry had started to exploit new technologies. The world's first online banking services started in 1995. By the end of 1996, there were only about 20 such services worldwide – and three of them were Estonian.

'We've come from the Stone Age to the IT Age,' comments Olari Ilison of the IT department of Hansabank, the country's largest financial services provider – and also the largest IT organization in the country. 'Western banks are struggling with old systems which are difficult to upgrade and adapt to Internet banking, but we leapfrogged the mainframe era' (Charles 2004: 20). 'Hansabank has contributed revolutionary inputs to the whole banking business in Europe, including e-banking,' adds Aivar Roop, the bank's EU and Structural Funds manager (interview, July 2004).

The nation's size has worked to its advantage in the field of information technologies. 'As Estonia is a small country, it's much easier for its local companies and organizations to change their IT systems than it is for older multinational organizations,' writes Peter Priisalm, CEO of Estonia's largest specialist IT company, MicroLink. (Priisalm 2004: 5)

Estonia's IT advances have inspired a certain amount of journalistic and academic hype. In 2004, Ben Aris in *The Guardian* described Estonia as 'the most intensely wired country in the world'. The same year, a study of the global development of e-government conducted by researchers at Harvard University placed Estonia in fifth place.

At the end of April 2005, the Economist Intelligence Unit's sixth annual ranking of the 'e-readiness' of 65 different countries – in which Denmark, the United States and Sweden took the top three spots – placed Estonia at number 26, just ahead of fellow new EU member Slovenia. Denis McCauley, Director of Global Technology Research at the Economist Intelligence Unit, predicted that Estonia 'would continue to make gains based on the amount of private and public funding going into [its] Internet development' (Pruitt 2005).

According to the International Telecommunication Union, Estonia reported 33 per cent of its population as Internet users in 2003 – a figure 2 per cent higher than Ireland's (Fuller 2004). That same year, TNS Emor pollsters reported that as many as 45 per cent of Estonian residents aged 15 to 74, or around 576,000 people, used the Internet, and that this figure had risen by 59,000 since the previous year. More recently, Ernsdorff and Berbec (2007: 174) report that '52 per cent of the Estonian population uses the Internet, [and] 35 per cent have their own computer at home'.

In 2003, a World Economic Forum Report ranked Estonia in eighth position (out of 82 countries) for its methods of putting the Internet to practical use. It came in at number three for e-government, and at number two for Internet banking. The number of Estonians who choose to bank online has risen to more than 700,000 – more than half the total population. The government is also encouraging the online use of other financial services: in 2003, more than 130,000 Estonians chose to file their tax returns over the Internet.

Estonia's IT progress has included the development by Estonian companies of such high-profile software projects as Skype and Kazaa. Yet, as the Russian cyber-attacks upon its state and commercial websites in May 2007 demonstrated, this emphasis on new media technologies may open the country to risk – both from without and from within.

In July 2004, *Public Sector Technology and Management* reported that Estonia had spent about 1 per cent of its state budget on public sector IT development over the previous ten years. However, Estonia's laissez-faire economic principles have resulted in much of the responsibility for e-development – both infrastructurally and educationally – falling to the private and voluntary sectors.

One example of this is in the field of wireless Internet services. In 2000, the country had three 'wi-fi' areas. By 2004, it had 340. The campaign to spread wireless Internet coverage across Estonia was spearheaded by a self-employed volunteer called Veljo Haamer. Haamer's project has received some funding from private companies and local governments, particularly in rural areas where wireless coverage is seen as an inexpensive way to increase Internet access, but no support from central government. Despite his project's success, Haamer does not see IT development on its own as a panacea for his country's social problems: 'Technology itself doesn't solve problems. Technology is only a tool, not a solution' (Charles 2004: 20).

The most impressive contribution to Estonia's e-development was the privately funded Look@ World project, which trained 102,697 people in basic IT skills between 2002 and 2004. In recent years, however, government interest in this programme has diminished.

Mart Laar – an energetic free-marketeer and IT enthusiast – served as Prime Minister from 1992 to 1994, and from 1999 to 2001. Despite Laar's dynamism, subsequent coalition administrations have lacked the political will to continue to implement Laar's ambitious programmes of technological development.

'When we started, the Prime Minister was Mart Laar,' Look@World Chairman Alar Ehandi has said. 'He did a lot to support us. The current government is very much for the information society – in words – but they don't do so much. There are more people who want training. The private sector has invested nearly 3,000,000 euros. Now it's the government's turn' (Charles 2004: 20).

This view has been echoed by Tex Vertmann, who served as Communications Adviser to four Estonian Prime Ministers – Mart Laar, Siim Kallas, Juhan Parts and Andrus Ansip. 'Mr Laar was enthusiastic about e-services, e-democracy and e-society,' Vertmann has said. 'Mr Kallas and Mr Parts were more focused on developing knowledge-based society than on the e-thing' (Charles 2004: 20).

E-government

In cooperation with the United Nations Development Programme, the Soros Foundation and the Open Society Institute, Estonia established a non-profit organization called the E-Government Academy in 2002.

In an interview with BBC News (7/5/04), Ants Sild, a programme manager at the E-Government Academy, explained: 'What we mostly teach [...] is understanding what your goals are as a government, and then figuring out how technology can help you achieve those goals.' One is forced to wonder in this connection whether the goals of government are always necessarily consistent with the interests of its electorate.

In 2002, the TNS survey of 'Government Online' reported that 21 per cent of Estonians transacted government-related business online, 1 per cent below the Swedes, and 1 per cent above the Finns and the Danes.

In 2004, the Economist Intelligence Unit (EIU) named Estonia, Slovenia and the Czech Republic as the leaders in e-government of the new EU Member States: 'Although held back by connectivity problems, these countries have gone well beyond e-government window-dressing, and compare favourably in many areas with the rest of the European Union, particularly in shifting public service delivery online' (Pruitt 2004). However, the EIU's report warned that Estonia's fixed-line penetration rate stood at only 46 per cent, while its broadband penetration was a mere 3 per cent.

The European Commission's fifth annual survey of online government services in Europe, published in March 2005, showed that, while most of the European Union's then ten newest Member States scored in the lower half of the ranking – with average levels of e-government equivalent to those enjoyed by the EU's older Member States in 2003 – Estonia alone of the new members appeared in the upper half (European Commission 2005). Indeed, according to Ernsdorff and Berbec (2007: 171), 'Estonia stands as the e-government leader in Central and Eastern Europe and as third in the world in e-government systems.'

The Estonian government's much-vaunted paperless Cabinet meetings are said to have saved $100,000 a year in photocopying costs alone (added to a $200,000 annual saving made by inter-ministerial online memoranda), and to have reduced twelve-hour Cabinet sessions down to 45 minutes – or even, in one case, down to 14 minutes. As the government proudly proclaims these figures, one might however ask to what extent a 14-minute Cabinet meeting fosters the processes of mature democracy and administrative accountablity.

This craze for paperlessness has, since 1 January 2007, encompassed the publication of legislation: since that date, the official government organ ceased its print publication (save for five paper copies) and now exists in an almost exclusively electronic form. For Marshall McLuhan the adoption of the phonetic alphabet by European cultures allowed for a sudden and massive expansion of public literacy; the resultingly literate civilization afforded a structure in which all individuals had direct access to – and therefore were equal before – 'a written code of law' (McLuhan 2001: 91). Estonia's decision to consign legislative and governmental records to a domain to which a third of the population lacks access might be seen as reversing McLuhan's politically progressive process. A system in which access to legislation requires degrees of technological expertise and facilities that are not available to the entire population appears no longer to meet McLuhan's basic conditions for modern civil society.

One of the more controversial aspects of Estonia's adventures in virtual administration was established in 2001 as the flagship project of its system of e-government. *Täna Otsustan Mina* ('Today I Decide') – or 'TOM' – is a website on which Estonian citizens can present proposals for legislation. If a proposal receives sufficient support, it is discussed by the government. Although the portal boasts some 6,000 registered users, there are only 10 or 20 active members.

The TOM portal has prompted a number of minor changes in Estonian legislation and governance. One of these was a proposal to put the clocks forward in the spring and back in the autumn. Another was an amendment to the law on the possession of dangerous weapons – an exception which permitted students of Tartu University (the country's oldest and most prestigious seat of learning) to carry swords on ceremonial occasions.

It is notable that the first of these was enacted in order to bring Estonia into line with the time zone of its richer northern neighbour, Finland, a nation to whose prosperity Tallinn's middle classes self-consciously aspire. It may be seen not only as a concern of the country's economically advantaged cosmopolitans and internationalists, but also in the specific interests of the commercial enterprises in north-western Estonia who do much business with the Finns. It also virtually goes without saying that the ceremonial sword-carrying rights of students at the country's elite university hardly provide evidence for this portal's stated intention to provide top-level governmental access for the Estonian people en masse.

According to Ernsdorrf and Berbec (2007: 176), 'the TOM portal was a success at its launch in July 2001 when 359 proposals were forwarded up to the end of that year; this enthusiasm was however not maintained and this is reflected by only 49 proposals being submitted in 2005'.

In fact, the website is generally considered an object of national ridicule, embarrassment or indifference. Mart Parve, technology correspondent for Estonia's most popular daily newspaper, *Postimees*, has called the initiative farcical, and has characterized its regular users as 'geeks and freaks'. Parve has added that 'E-government is not employed at the level it should be. We're very interested in new technologies, but we don't use them properly' (Charles 2004: 20).

As Nixon (2007: 29) points out, 'a range of studies shows that the number of e-government projects that can be considered as total or partial failures ranges [...] from 60 to 85 per cent of all projects'. However, this issue may be seen not only in terms of its failure – even of its absurdity – for there are potentially more sinister intentions at play. As Catherine Needham (2004: 65) notes, 'direct consultation of citizens can be a resource for the executive branch of government, used to sideline the representative claims of the legislature by giving the executive an independent channel to public opinion'.

Needham's anxiety as to the circumvention of parliamentary authority by the executive branch, while valid in itself, neglects to recognize the democratic mandate of that executive, and therefore fails to envisage the possibility of the significance of that mandate itself being marginalized. As Ernsdorff and Berbec (2007: 177) report, Estonia's TOM website has now been sidelined and a new portal is tacitly acknowledged by the country's political elite as the primary arena for the proposal and discussion of legislation. This website is run by an independent body, the Estonian Law Centre Foundation. Public opinion and legislative influence is now mediated neither by parliament nor even by a public or publicly accountable organization. Estonia appears to be leading the way in this new Europe: the *laissez-faire* diminution of the public sector is balanced by the increasing domination of the private.

E-voting

In May 2005 the Estonian parliament passed legislation to introduce online voting at Estonia's local elections in October 2005. According to *The Baltic Times* newspaper (11/5/05): 'Estonia would become the only country in the world where people could vote through the Internet from home. Although online voting is widespread in other countries, a voter must conduct his E-vote at a polling station computer.' On 12 May, the Associated Press added: 'Voters will need an electronic ID card, an ID-card reader and internet access. [...] It is estimated that nearly 1 million of Estonia's 1.4 million residents already have an official electronic ID card. The ID cards, launched in 2002, include small microchips and offer secure e-signing through a reader attached to their computers.'

According to Aleksei Gunter, a leading journalist at *Postimees*, 'at the 2005 local elections, most of the e-votes went to the Reform Party. That was somewhat predictable, because the young and the well-off, who obviously have the means and the interest to use new technologies, favour that party' (interview, January 2007). In fact, according to the government's own report on that exercise in e-democracy, 'the Reform Party handed out ID card readers during their election campaign' (Madise et al. 2006: 41). As Ernsdorff and Berbec (2007: 178) report, 'some political parties considered e-voting an opportunity to increase their support, while others conceived it a threat'. Indeed, the then President Arnold Rüütel attempted to veto the legislation which permitted online voting, but was eventually overruled by the Supreme Court.

On 28 February 2007, Estonia extended e-voting to its national parliamentary elections. According to *The Baltic Times* newspaper (7/3/07), 'in what was hailed as the world's first full-scale internet election, a total of 30,243 voters chose to log their votes online.' The total number of votes cast at the election was 550,213 and the total number of eligible voters circa 940,000.

Ernsdorff and Berbec (2007: 171) have written that Estonia 'is setting an example in e-democracy throughout the European Union, being the first country in the world to enable all its citizens to vote over the Internet in political elections'. One might, however, call into question Ernsdorff and Berbec's use of the word 'all'.

It has been estimated that nearly two-thirds of Estonians currently use the Internet. These people represent, for the most part, the country's educated urban middle class. E-voting means that this sector of the population (i.e. those who tend to be supporters of the Centre Right coalitions that invariably govern Estonia) will find it easier to exercise their democratic rights than those on the other side of the digital divide.

Voter-mobilization is, of course, a key factor in the winning of elections. 'Recent voting studies emphasize the importance of voter mobilization by political candidates,' write Oberholzer-Gee and Waldfogel (2005: 74). 'You need to [...] mobilize them [voters] to turn out on Election Day,' add Trost and Grossmann (2005: 128). In facilitating the voting process for their typical supporters, Centre Right parties are therefore afforded an electoral advantage by electronic democracy. This is a hypothesis with which even the Prime Minister's former Communications Adviser, Tex Vertmann, has 'theoretically' agreed (Charles 2004: 20). Ülle Madise (2007), Director of Audit of Estonia's State Audit Office, has claimed that online voting offers 'no advantage for e-voters' – but, if that were indeed the case, one wonders why the state would bother with the trouble and expense of it at all. As Trechsel (2007: 37) points out, nearly 86 per cent of Estonian e-voters who chose to vote online did so because they found it more convenient than voting by traditional methods.

In fact, even the founding father of the Estonia's Tiger Leap Initiative, Linnar Viik, has expressed doubt over these experiments in electronic democracy: 'e-democracy doesn't have a real impact on the democratic process. Democracy in Estonia is like a small child. I can compare it to my five-year-old son. He can talk, he knows some manners, he knows how to pee – but he's still learning' (Charles 2004: 20). Or, as Ernsdorff and Berbec (2007: 178) – in an otherwise remarkably optimistic essay – admit, 'e-voting has never been the result of popular demand but rather a result of the imposition of yet another initiative by a young Estonian political elite'.

However, Estonia's Social Affairs Minister (from April 2005 to April 2007) Jaak Aab (in an interview conducted for this study in January 2007) argues: 'I believe that online voting encourages people to take an active part in democracy, because it gives an additional possibility to vote. It is especially important for people who cannot or have lower motivation to go vote to the designated voting place. I am not concerned that it may primarily encourage participation among the educated middle classes, because Estonia doesn't have a big gap in Internet use, as lots of other European countries do. Research shows that in 2006 spring, 60 per cent of Estonians (aged 6 to 74) were using the Internet. The Estonian government's aim is to provide the Internet to all Estonian people.'

There appear to be a number of holes in Aab's argument. His first proposal – that e-democracy encourages participation – appears to contradict the evidence of various empirical studies. Gibson et al. (2004: 3) cite, for example, Scheufele and Nisbet's 2002 survey, in which 'none of the modes of Internet use [...] was found to have any significant effect on individuals' proclivity to engage in politics'.

Aab's dismissal of the education gap as irrelevant to Estonia is extraordinary, not only in the light of the country's massive socio-economic divide, but also because it specifically contradicts the findings of his government's own report on the 2005 elections – 'there were more people with high education [...] among actual e-voters' (Madise et al. 2006: 30) – and Breuer and Trechsel's *Report for the Council of Europe*. Breuer and Trechsel (2006: section 7) find that 'e-voting in Estonia is not as seducing for elderly people as it is for younger generations', that 'language remains a problem in a linguistically divided society' (minority Russian-speakers are less likely to use the system than majority Estonian-speakers), and 'computing knowledge remains a hurdle for e-voting'. Although Breuer and Trechsel reject general educational status as a particular factor in citizens' proclivities towards online voting, the specific case of IT-education (which is of course related to quality and currency of general education) is seen as a crucial – and therefore divisive – issue here.

Indeed, Trechsel's *Report for the Council of Europe* on the 2007 elections goes on to note that 'the share of highly educated voters was almost 20 percentage points higher among e-voters than among traditional voters' (Trechsel 2007: 43). Trechsel's 2007 report also stresses that, in terms of economic status, 'the highest-income category is heavily overrepresented among e-voters' and that 'a very large part of the Russian speaking community [refrained] from using this tool' (Trechsel 2007: 44, 6). Trechsel's study demonstrates that more than 62 per cent of voters who elected not to vote online did so because they lacked the necessary facilities (Trechsel 2007: 38). He also points out that 'e-voters do not only differ [from traditional voters] with regard to their socio-demographic and economic profiles, but they also do so [...] with regard to their political preferences' (Trechsel 2007: 49).

To the extent that socio-economic status can be elaborated upon geographical lines, it seems significant that, with the exception of the university city of Tartu, the areas of Estonia which, according to the report of the Estonian National Electoral Committee (2007), demonstrated the highest use of electronic voting among the national turnout were Tallinn itself and its neighbouring counties in the affluent north-west of the country. With barely more than a third of Tallinn's score, the economically depressed county of Ida-Viru on Estonia's eastern border with Russia showed the lowest rate of adoption of the electronic system.

Further to these concerns as to the equity of the electronic voting system, the Organization for Security and Co-operation in Europe's report also highlighted the lack of 'oversight of the internet voting process by political parties or civil society' and went so far as to question 'whether [in future] the internet should be available as a voting method, or alternatively whether it should be used only on a limited basis or not at all' (OSCE 2007: 2). This lack of enthusiasm has not, however, prevented Estonia forging ahead with a plan to introduce voting from mobile telephones in time for its municipal elections in 2009 (Alas 2007). It is perhaps notable, however, that its Baltic neighbour Lithuania has recently rejected proposals for electronic elections (Vaiga 2008).

According to the recommendation on *Legal, Operational and Technical Standards for E-Voting* adopted by the Committee of Ministers of the Council of Europe on 30 September 2004, 'measures shall be taken to ensure that the relevant software and services can be used by all voters'. When Jaak Aab suggests that his government intends (one day) to provide full Internet access to their entire electorate, one might therefore ask whether online voting should be implemented before that day has come. Indeed, that day seems further off than Aab implies: although he suggests that 60 per cent of his compatriots have Internet access, he neglects to mention that, for the vast majority, this access does not include the card-reader necessary for online voting. As Ernsdorff and Berbec (2007: 180) emphasize, 'one prerequisite for popular e-voting had certainly not been satisfied, namely that of the spreading of specific electronic ID card readers. [...] They are not common for personal use and furthermore, they are expensive.'

According to the website of the 22nd Chaos Communication Congress, Tarvi Martens was 'the guy who made e-voting possible for the whole nation first time [sic] in the history'. From 1993 to 1997 Martens headed Estonia's Data Communication Department, where he championed the introduction of a national electronic identity card. Martens then moved to Sertifitseerimiskeskus (SK), the private company responsible for Estonian identity cards, electronic signatures and card-readers. Since 2003, Martens has worked with the National Electoral Committee to implement an online voting system. He is Chief Operating Officer of SK and the Project Manager for Estonian e-voting. Martens comments that 'the increasing number of e-voters is of course encouraging. I see two main factors behind it: (a) an increasing awareness of ID-card electronic usage, and (b) a steady, trustworthy and transparent e-voting system which produces increasing confidence in users' (interview, March 2007).

Despite Martens's confidence in the system, he admits that 'we do not possess exact data about number of card-readers installed among ID-card holders'. This tallies with the official government report on *Internet Voting at the Elections of Local Government Councils on October 2005* (Madise et al. 2006: 8) which reveals that 'there is [...] no reliable data on the distribution of card-readers in Estonia'. However, Martens's Marketing Manager Andres Aarma was able to provide more detail on the subject: 'Our estimate for the total number of readers installed is currently around 70,000–80,000. How many of those are in personal use and how many in organizational use we do not know. In the end of 2006 we concluded an agreement with German technology company OMNIKEY which won the international tenders for procurement of up to 600,000 readers between 2007 and 2009. The aim is to enable everyone affordable access to the public key infrastructure' (interview, January 2007).

Estonia initiated an online voting system at a time when nobody knew how many people had access to the technology which would allow them to vote from home – although it probably was not many more than the 3.2 per cent of the electorate who actually used the system. But at least the people who recommended the system in the first place have secured a deal to sell the technology necessary to make it work.

In this context, there is something chilling about the final words of a presentation given by Tarvi Martens (2007) on Estonian e-voting: 'there's no way back'.

Conclusions
Where then might this example lead us?

Certainly (obviously) not towards an undilutedly cyberoptimistic perspective. The Estonian example demonstrates that, if nothing else, technological developments do not necessarily result in greater levels of participatory citizenship, democratic accountability or social justice.

In January 2003 Donald Rumsfeld famously suggested that Estonia and its post-Communist neighbours in central and eastern Europe epitomised what he called a 'New Europe'. If indeed they do represent the latest stage of European development, then perhaps the situation of Estonia, ostensibly the most progressive of these newer EU Member States, may also reveal something of the future of Europe itself. It may therefore be the case that the current state of Estonia – a nation whose recent history has been determined more than most by the latest developments in media technologies, their formats, their convergences and their ownerships – may speak to us of the shape of things to come.

Rather than fostering democracy, consensus and citizenship, the influence of media forms upon European societies (upon 'European society', if one can speak of such a thing) may be, as the Estonian example suggests, to reinforce entrenched structures of political, economic and ideological power. If that turns out to be the case, then the role of academic meditations upon this entire field, such as all those contained within this collection, may prove to be unprecedentedly critical.

References
Alas, J. (2007), 'Thumbs up for mobile voting', The Baltic Times, 3 October 2007.
Aris, B. (2004), 'Technological Tiger', The Guardian, 22 April 2004.
Åström, J. (2004), 'Digital democracy', in Gibson, R., Römmele, A., and Ward, S. (eds.), Electronic Democracy, Abingdon: Routledge, pp. 96–115.

Baltic Times (2005), 'Online voting raises concern, gives new coalition first challenge', 5 May 2005.

Baltic Times (2007), 'Card readers the only challenge in e-election', 7 March 2007.

Breuer, F., and Trechsel, A. (2006), *Report for the Council of Europe: E-Voting in the 2005 local elections in Estonia*, Strasbourg: Council of Europe.

Bynum, T. and Rogerson, S. (2004), 'Global Information Ethics: Editors' Introduction', in Bynum, T., and Rogerson, S. (eds.), *Computer Ethics and Professional Responsibility*, Oxford: Blackwell Publishing, pp. 316–318.

Charles, A. (2004), 'Estonia – the State of the E-State', *The Baltic Times*, 22 July 2004.

Ernsdorff, M., and Berbec, A. (2007), 'Estonia: The short road to e-government and e-democracy', in Nixon, P., and Kautrakou, V. (eds.), *E-government in Europe*, Abingdon: Routledge, pp. 171–183.

Estonian National Electoral Committee (2007), *Parliamentary elections 2007: Statistics of e-voting*. Tallinn: Estonian National Electoral Committee.

European Commission (2005), *Online government is now a reality almost everywhere in the EU*, Brussels: European Commission, 8 March 2005.

Fuller, T. (2004), 'In Estonia, E-banking, E-commerce, E-government', *International Herald Tribune*, 13 September 2004.

Gibson, R., Lusoli, W., Römmele, A., and Ward, S. (2004), 'Representative democracy and the Internet', in Gibson, R., Römmele, A., and Ward, S. (eds.), *Electronic Democracy*, Abingdon: Routledge, pp. 1–16.

McLuhan, Marshall (2001), *Understanding Media*, London: Routledge.

Madise, Ü., Vinkel, P., and Maaten, E. (2006), *Internet Voting at the Elections of Local Government Councils on October 2005*, Tallinn: Estonian National Electoral Committee.

Madise, Ü. (2007), *Internet Voting in Estonia Free and Fair Elections*, Tallinn: Estonian National Electoral Committee.

Margolis, M. (2007), 'E-government and democratic politics', in Nixon, P., and Kautrakou, V. (eds.), *E-government in Europe*, Abingdon: Routledge, pp. 1–18.

Martens, T. (2007), *Internet Voting in Practice*, Tallinn: Estonian National Electoral Committee.

Mikecz, R. (2005), 'Ambition versus Pragmatism', in Charles, A. (ed.), *EU Enlargement – One Year On*, Tallinn: Audentes University, pp. 146–156.

Needham, C. (2004), 'The citizen as consumer: e-government in the United Kingdom and the United States', in Gibson, R., Römmele, A., and Ward, S. (eds.), *Electronic Democracy*, Abingdon: Routledge, pp. 43–69.

Neumann, P. (2004), 'Computer Security and Human Values', in Bynum, T., and Rogerson, S. (eds.), *Computer Ethics and Professional Responsibility*, Oxford: Blackwell Publishing, pp. 208–226.

Nixon, P. (2007), 'Ctrl, Alt, Delete: Rebooting the European Union via e-government', in Nixon, P., and Kautrakou, V. (eds.), *E-government in Europe*, Abingdon: Routledge, pp. 19–32.

Nixon, P., and Koutrakou, V. (2007), 'Introduction', in Nixon, P., and Kautrakou, V. (eds.), *E-government in Europe*, Abingdon: Routledge, pp. xviii-xxviii.

Oberholzer-Gee, F., and Waldfogel, J. (2005), 'Strength in Numbers: Group Size and Political Mobilization', in *Journal of Law and Economics* 158, Chicago: University of Chicago Press, 73–91.

OSCE (2007), *Republic of Estonia Parliamentary Elections 4 March 2007*, Warsaw: OSCE / Office for Democratic Institutions and Human Rights.

Pleace, N. (2007), 'E-government and the United Kingdom', in Nixon, P., and Kautrakou, V. (eds.), *E-government in Europe*, Abingdon: Routledge, pp. 61–74.

Priisalm, P. (2004), Viewpoint, in Charles, A. (ed.), *The International 2*, Tallinn: Audentes University, p. 5.

Pruitt, S. (2004), 'Poor infrastructure hinders E-government in new EU', *Network World Fusion*, 1 October 2004.

Pruitt, S. (2005), 'Europe makes greatest gains in E-readiness', *IDG News Service*, 20 April 2005.

Raab, C., and Bellamy, C. (2004), 'Electronic democracy and the "mixed polity"', in Gibson, R., Römmele, A., and Ward, S. (eds.), *Electronic Democracy*, Abingdon: Routledge, pp. 17–42.

Trechsel, A. (2007), *Report for the Council of Europe: Internet voting in the March 2007 Parliamentary Elections in Estonia*. Strasbourg: Council of Europe.

Trost, C., and Grossmann, M. (2005), *Win the Right Way*, Berkeley: Public Policy Press.

UN World Public Sector Report (2003), *E-Government at the Crossroads*, New York: United Nations.

Vaiga, L. (2008), 'Lithuania says "no" to E-voting', *The Baltic Times*, 23 January 2008.

CONTRIBUTORS

Richard Caddell is a Lecturer in Law at Swansea University. He is the editor-in-chief of *Blackstone's Statutes on Media Law* (OUP) and is a regular contributor on defamation and media law issues for a number of leading journals, including *Communications Law* and the *Cambridge Law Journal.*

Dr Alec Charles has worked as a documentary-maker for BBC Radio, and has taught at universities in the United Kingdom, Japan and Estonia, where he held the position of Professor of Media at Audentes University in Tallinn, and worked as a freelance reporter for *The Baltic Times.* He is the editor of *Transatlantic Cooperation: America, Europe and the Baltics* (2004) and *EU Enlargement – One Year On* (2005). His recent publications include papers in *British Journalism Review* and *Science Fiction Studies.* He is currently Senior Lecturer in Media and Field Chair of Art & Design at the University of Bedfordshire, and acts as a consultant for *Diena*, Latvia's largest newspaper publisher, on its journalism training programme.

Dr Gabriela E. Chira is a Postdoctoral Fellow at the University of Victoria, Canada, and has also worked as a journalist in Brussels. She completed her Ph.D. at the Universite de Nice-Sophia Antipolis, France, with a dissertation on the pre-EU accession transformation of media in central and eastern European countries.

Lenka Waschková Císařová works as a Lecturer in the Department of Media Studies and Journalism at Masaryk University in Brno, the Czech Republic. She is Editor-in-Chief of *Mediální studia/Media Studies*, an academic journal based in the Czech Republic.

Oliver Daddow lectures in the Department of Politics, International Relations and European Studies at Loughborough University. His research interests are in British foreign policy, European integration and critical historiography. He is the author of *Britain and Europe since 1945* (2004) and the editor of *Harold Wilson and European Integration* (2003), and has published many journal articles and book chapters in the fields of Euroscepticism, historical theory and British foreign policy.

Professor Hedwig de Smaele is Professor in Communication Sciences at the Catholic University of Brussels. She has previously worked as a Research Fellow and Postdoctoral Researcher at the Research Foundation, Flanders, and as a Lecturer in Politics and Mass Media at Ghent University's Department of Communication. She completed a Ph.D. in political and social sciences on the transition of mass media in Russia from Communism to post-Communism. Recent research projects include a study of the Russian mass media and information climate, audio-visual policy in the enlarged European Union, the impact of EU media policy on the programme schedules of European broadcasters, media and democratization processes, and political communication in new democracies. She has published papers in such journals as the *European Journal of Communication* and *Trends in Communication*.

Dr Andrea Esser is a Senior Lecturer in the media and cultural studies team at Roehampton University. Her research interests include the sociology of television and the transnationalization of the media in the context of European integration. Her work explores both the continuity of the market and the dynamics of change.

Dr Julie Firmstone is Lecturer in Communications Research at the Institute of Communications Studies, University of Leeds, and an Associate Director of the Centre for European Political Communications. She is currently co-applicant of an ESRC/ESF project that examines debates over the EU Constitutional Treaty and the future of Europe. The project explores the role of civil society organizations in mediating the preferences of citizens to the European Union, and examines public claims-making in the media over issues related to the future of Europe. Her research has also investigated the representation of European issues in the media, journalism and the European Union, and newspapers' editorial opinions on European integration.

Neil T. Gavin is Senior Lecturer in the School of Politics and Communication Studies, Liverpool University, and has formerly taught at York University and London School of Economics and Political Science. He has served as editor of *The Economy, Media and Public Knowledge* and co-editor of *Britain Votes 1997*, and has recently published the Palgrave monograph *Press and Television in British Politics: Media, Money and Mediated Democracy*.

Davy Geens is a Researcher at the Centre for Media and Culture Studies of the Department of Media and Communication Studies of Vrije Universiteit in Brussels. He graduated from the same university in 2004 with a Master's degree in Media and Communication Studies; his thesis explored the representation of the European Union in editorials in the Flemish daily press. After he obtained a Master's degree in International Relations and Diplomacy from the University of Antwerp, he completed a four-month internship in the European Parliament at the Directorate-General for Information.

Jim Hall served as Course Leader of the BA Journalism programme at University College Falmouth, and wrote extensively on journalism, creative writing and multimedia for such publications as *Convergence* and *Journalism Studies*. His study of *Online Journalism* (Pluto Press, 2000) remains a seminal account of the subject. Jim Hall died in October 2008.

Mark Hayward teaches in the Department of Global Communications at the American University of Paris. His research looks at the globalization of Italian media. He has also published work on UNESCO and international cultural policy.

David Hutchison is Research Fellow in Media Policy at Glasgow Caledonian University. Among his publications are *The Modern Scottish Theatre* (1977) and *Media Policy* (1999); he has also co-edited a multi-authored volume on *The Media in Scotland* (2008). He has served as a member of the BBC's General Advisory Council and of the Scottish Film Council.

Yasmin Ibrahim is Senior Lecturer in the Department of Information and Media Studies at the University of Brighton. Her research interests include the new media and empowerment in non-democratic states, risk communication, political communication and alternative media.

Valentina Marinescu is a member of the Faculty of Sociology and Social Work at the University of Bucharest in Romania.

Dr Monika Metyková is a Postdoctoral Researcher at University of Sunderland's Centre for Research in Media and Cultural Studies. She is currently working on a project on eastern European migration to the United Kingdom. Her recent publications include 'Establishing Public Service Broadcasting in the Slovak Republic (1993–2004): From State Control to the European Single Market', in *Trends in Communication*.

Professor Paschal Preston teaches in the School of Communication, Dublin City University. He founded the Communication, Technology and Culture Research Centre in DCU, an interdisciplinary research unit focused on socio-economic and policy aspects of new ICTs, with a particular interest in media sector developments. His publications include *Reshaping Communication: Technology, Information and Social Change* (2001).

Dr Inka Salovaara-Moring is Post-doctoral Researcher of the Academy of Finland, University of Helsinki. She is currently editing a book on the research project *European Public Sphere: Uniting or Dividing?* and has started up her own research project *Beyond East and West: Comparing Media Geographies of New Europe* funded by the Academy of Finland.

Russell Sandberg is an Associate Tutor at Cardiff Law School and an Associate of both the Centre for Law and Religion and the Centre for the Study of Islam in the United Kingdom, Cardiff University. He has written widely on religion and human rights, discrimination law and Church-State relations.

Rudiger Theilmann has lectured at the Department of Communications and Journalism at the University of Hohenheim, and at the University for Design, Schwäbisch Gmünd, in Germany, and at Audentes University in Estonia. He has conducted empirical research studies for the University of Munich, the South Western Broadcasting Company and the Bavarian Broadcasting Company, and has worked as a product manager in the international trade agency Augusta. He is currently Senior Lecturer at Leeds Metropolitan University.

Dr Kristel Vandenbrande is Lecturer in Politics and Popular Media, Media and Citizenship, and Qualitative Research Methodologies, at the Department of Media and Communication Studies of Vrije Universiteit in Brussels. She is a member of the Centre for Media and Cultural Studies at the same university, and also lectures in journalism at the Erasmushogeschool in Brussels.

Liliana Vitu is Program/Communications Officer for the Moldova Representative Office of the Eurasia Foundation in Chisinau.

Dr Friederike von Franqué completed her Ph.D. on *Media Assistance as Foreign Policy. Motives, Objectives and Implementation by International Organizations in Bosnia-Herzegovina and Kosovo* at the Institute for Peace and Security Studies in 2007. She has worked for the European Parliament, and now works as a freelance consultant for media intervention and security issues in Frankfurt, Germany.

Dr Eylem Yanardagoglu is a post-doctoral fellow for the *Framework 6th Project- Eurosphere: Diversity and the European Public Sphere* at Sabanci University in Istanbul, Turkey, and has taught in the department of Sociology at City University in London. She completed her postgraduate studies in Sociology and Journalism at the Middle East Technical University in Ankara and at City University.